Theology as an
Ecclesial Discipline

Theology as an Ecclesial Discipline

Ressourcement and Dialogue

J. AUGUSTINE DI NOIA, OP

EDITED BY JAMES LE GRYS

The Catholic University of America Press
Washington, D.C

Chapter 1, Originally published in *Blackwell Companion to Catholicism*,
ed. James J. Buckley and F. C. Bauerschmidt (Cambridge: Blackwell, 2007), 238–50.
© 2007 by Blackwell Publishing Ltd.
Chapter 2, Originally published in *Modern Theology* 9 (1993): 403–18.
Chapter 3, Originally published as "*Metodo teologico e magistero della chiesa*," PATH
(Pontificia Accademia Theologica) 3 (2004): 57–68. This English translation published as,
"Theological Method and the Magisterium of the Church," *Dominicana* 64 (2011): 51–61.
Chapter 4, Originally published in *Pro Ecclesia* 10 (2001): 329–45, with Bernard Mulcahy,
OP.
Chapter 5, Originally published in *Called to Holiness and Communion: Vatican II on the
Church*, ed. Steven C. Boguslawski, OP, and Robert L. Fastiggi (Scranton, PA: University of
Scranton Press, 2009), 321–39.
Chapter 7, Originally published in *The Thomist* 73 (2009): 111–27.
Chapter 9, Originally published in *Speaking the Christian God: The Triune God and the
Challenge of Feminism*, ed. Alvin F. Kimel, Jr. (Grand Rapids, MI: Eerdmans, 1992), 162–87.
Reprinted by permission of the publisher.
Chapter 10, Originally published in *Nova et Vetera* 2 (2004): 267–77.
Chapter 12, Originally published in *The Thomist* 73 (2009), 281–98.
Chapter 13, Originally published in *The Thomist* 81 (2017): 345–59.
Chapter 16, Originally published in *Either/Or: The Gospel of Neopaganism*, ed. Carl E.
Braaten and Robert W. Jenson (Grand Rapids, MI: Eerdmans, 1995), 37–48. Reprinted by
permission of the publisher.
Chapter 17, Excerpt from *Nicene Christianity* by Christopher R. Seitz, ed., copyright ©
2001. Used by permission of Brazos Press, a division of Baker Publishing Group
Chapter 18, *Pro Ecclesia* 13 (2004): 58–69.

ISBN: 978-0-8132-3790-9 paper
ISBN: 978-0-8132-3849-4 case
eISBN: 978-0-8132-3791-6

Cataloging-in-Publication Data is available from the Library of Congress

Contents

Contents

Preface

The practice of theology depends in part on asking the right questions. Not any sort of question will do, but well-formulated ones that arise from and are shaped through reflection on the Word of God in Scripture and Tradition. Not idle questions, nor questions framed entirely by our own experience or the great issues of our times, but good theological questions that arise in our pondering of the scriptural witness. Indeed, one of the things we are taught by contemplating the Word of God is how to ask the right questions. Historically, it has been the case that *lectio* gave rise to *quaestio*, and it largely continues to be so today. Good theological questions focus the mind of the inquirer on the endlessly intelligible self-revelation of God to which the Sacred Scripture bears witness. Our own questions and the great questions of our times have a place, of course, as long as they are purged of the ideological outlooks that can suppress or obscure the questions that the *sacra pagina* itself presses upon us.

We find that our questions have inner finalities, and so, sometimes inquiries we thought to be distinct converge unexpectedly toward one another. That should not surprise us. For they arise from a desire to fathom the fathomless mystery of God. The more tenaciously we travel along the paths they map out, the more surely do our questions deepen our knowledge of God and everything else in the ambient light of the divine reality. If sometimes there seems to be darkness at the far reaches of our quest for understanding, it will usually be because of the limits of our capacity to see rather than the obscurity of divine revelation itself. The path of theological inquiry leads not toward an inevitable perpetual darkness, but to the unending light where God dwells.

The questions that occupy theologians connect at many points with questions in other fields of inquiry, especially philosophy, the physical and biological sciences, psychology, and history. The presumption among Catholic theologians is that such connections should be pursued with due regard for the proper finalities of other fields of study as well as the principles and methodologies that distinguish them from each other, and from theology.

The first set of essays gathered together in this book directs the reader's attention precisely to questions that trace the distinctive features of the theological field. What are the principles and scope of the field of theology as practiced by believers in an ecclesial context? Are historical-critical methods of exegesis compatible with a properly theological interpretation of the Scriptures? How can theology have a place in the academy as an intellectual discipline if the Magisterium limits the scope of its inquiries? These questions take on a certain concreteness when considered in the context of the experience of two Dominican institutions where I once taught theology.

Although autobiography is by no means at center stage in these chapters, the second part of *Theology as an Ecclesial Discipline* does begin with some educational experiences that molded the author's understanding of the impact of modernity on the kinds of questions that preoccupy contemporary Protestant and Catholic theologians. Can the names Father, Son and Holy Spirit be replaced by more inclusive titles in doctrine and liturgy? By placing humanity at the center of theological investigation, is Christian humanism really distinct from secular humanism? How can we be guilty of a sin committed by our first ancestors, even if we knew who they were? Can the Christian vision of procreative human sexuality survive the cultural onslaught of the sexual revolution? These are just a few of the questions that have emerged at the frontiers where Christian confession intersects with the secular individualism that prevails in society and culture today.

The questions in the third part of this book arise from Catholic dialogue with non-Christian religions, with other Christian communities, or with conceptions of a cosmos in ecological crisis. Is there a future for Catholic theology of religions? How can people who do not believe in Christ be saved? Is the cosmos a safe environment for human beings, or, alternatively, how can the cosmos be protected from human depredation? Can the concept of "church" stretch far enough to encompass Christian communities that see themselves as strictly local and independent bodies?

These chapters first consider theological questions internal to the very nature of theology; then, questions prompted by the challenges of modernity; and finally, questions arising out of the encounter with other religions, with other Christian communities, and with a scientific understanding of the world. Some of the essays that have become chapters in this volume have never been published before. Most have appeared (or, as Karl Rahner once quipped in the preface to a volume of his own essays, disappeared) in journals or anthologies. All represent, to one degree or another, accumulated debts that can barely be recalled and much less acknowledged—except for John Martino, acquisitions editor of The Catholic University of America Press, and James Le Grys, who has served as the book's editor, without whose determination and dedication this volume would not have seen the light of day.

J. Augustine Di Noia, OP
Feast of St. Augustine
August 28, 2023

PART I

The Nature and
Practice of Theology in Its
Ecclesial Context

CHAPTER 1

The Practice of Catholic Theology

Readers of the final chapters of the Gospel of St. Luke are treated to the remarkable story of an encounter between the risen Christ and two disciples on the road to Emmaus. The two disciples do not recognize Jesus as he joins them on their journey and are amazed at how little this stranger knows about the troubling "events of the past few days." As they walk along, they inform him of the events surrounding the trial and execution of Jesus of Nazareth in Jerusalem. After hearing them out, Jesus rebukes them for being "foolish . . . and slow of heart to believe all that the prophets have declared!" "Was it not necessary that the Messiah should suffer these things and then enter into his glory?" Jesus asks. Then, "beginning with Moses and all the prophets, he interpreted to them the things about himself in all the scriptures" (see Lk 24:13–35).

Among the many interesting features of this story, there is something particularly instructive for our purposes here. The way that Christ poses the question and then goes about answering it sheds light on very basic elements of the field of inquiry that has come to be called theology and that is our subject in this essay.

Originally published in *Blackwell Companion to Catholicism*, ed. James J. Buckley and F. C. Bauerschmidt (Cambridge: Blackwell, 2007), 238–50. © 2007 by Blackwell Publishing Ltd.

THEOLOGY AS *FIDES QUAERENS INTELLECTUM*

Why was it necessary for Christ to suffer? The question is a cogent and difficult one, and once we start thinking about it we find ourselves asking additional questions. Why did Christ have to suffer *these things*? We believe that Christ died to save us from our sins, but how does dying in this way do that? Is the shedding of blood on the cross like the shedding of blood in the animal sacrifices recounted and prescribed in the Bible? When God is brought into the picture, as he must be, the questions multiply. If God is all-powerful, can we say that any particular course of action is "necessary" for him? If God is all-good, then how could he have allowed his beloved Son to suffer so much? And so on.

Several things about this series of questions are noteworthy. For one thing, we see almost immediately that the initial question cannot be considered in isolation. In order even to think about it, we need to raise other questions as well. Quite significant is Christ's approach to answering the question as posed: from this, we learn that the Bible is the first place to look in trying to get answers to questions like these. Fairly early in our inquiry, we are likely to wonder what the Church, either in an official manner or within the broad context of her tradition, has thought and said about these questions. We find that the answers to some of our questions have already been formulated as doctrines of the Church. We recognize that our questions have been asked before by others, some of whom have had very interesting things to say about them. Eventually, we sense that questions in one area of our faith intersect with others. The question about why it was necessary for Christ to suffer is connected with questions about who Christ is, who God is, and who we are. Sometimes the questions that arise here lead to questions in other fields. We might wonder, for example, whether Christ's dying for our sake is in any way analogous to sacrificial death in other religious traditions.

Before proceeding further, we should take note of the possibility, despite the implicit scriptural warrant, of a principled objection to posing questions of this type. Someone might protest that the mysteries of Christian faith invite devotion and worship, not scrutiny. Although most Christians have taken to heart the cautionary nature of this objection, they have nonetheless been convinced that intellectual probing can itself be regarded as a form of worshipful response to the mysteries of faith. Because not only our hearts are called to adoration, but also our minds, scrutiny can be a form of worship. Because it has God and his mysteries as its object, theology can appropriately be done "on one's knees."[1]

The series of questions we have been considering shows *fides quaerens intellectum* in action. The phrase *fides quaerens intellectum*—"faith seeking understanding"—was coined by St. Anselm of Canterbury (1033–1109), who was himself reframing some ideas of St. Augustine (354–430). It has ever since been widely regarded as an apt description for the sorts of inquiries that are practiced in theology.[2] Naturally, the phrase does not mean that raising questions of the type we have been considering automatically constitutes an inquiry as theological. The point is rather that faith by its very nature gives rise to a desire for deepened understanding, one that can, however, be pursued at a variety of levels of intensity and rigor. Built into faith is an intellectual restlessness[3] and sense of wonder[4] that drives inquiry.

Theology as such emerges, it seems clear, with the recognition that large bodies of questions can be related to one another and can usefully be ordered and addressed consecutively. By applying some systematic principles and careful reasoning, this kind of inquiry can

1. See Hans Urs von Balthasar, *Word and Redemption,* trans. A. V. Littledale (New York: Herder & Herder, 1965).
2. See G. R. Evans, ed., *The Medieval Theologians* (Oxford: Blackwell, 2001); Evans, *The First Christian Theologians: An Introduction to Theology in the Early Church* (Oxford: Blackwell, 2004).
3. See Romanus Cessario, OP, *Christian Faith and the Theological Life* (Washington, DC: The Catholic University of America Press, 1996).
4. See Aidan Nichols, OP, *The Shape of Catholic Theology* (Collegeville, MN: Liturgical Press, 1991).

provide an overall deepened understanding of the faith either for oneself or to form others in thinking about the Christian faith. Theology in the Catholic sense of the word can best be understood as an umbrella term for inquiries that pursue this deepened understanding of faith through the application of properly systematic and disciplined intellectual procedures such as are found in philosophy, the physical and social sciences, and in history and the humanities.[5]

THEOLOGY IN ACCORD WITH REVELATION

It has been precisely in connection with sorting out the similarities and differences between theology and other scholarly inquiries that its status as a distinctive field of study has come to be clarified and secured.

Although it is true that the types of interpretation and reasoning through which theology approaches its characteristic questions are like those found in other disciplines, the very fact that it presupposes faith seems to render it quite unlike other disciplines. To be sure, all fields of inquiry have to presuppose something or other in order to get started, even if nothing more than a given subject matter. But, unlike the given in other fields, theology seems to have to accept not only a particular given but what to think about this given as well. It is not only that certain materials—scriptures, tradition, doctrines, etc.—are to be received in faith, but also that their fundamental meanings must be accepted in faith as in some sense already fixed. The very language we use betrays this: to say that we accept something "on faith" implies just the opposite of what we assume intellectual inquiries to be about—involving, as they do, an openness to finding out what is the case, rather than an acceptance a priori of some account of what is the case. Because theology seems to require as a starting point accepting beforehand an account of what is the case, it seems quite unlike other intellectual inquiries whose

5. See Yves Congar, OP, *A History of Theology*, trans. Harvey Guthrie, SJ (Garden City, NY: Doubleday, 1968).

methodologies it apes. A more properly scientific approach to these materials and the questions they raise would be to expose them precisely to philosophical, historical, social, anthropological, and other types of inquiry—independently of the specifically religious commitments and expressions which these materials support in the life of those communities where they are taken on faith.

These issues have a modern ring to them and indeed they have been raised with particular force in modern times. But in fact, they arose well before modern times, serving to stimulate sustained reflection about the distinctive nature of theology in comparison with other scholarly pursuits. St. Thomas Aquinas (1224–74) gave a great deal of thought to these issues and his insights, at least in their essential drift, have been widely influential for all subsequent Catholic theology.[6]

Presupposed to all the specific questions that reflection on the Bible and the Christian creeds elicits is a fundamental conviction about who God is and what he intends. This conviction is an essential feature of catholic Christian faith in almost all its varieties. It is the conviction that God is Father, Son, and Holy Spirit, a communion of life and love, and that he desires to share this communion of trinitarian life and love with persons whom he creates. Indeed, it would be true to say that no one has ever desired anything more than the triune God desires to share this communion with creaturely persons. God himself has disclosed to us (for how could we otherwise have known about it?) that this divine desire—more properly, intention and plan—lies at the basis of everything that God has done in creation, incarnation, redemption, grace, sanctification, and glory.[7]

6. See St. Thomas Aquinas, *Summa Theologiae* I, a. 1, in *Christian Theology, Summa Theologiae, volume 1*, trans. Thomas Gilby, OP (New York & London: McGraw-Hill, and Eyre & Spottiswood, 1964); Aquinas, *In Boethius de Trinitate*, q. 6, a. 3, in *Saint Thomas Aquinas: Division and Methods of the Sciences. Questions V and VI of his Commentary on the De Trinitate of Boethius*, 4th ed., trans. Armand Mauer (Toronto: Pontifical Institute of Medieval Studies, 1986).

7. See Bruce D. Marshall, *Trinity and Truth* (Cambridge: Cambridge University Press, 2000).

To look at everything through the eyes of faith—to adopt, as it were, a "God's-eye view"—is to see everything in the light of this divine plan of salvation. To be able to do this is itself a divine gift involving the transformation of ordinary human capacities for knowing and thinking through what the Catholic tradition has called the infusion, at Baptism, of the theological virtue of faith. When we look at things in faith—in the way God himself has taught us to do—we understand why we were created, why the Word became flesh, why Christ died and rose from the dead, how the Holy Spirit makes us holy, and why we will see God face to face. We were created so that God could share his life with us. God sent his only-begotten Son to save us from the sins that would have made it impossible for us to share in this life. Christ died for this and, rising from the dead, gave us new life. To become holy is to be transformed, through the power of the Holy Spirit at work in the Church, into the image of the Son so that we may be adopted as sons and daughters of the Father. Glory is the consummation of our participation in the communion of the triune God—nothing less than seeing God face to face.

Faith, then, involves a kind of sharing in God's own knowledge of himself, and of things that he has done and is doing in creation and redemption. But it is, in a crucial sense, a *kind* of sharing. The triune God is one in being, action, *and* knowledge. He comprehends in a single act of knowledge the fullness of his Truth and Wisdom. Through the gift of faith, the believer is rendered able to participate in this divine vision, but always and only according to human ways of knowing. We know God truly, but not in the way that he knows himself. Human understanding of the single mystery of divine truth is thus necessarily plural in structure. In this sense, we can speak both of the "mystery of faith"—referring to the single reality of the triune God who is one in being and action and known by us through the gift of faith *and* of the "mysteries of faith"—referring to our way of grasping the diverse elements of the single mystery of God's plan as we experience them in the life of the Church. All the mysteries of faith are facets of the single mystery of faith, which is nothing less than the triune God himself.

Catholic tradition uses the term "revelation" to describe the action and the content of this comprehensive divine disclosure. For the complex grace-enabled human response to this disclosure, the specifically knowledge-related term is faith. The elaboration of this knowledge is called theology.

The existence of the body of knowledge to which revelation gives rise—sometimes called the deposit of faith—warrants the constitution of a field of study distinct from philosophy and the other cognate disciplines that typically investigate these areas of human experience (belief in God, religion, ritual, etc.). It also warrants the distinctiveness of the approach to the materials or sources in which this revelation is found and establishes a vantage point from which to view all other fields of knowledge. The whole body of questions that can arise in theology are studied within the framework of a distinctive field of knowledge constituted by divine revelation.

According to this account, Aquinas was able to secure the scientific status of theology with reference to the model of scientific inquiry he found laid out in Aristotle's logical works.[8] That theology derives its principles from a higher knowledge is not a factor peculiar only to theology. Aquinas noted that other so-called subalternated or subordinate disciplines do the same. Music, for example, depends on principles established not by itself but by arithmetic, while medicine on those established by chemistry and biology. Thus, we could say that music is subalternated to mathematics, since music depends on timing, intervals (of pitch), and other qualities which are measured by mathematics. This does not mean that doing calculus is more noble than playing the French horn, but only that musicians need arithmetic if they are to make headway in some of their

8. See Marie-Dominique Chenu, OP, *Is Theology a Science?* trans. A. H. N. Green-Armytage, (New York: Hawthorne Books, 1959); Edward Schillebeeckx, OP, *Revelation and Theology*, Volume I, trans. N. D. Smith (New York: Sheed and Ward, 1967).

own proper business, e.g., composing harmonies. Nor does it mean that one could reasonably demand that a musician answer questions about higher mathematics, nor that a mathematician must be able to play a musical instrument. It does mean, however, that one discipline depends on the other in such a way that the lower draws its principles from the higher.

According to Aquinas, the fact of such derivation or subalternation does not render the dependent science less scientific. While it is true that theology's principles are per se indemonstrable and thus not knowable in the way that the arithmetical principles of music are, does not rule out the scientific character of theology. Theology is like a derived or subordinate science with respect to the higher knowledge which is the *scientia dei* (God's own knowledge) as such.

For Aquinas, this permits in theology an inquiry of the highest possible degree of rigor—scientific in the sense described by Aristotle in his *Posterior Analytics*. But Aquinas's account is useful for describing the more broadly scientific or scholarly character of a whole range of practices and types of inquiry that fall under the broad umbrella of theology in its current forms. The level of conceptual precision that one is seeking in part determines the degree of rigor and the nature of the methodologies one employs in the study of the questions to which faith gives rise. Approaches that are more analogous to history, literary studies, and sociology than they are to philosophy can have a properly theological character if they are pursued within this framework of a principled acceptance, in faith, of the body of knowledge defined by revelation and thus constitutive for this field of study as such.

This account by no means excludes the possibility that the methods of philosophy, history, literary studies, sociology, or other disciplines could be applied to Christian materials independently of their status as vehicles of divine revelation. In other words, Christian materials can be considered under other descriptions—for example, as literary products or historical monuments—and can be studied with the formal interests associated with history or literary criticism. But in order for such studies to be properly theological, these materials must be viewed under a certain description—namely, as materials bearing revealed content—and with a specified formal interest—namely, as *fides quaerens intellectum*. Theology's distinctiveness as a science or independent discipline, as well as its scientific or scholarly character, are secured with reference to the body of knowledge created by revelation and in principle unknowable apart from it. While it is unlike other disciplines in taking this body of knowledge on faith, it is like many other disciplines whose principles are derived from other disciplines. In addition, it is like all other disciplines in possessing a formal interest in a particular body of knowledge and studying this body of knowledge with principles and methods appropriate to it.

THEOLOGY AND ITS SOURCES

In any scholarly discipline, it is important to know where to look for the answers to our questions. Hence, in Catholic theology as in many other humanistic disciplines, the term "sources" is a handy one for designating the specific body of materials to be consulted and pondered in every theological inquiry.

If theology arises from faith in divine revelation, then it follows that its principal sources will be those in which this divine revelation is found and expressed. According to Catholic teaching, divine revelation is fully and definitively given in Christ who, as the incarnate Word, reveals God and his mystery to humankind. The Second Vatican Council states that Christ "commissioned the Apostles to preach to all men the Gospel which is the source of all saving truth and moral teaching.... This commission was faithfully fulfilled by the Apostles who, by their oral preaching, by example, and by observances handed on what they had received from the lips of Christ, from living with Him, and from what He did, or what they had learned through the prompting of the Holy Spirit. The commission was fulfilled, too, by those Apostles and apostolic men who under the inspiration of the same Holy Spirit committed the message of salvation to writing."[9]

The Sacred Scripture is "the message of salvation" as committed to writing and comprises, as earlier chapters of this Companion recount, the books of the Old and New Testaments. "Tradition" is a term used in an active sense to describe the handing down or transmission of the revelation received by the Apostles, and in a passive sense to describe everything that is transmitted in the creeds, institutions, liturgy, and other constituents of the Church's life.

In the Catholic view, Scripture and Tradition emerge from the same divine source and are inseparable. They are not two parts of a whole revelation, but rather are both faithful witnesses to the one revealed Word. The Apostles handed on "everything which contributes toward the holiness of life and increase in faith of the people of God; and so the Church, in her teaching, life, and worship, [by the help of the Holy Spirit] perpetuates and hands on to all generations all that she herself is, all that she believes."[10] But the Bible, relative to the continuing oral and practical Tradition, is fixed in a way that the latter is not: the text of the Bible is inspired and authored by God (even though he uses human beings as instruments). Scripture is the *norma normans non normata* of Christian faith and practice, and thus the rule or measure for authentic Christianity. This does not mean, however, that the Bible is "self-interpreting" or revelatory on an entirely literal level. As the *Catechism of the Catholic Church* puts it,

the Christian faith is not a "religion of the book." Christianity is the religion of the "Word" of God, a word which is "not a written and mute word, but the Word which is incarnate and living." If the Scriptures are not to remain a dead letter, Christ, the eternal Word of the living God, must, through the Holy Spirit, "open [our] minds to understand the Scriptures."[11]

9. Vatican Council II, *Dei Verbum* (November 18, 1965), 7, in *Vatican Council II: Constitutions, Decrees, Declarations*, ed. Austin Flannery, OP (Northport, NY: Costello Publishing Company, 1996).

10. *Dei Verbum*, 8.

11. *Catechism of the Catholic Church*, 2nd ed., (Vatican City: Libreria Editrice Vaticana, 1994 and 1997), §108.

According to Catholic teaching, Scripture and Tradition make up one deposit of revelation, entrusted to the whole Church. The authentic interpretation of this deposit belongs to the Magisterium of the Church. In this context, the term "Magisterium" (derived from the Latin word *magister* or teacher) designates the official teaching authority of the Church, exercised by the pope and bishops who are the successors of the Apostles and who determine that what is proposed for belief or practice accords with revelation in Scripture and Tradition. This authority is exercised in the name of Christ. The position of the Magisterium with respect to revelation is thus one of service. The Magisterium "listens devoutly," "scrupulously guards," and "faithfully explains" the Word of God, and "draws from this fountain of the living word everything that it proposes to the belief of the faithful as divinely revealed."[12] Scripture, Tradition and the Magisterium "are so connected and associated that one of them cannot stand without the others."[13]

It is not hard to understand, then, why we can say that the primary sources of Catholic theology are Scripture and Tradition, as interpreted by the Magisterium. We will have more to say about Scripture and the Magisterium in the following sections of this essay. At this stage, some general comments about the sources of theology are in order.

Among the principal witnesses to Tradition, Catholic theologians generally concur in listing the following sources: the Fathers of the Church; ecumenical and local councils; papal Magisterium; liturgy and Christian art; the leading doctors, theologians, and canonists of the Church, past and present; and the sense of the faithful. Among the non-theological sources which can be consulted, it has been customary for Catholic theologians to include natural reason, the works of philosophers and jurists, and, more broadly, history and human tradition.

The breadth and comprehensiveness of this traditional list of

12. Vatican Council II, *Dei Verbum*, 10.
13. *Dei Verbum*, 10.

"sources" suggest something of the wide-ranging character of the Catholic conception of theology. Revelation and everything else viewed in the light of revelation: these are the materials to be studied and pondered by *fides quaerens intellectum*. These sources do not of course each possess equal weight or authority in theological inquiry and argument. As the primary vehicles of divine revelation, Scripture and Tradition, as interpreted by the Magisterium, are the privileged or primary sources of all theological inquiry.

The task of determining what the primary sources have to tell us about the particular set of questions we may be considering has, since the seventeenth century, been termed "positive theology" to distinguish it from the task of reflecting on these data in a systematic way in "scholastic" or "speculative" theology.[14] While this terminology is no longer widely used, what might be called the "positive function" of theology remains a fundamental one. An essential phase of every theological inquiry is to establish what the primary sources have to say about the questions that are being addressed. The degree of comprehensiveness and precision that is being sought in the outcome of a particular inquiry to a certain extent determines how extensive this "positive" phase of a theological inquiry needs to be.

"Historical theology" or the "history of doctrine" are the terms normally used to designate the study of the witnesses of Tradition. This is a vast field, comprising many different historical periods and a wide variety of scholarly specialties. Earlier chapters of this Companion provide some indication of the range of materials in this phase of theological inquiry. The terms "biblical exegesis" or "hermeneutics" designate the positive phase of a theological inquiry which has Sacred Scripture as its object. Let us turn to that now.

---

14. See René Latourelle, SJ, *Theology: Science of Salvation*, trans. Sr. Mary Dominic (Staten Island, NY: Alba House, 1979).

THEOLOGY AND SCRIPTURE

Vatican Council II described the relationship of theology and Scripture in words that every theologian would embrace: "The study of the sacred page [Sacred Scripture] should be the very soul of theology." Theology is "powerfully strengthened and constantly rejuvenated" by the Scripture "as it searches out, under the light of faith, all the truth stored up in the mystery of Christ."[15] A central task in every theological inquiry is the determination of what the Scripture has to tell us about the particular question or set of questions which we happen to be addressing. Because our inquiry is a theological one, our reading and study of the Scripture proceeds "under the light of faith," assumes the revealed and inspired character of the passages under consideration, and views them within the perspective of a tradition of doctrinal formulation, theological interpretation, and liturgical usage.

The Catholic Church has generally understood the word "exegesis" to refer to scriptural reading and interpretation conducted within this perspective. The *Catechism of the Catholic Church* provides a handy summary of the Catholic understanding of the kind of interpretation of the Bible which serves properly theological inquiry. It involves using the best critical tools and methods available and reading the Scripture within the context of the Catholic faith. According to the *Catechism*, the hermeneutical criteria for proposed by Vatican Council II for genuinely Catholic theology are as follows:

1. *Be especially attentive "to the content and unity of the whole Scripture."* Different as the books which comprise it may be, Scripture is a unity by reason of the unity of God's plan, of which Christ Jesus is the center and heart, open since his Passover.[16]

2. *Read the Scripture "within the living tradition of the whole Church."* According to the sayings of the Fathers, Sacred Scripture is written principally in the Church's heart rather than in documents

15. Vatican Council II, *Dei Verbum*, 24.
16. *Catechism of the Catholic Church*, §112.

and records, for the Church carries in her Tradition the living memorial of God's Word, and it is the Holy Spirit who gives her the
spiritual interpretation of the Scripture ("according to the spiritual
meaning which the Spirit grants to the Church").[17]

3. *Be attentive to the analogy of faith.* By "analogy of faith" we mean
the coherence of the truths of faith among themselves and within
the whole plan of revelation.[18]

In summary, then, the theological interpretation of the Bible must
take account of its unity, divine authorship, or constant reference
to Christ.

This ecclesial kind of reading has been rendered more difficult
and complex by the emergence in roughly the seventeenth century of a style of historical-critical interpretation that has come to be
seen in hindsight as an alternative way of reading the Bible.[19] As we
have understood the matter so far, the theological way of reading the
Bible can be described as an endeavor to read it precisely as *scripture*—viz., as God's word heard and read in a community of faith.
Historical-critical forms of exegesis, on the other hand, are best described as part of an endeavor to read the Bible as *text*—viz., as a literary product, considered independently of its status as the Church's
scripture, whose historical sources and diverse meanings are susceptible of study and interpretation according to the same scholarly
methods as are applicable to other ancient texts.

A properly theological exegesis needs to be distinguished from
two other kinds of inquiries identified by the term "exegesis," viz.,
historical and literary exegesis. Historical exegesis is essentially reconstructive. Adopting critical methods applicable to texts of all
kinds—not just the Bible—the aim is to identify the events and
sources *behind* the text under examination. The main emphasis of
this kind of criticism is historical, and its practitioners are concerned

17. *Catechism of the Catholic Church*, §113.
18. *Catechism of the Catholic Church*, §114.
19. See David H. Kelsey, *The Uses of Scripture in Current Theology* (Philadelphia: Fortress Press, 1975).

with establishing, by the standards common among modern historians, what realities *probably* gave rise to the text being studied. Literary exegesis, on the other hand, aims to establish what the text means *as written by its author*. This includes establishing what its author may have *meant* to convey to his contemporaries to whom he wrote.

Together these types of exegesis yield literary and historical judgments about the biblical texts *without* reference to the status of Bible as Scripture, understood as inspired by God and containing the revelation he intends to be received by the Church. Ordinarily, literary and historical exegesis enhance one another and influence the third type of exegesis, which is properly theological and which considers the text at hand not simply *as text* but precisely *as Scripture*. Theological exegesis takes cognizance of the text as identified by its place, not only within the whole scriptural corpus, but within and according to patterns of interpretation which logically and imaginatively *precede* commentary on that text *as normative for the community*. Thus, theological exegesis examines texts inasmuch as they relate to faith, doctrine, theology, and liturgy.[20]

This is not to say that theological interpretation is properly separable from historical or literary study. On the contrary, historical and literary exegesis serve to ground and limit theology's historical and literary assertions about a given text and influence the theological interpreter's rational and imaginative construal of revelation as a whole. Yet whatever impact literary or historical studies may have on theological exegesis as such, it is not the case that they supply a hermeneutical context sufficient for the task of theology. The use of Scripture as a rule or authority requires (absolutely speaking) an interpretive horizon or principles by which the reader can sift and make sense of the texts at hand. All Christian communities share a conviction that the theological exegesis must take as authoritative the trinitarian, Christological and soteriological patterns discernible

20. See Stephen E. Fowl, *The Theological Interpretation of Scripture* (Oxford: Blackwell, 1997).

in the Scripture and, at least in part, formulated as doctrinal rules by the great ecumenical councils.

A book composed under the influence of the Holy Spirit is still a book, with a language, genre, historical setting, and other dimensions which cannot all be entirely accidental to the meaning of the text. It is plain that a knowledge of the "humanity" of Scripture—everything from its vocabulary and grammar to its poetic devices and the circumstances of its composition—can be helpful for understanding the biblical texts *as Scripture*. At the same time, historical and literary inquiries have an integrity and purposes of their own and exegetical studies of the Bible as *text* have a legitimacy independent of the theological uses to which their results may be put. But this implies that theological exegesis possesses its own integrity as an intellectual inquiry (or, as medieval theologians would have said, a science), with a distinctive set of principles which must guide its appropriation of the results of historical and literary studies.

THEOLOGY AND THE CHURCH

With Scripture and Tradition, the Magisterium of the Church is among the primary sources for theology. The dependence of theology upon the Magisterium needs to be located within in the broad context of the life of Church. For the Church is the locus of a truth which she did not generate but which she received as a gift whose center is the truth of Jesus Christ. The function of the Magisterium is to guard and teach this truth in its entirety which the Church received as a gift and is bound to hand on. Both the Magisterium and theology are servants of a prior truth, received in the Church as a gift.

The gift of truth received in the Church thus establishes the framework for the actual practice of the discipline of theology. This ecclesially received truth, as articulated in the deposit of faith and handed on by the Magisterium, constitutes not an *extrinsic* authority that poses odious limits on an inquiry that would otherwise be free but an *intrinsic* source and measure that gives theology its identity and finality as an intellectual activity. "Is theology for which the Church is no longer meaningful really a theology in the proper sense of the word?"[21] Examined independently of the assent of faith and the mediation of the ecclesial community, the texts, institutions, rites and beliefs of the Catholic Church can be the focus of the humanistic, philosophical and social scientific inquiries that together constitute the field of religious studies. But Catholic theology is a different kind of inquiry. Its precise scope is to seek the intelligibility of a truth received in faith by the theologian who is himself a member of the ecclesial community that is "the place of truth."[22]

A theological inquiry is thus free to seek the truth within limits imposed, not by an intrusive external authority, but by the nature of his discipline as such. "Freedom of research, which the academic community holds most precious, means an openness to accepting the truth that emerges at the end of an investigation in which no element has intruded that is foreign to the methodology corresponding to the object under study."[23] The acceptance of the authority of Scripture and doctrines in theology is "not a limitation but rather the charter of its existence and freedom to be itself."[24] The freedom of inquiry proper to theology, is the "hallmark of a rational discipline whose object is given by Revelation, handed on and interpreted in the Church under the authority of the Magisterium, and received by faith. These givens have the force of principles. To eliminate them would mean to cease doing theology."[25] The principles of theology are derived from revelation, as we have seen, and constitute the discipline as such. In accepting them, the theologian is simply being true to the nature of his subject, and to his vocation as a scholar in this field.

21. Joseph Ratzinger, *Principles of Catholic Theology*, trans. Sr. M. Frances McCarthy (San Francisco: Ignatius, 1987), 323.

22. See Walter Kasper, *Theology and Church*, trans. Margaret Kohl (New York: Crossroad, 1989).

23. Congregation for the Doctrine of the Faith, *Donum Veritatis* (Instruction on the Ecclesial Vocation of the Theologian), §12, *Origins* 20 (1990), 117–26.

24. Avery Dulles, SJ, *The Craft of Theology: From Symbol to System* (New York: Crossroad, 1992), 168.

25. Congregation for the Doctrine of the Faith, *Donum Veritatis*, §12.

The Catholic understanding of theology and its relation to the Magisterium is contested wherever what has been called the "individualistic foundational rationalism" of modernity holds sway.[26] But, as we have seen, the Church has a solid, well-substantiated, and historically warranted rationale for its account of the nature of theology as an intellectual discipline of a particular sort, and of the inner connection between this discipline and magisterial teaching. It is central to the convictions of the Catholic Church, and indeed of the Christian tradition as such, to give priority to a theonomous rationality—one that is exercised within the liberating order of divine truth—rather than to an autonomous rationality whose only measure is human reason. While it is true that the basis for this understanding is itself a properly theological one that is rooted in fundamental Christian convictions about the gift of truth and its reception in the ecclesial community, in the light certain postliberal intellectual trends, the Church's claims for the community-and tradition-dependent character of theology are more readily intelligible.[27] Whatever other challenges it may pose, the postliberal intellectual climate is, to a certain extent, more favorable to the defense of the principle of theonomous rationality that is crucial for the Catholic understanding of theology.

It would be a mistake to exaggerate the singularity of the dependence of Catholic theology on the authority of the Magisterium. Authoritative criteria and professional bodies exist in almost all intellectual disciplines. Authorities function to maintain the quality and standards of many of these disciplines. "The acceptance of a certain degree of authority—which those subject to it regard as more or less legitimate, which they accept more or less easily, and which they challenge only exceptionally—is the normal state of affairs."[28]

---

26. George A. Lindbeck, *The Church in a Postliberal Age* (Grand Rapids, MI: Eerdmans, 2002), 7.

27. See George A. Lindbeck, *The Nature of Doctrine* (Philadelphia: Westminster Press, 1984).

28. Richard T. DeGeorge, *The Nature and Limits of Authority* (Lawrence: University Press of Kansas, 1985), 1.

In this sense, the Catholic understanding of the relationship of theology to the Magisterium has formal parallels to other academic disciplines in which authorities serve to foster rather than undermine intellectual and scholarly integrity.

THEOLOGY AND ITS SUB-FIELDS

The tendency for related questions to be considered together has been a factor over the centuries in the emergence of sub-fields and specializations in Catholic theology. The many questions concerning the Blessed Trinity, for instance, or creation, or Jesus Christ, or the Church have been grouped and considered together (as the titles of the following chapters of this section of the *Companion* indicate). So it has happened that one set of theological sub-fields is topical, comprising the areas of Christology, anthropology, ecclesiology, canon law, and so on.

Another set is more functional, concerned with determining what the sources have to say about the main questions of theology.[29] Thus, the exegetical and historical functions of theology have given rise to a number of sub-fields, such as Old Testament and New Testament exegesis, biblical theology, patristic theology, history of doctrines and historical theology, and liturgical theology. In appropriating the results of inquiries in these sub-fields, the challenge to maintain a properly theological perspective is a continual one.

It is common now for individual theologians to concentrate their work on the questions that arise in one or another of the particular sub-fields that have now become stable features in the organization of theological studies, teaching and research. With this degree of specialization, there is always the threat of the fragmentation of theology. But the unity of theology will be sustained wherever its various sub-fields are viewed not as distinct disciplines but as integral parts of a single discipline with the same principles and the same

---

29. See Bernard J. F. Lonergan, SJ, *Method in Theology* (New York: Herder & Herder, 1972).

dependence on revelation and the Church. While theologians specialize in certain groups of questions, there is a widespread recognition of the need to acknowledge and maintain the fundamental unity of the discipline.

The broadest division of labor is mapped out under the rubrics of fundamental theology, dogmatic theology, moral theology, spiritual theology and pastoral theology. With roots in earlier periods of theological history, this division emerges clearly in the seventeenth century and reflects a natural grouping of the characteristic questions raised in theology. Some observations on this division of labor are in order.

For the most part, divine revelation in Scripture and Tradition, and thus the Church's teaching, are directed to leading us to salvation and holiness—to the present and future enjoyment of ultimate communion with the Blessed Trinity and with other persons in lives of ever-deepening charity. Through her teaching activities, the Church seeks to cultivate the intellectual and moral dispositions necessary for this enjoyment, to enhance understanding of its profound meaning, and to commend it to others. The whole ensemble of Catholic doctrine—the deposit of faith—embraces all the teachings that together serve to shape and direct our lives toward holiness. As the *Catechism of the Catholic Church* demonstrates, such doctrines answer questions about what must be believed, which courses of action should be pursued and which shunned, which interior dispositions must be cultivated and which avoided, and so on, in order to enjoy the life of ultimate communion to the full. Dogmatic theology concentrates mainly on questions about what Christians believe (the Creed), while moral and spiritual theology concentrate on questions about Christian life.

The work of **dogmatic theology** (also known as systematic theology) is chiefly to elaborate a penetrating knowledge of faith by identifying the mutual connections among the mysteries of the faith. There is a conviction at work here, as we have seen, that the entire ensemble of the mysteries and doctrines of the Catholic faith possesses an internal intelligibility that reflects the divine truth itself and that can be exhibited through contemplative prayer and theological inquiry. It is this intelligibility that dogmatic theology seeks above all else.

The task of **moral theology** and **spiritual theology** is a related one, except that it concentrates on those doctrines that concern the conduct of Christian life (holiness, the commandments, virtues, beatitudes, gifts of the Holy Spirit, and so on) and connects them with the all-embracing mysteries of trinitarian communion, incarnation, redemption, grace, and ecclesiology, as well as theological anthropology.

Much of the present chapter has been concerned with the sub-fields of **fundamental theology** and theological methodology. Typically, the questions that get attention in fundamental theology are those concerned not with *primary doctrines* (what must be believed and undertaken in order to grow in the life of grace and charity), but with *governing doctrines* (how it can be known reliably that such things should be believed and undertaken).[30] Governing doctrines concern such questions as the following: Is this really a doctrine of our community? What procedures do we have for deciding? Is this doctrine more important than other doctrines? Is it consistent with them? Is it appropriate to develop understandings that seem implicit in our doctrines? Should these also be considered as doctrines? Who in the community is authorized to decide?

The history of the Catholic Church has afforded many occasions for developing and invoking governing doctrines. But in recent times the sub-field of fundamental theology, along with its close relatives, apologetics, and foundational theology, have been of increasingly prominent interest to theologians.[31] One reason for this development is that questions of the authenticity of the primary Catholic

30. See William A. Christian, *Doctrines of Religious Communities* (New Haven, CT: Yale University Press, 1987).

31. See Gerald O'Collins, SJ, *Fundamental Theology* (New York: Paulist Press, 1981); Karl Rahner, SJ, *Foundations of Christian Faith*, trans. William V. Dych (New York: Seabury Press, 1978).

doctrines have been pressed upon the Church almost without interruption for the past two hundred years. Thus, for example, more explicit attention has been devoted to the doctrine of revelation during this period than in all the previous centuries taken together. Throughout this period, the Church has gradually formulated a range of previously implicit governing doctrines to affirm that her primary doctrines authentically express what is contained in Scripture and Tradition, that Scripture and Tradition themselves constitute the single source of revelation, that revelation involves a real divine communication mediated by Christ, the prophets and apostles, that the scriptural record of this revelation is divinely inspired, that the liturgical and doctrinal tradition embodies communally authorized readings of the Scripture, and that the Church under the Successor of Peter is divinely guided in its formulation of primary doctrines of faith and morals. In addition, the increasingly explicit formulations of the doctrine of the Magisterium over the past two centuries is part of the evolution that represented a response to the growing need for a clear articulation of the governing doctrines of the Catholic faith. In circumstances in which the authenticity of Catholic doctrines was a matter of persistent and unrelenting controversy, it was natural that doctrinal developments addressing this issue should take place along several fronts at once: the nature of revelation, the interpretation of Scripture, the authority of Tradition, and the scope of the Church's teaching office.

Pastoral theology is the systematic reflection on questions concerning the activity of the Church in building up the Body of Christ in society and is thus closely related to other sub-fields like missionary theology, ecumenical theology, theology of religions, and political theology. In this connection, it should be noted that new cultural and social situations, new theories, and new scientific discoveries are among the factors that can give rise to new questions for the Church and for theologians. Late twentieth-century theology saw the emergence of many new types of theological inquiry keyed to a range of

social, cultural, philosophical, and scientific contexts.[32] A crucial
challenge for theologians who reflect on these questions in a formal way is to maintain a properly theological perspective—one that
gives priority to the truth of revelation as the Church understands
and confesses it.[33]

32. See Fergus Kerr, *Twentieth Century Catholic Theology: From Chenu to John Paul II*
(Oxford: Blackwell, 2006).
33. See Hans Frei, *Types of Christian Theology* (New Haven, CT: Yale University
Press, 1992).

CHAPTER 2

Communion and Magisterium

Teaching Authority and the Culture of Grace

THE SOCIAL SCIENCES

It is tempting to frame ecclesiological issues such as the nature of the Magisterium in the terms provided by the social sciences and, more narrowly, by management theory. As a vast and complex international community with a distinctive polity, the Catholic Church seems to invite analysis in just such terms.

Most of the 929 million members of the Catholic Church (about eighteen percent of the world's population) belong to the more than two hundred thousand parishes that comprise the Church's 1,851 dioceses. This community is served by about three thousand bishops, by well over four hundred thousand priests and deacons, and by many thousands of lay ministers.[1] The Catholic Church is unique among the world's religious communities in gathering this large, multi-layered membership in a hierarchically ordered worldwide communion. Leadership of the community is exercised by the bishops in union with the pope and grouped both in an international

Originally published in *Modern Theology* 9 (1993): 403–18.
1. *1993 Catholic Almanac*, ed. Felician Foy (Huntington, IN: Our Sunday Visitor, 1992), 367.

college of bishops and in national conferences. Without prejudice to the collegial structure of the episcopacy, Catholic polity understands papal ministry to involve a universal and immediate jurisdiction over the whole community. Among the chief roles exercised by the leadership of the pope and bishops in their overall governance of the community is the official proclamation of Catholic doctrine. The role of the Magisterium—as it came to be called in the last century—is to insure a common expression of faith in doctrine and life throughout the culturally and theologically diverse worldwide communion.

When undertaking analysis of complex religious phenomena such as those presented by Catholic polity, the social sciences typically deploy a range of basic concepts such as belief system or worldview, legitimacy and legitimation, ideology, organization, management, bureaucracy, and the like.[2] To be sure, there is little consensus among social scientists and theologians about how such concepts should be applied to religious communities. Depending on the theoretical commitments of its practitioners, social explanation of religion tends to fix on ideational or organizational factors, or on some combination of these. Thus, the sociology of knowledge views the Catholic community as a social construct that enshrines the all- encompassing rationale for the ethos and institutions of the wider social world of which the community is a part. In this perspective, the Magisterium is seen as one of the structures by which the community maintains and adjusts society's "sacred canopy."[3] In more empirically oriented sociology of religion, the Catholic community is studied as a type of organization with distinctive membership, management and bureaucratic arrangements, and specific patterns of

2. For a general orientation to the social explanation of religious communities, see the articles on the anthropological (Clifford Geertz), sociological (Robert N. Bellah) and psychological (James E. Dittes) study of religion, as well as Bryan R. Wilson, "Religious Organization," in *International Encyclopedia of the Social Sciences*, ed. David L. Sills (New York: Macmillan, 1968), Vol. 13, pp. 398–421 and 428–37.

3. An expression made famous as the title of Peter Berger's *The Sacred Canopy: Elements of a Sociological Theory of Religion* (Garden City, NY: Doubleday, 1966).

internal and external interaction. Here, magisterium is viewed largely as an aspect of community management: through appropriate bureaucratic structures, the leadership expresses and enforces a level of cognitive uniformity sufficient to insure the community's organizational stability and effectiveness.

Over the past three decades, the application of various methodologies of social analysis to the study of ecclesiology has generated a large body of work.[4] But the validity and fruitfulness of the entire enterprise have not gone uncontested.

Lately, John Milbank has argued persuasively that "all twentieth century sociology of religion can be exposed as a secular policing of the sublime."[5] Milbank contends that social explanation of religion—inevitably and in principle—represents an effort on the part of secular reason to circumscribe, encompass and control the religious, and particularly the Christian, realm. Whether or not Milbank's critique of sociology of religion can be sustained in all its details, it seems clear that no purely functional explanation can capture the specifically religious and theological meanings embedded in the structures of Catholic polity. Even exponents of such explanation are prepared to acknowledge this much.[6] But Milbank's point is a stronger one. He argues that functional explanations do not simply

4. For a general view of applications to Catholic ecclesiology, see James A. Ecks, "The Changing Church: Contributions from Sociology," *American Benedictine Review* 23 (1972): 385–96. For a pioneering and still influential Reformed theological appropriation of sociology of religion, see James M. Gustafson, *Treasure in Human Vessels* (New York: Harper & Brothers, 1961). For a full-blown sociological account of Catholic ecclesiology, see Patrick Granfield, *Ecclesial Cybernetics* (New York: Macmillan, 1973). For some examples of the application of social explanation to the exercise of authority in the Catholic Church, see Karl Gabriel, "Power in the Contemporary Church"; Wigand Siebel, "The Exercise of Power in Today's Church"; and Patrick Granfield, "Legitimation and Bureaucratisation of Ecclesial Power," in *Power in the Church*, ed. James Provost and Knut Wolf, *Concilium* 197 (Edinburgh: T&T Clark, 1988), 29–38, 39–49, 86–93. For applications to teaching authority, see Edward Schillebeeckx, OP, "The Magisterium and Ideology," and F.-X. Kaufmann, "The Sociology of Knowledge and the Problem of Authority," in *Authority in the Church*, ed. Piet F. Fransen (Leuven: Leuven University Press, 1983), 5–31.

5. John Milbank, *Theology and Social Theory: Beyond Secular Reason* (Oxford: Basil Blackwell, 1990), 106.

6. See Joseph A. Komonchak, "Ecclesiology and Social Theory: A Methodological Essay," *The Thomist* 45 (1981): 262–83.

complement properly religious and theological explanations, but supplant them. Far from being neutral tools of analysis for the study of religious phenomena, the explanatory concepts employed by the social sciences advance a secular redescription of these phenomena.[7]

Take the Magisterium, for instance. In functional explanations that fix on ideational factors, the Magisterium is seen as contributing to the overall maintenance of the prevailing ideology by which contingent social arrangements or privileged social status are seen to be in some sense transcendently warranted. In conjunction with analysis drawing upon organizational categories, the role of the Magisterium is understood in strictly pragmatic terms, as if cognitive uniformity were to be preserved no matter what the contents of the affirmations in question. The perceived credibility and legitimacy of the community's teacher-managers can thus seem to have greater weight than the truth of what they uphold. The ascendancy of one set of viewpoints over others in contention can come to be viewed chiefly as a function of bureaucratic power struggles in which self-interest and self-preservation are the chief objectives. Resisting innovation, the Magisterium is seen as the guardian of the status quo. Prevailing ideological interests strive to circumscribe the public expression of alternative opinions. When the Church is viewed largely in organizational terms, the Magisterium is understood to ensure that the community will maintain an adequate level of internal cohesion and a united front in its external relations. This managerial function is administered through a set of bureaucratic procedures that help to enforce conformity in public expression of the Christian faith by theologians or others. The bureaucracy devotes its attention to maintaining the stability of the organization, the privileged status of managers currently in power, and the curial positions of their appointees. Reform can be achieved through personnel diversification, improved procedures, and revised ideology.

When framed in such terms, social analysis of the Magisterium leaves little room for doctrinally shaped accounts in which primacy

7. See Milbank, *Theology and Social Theory*, 113–40.

is accorded to concepts of grace, revelation, communion, universal truth, and the like. Increasing fragmentation and specialization in the practices of Catholic theological inquiry and education render doctrinally ruled appropriation of sociological study of the Church difficult if not impossible. Indeed, theological descriptions of the role of the Magisterium will in turn themselves be susceptible to sociological redescription as forms of rationalization in which the community's prevailing beliefs and practices are justified and defended. This is the sort of difficulty Milbank has in view.

While the Catholic communion clearly has the form of a complex international organization, the triune God who is its source and focus is understood both to transcend and to encompass the social realities of the community. Although it must take a social form, the Catholic Christian community is essentially not a social construct but a divine creation.[8] It constitutes the visible expression of the divine grace by which created persons are drawn into communion with each other in the eternal communion of the uncreated Persons of the blessed Trinity. Precisely as a worldwide community, it is the sign of and summons to the universal communion which God foreordained as the destiny of humankind in Jesus Christ. For this reason, functional explanation of ecclesial structures cannot proceed independently of theological explanation. As social realities, ecclesial structures already embody a "supernaturalized" level of human existence: an imperfect, yet nonetheless real, participation in the divine life of trinitarian communion.

It follows that redescription in the terms of a fundamentally social (secular?) narrative cannot, without substantial loss, replace a properly religious and theological description of the role of the Magisterium—a description framed not by the culture of management but by the culture of grace. A Christian as distinct from a secular narrative of the Church and its polity will depict ecclesial communion as a gift of the triune God.

---

8. See Johann Auer, *The Church: The Universal Sacrament of Salvation* (Washington, DC: The Catholic University of America Press, 1993), especially 7–14.

TRINITARIAN COMMUNION

The fundamental core of the narrative the Church recounts is that the triune God has undertaken to be in communion with humankind. Christ himself affirms this: "If a man loves me, he will keep my word, and my Father will love him, and we will come to him and make our home with him" (Jn 14:23). The fundamental truth about this ultimate communion is that it is a personal one: each person is invited to enjoy the communion of the Persons of the blessed Trinity and, in this way, a transformed communion with all other persons.

The Church's narrative of human history and society is essentially trinitarian in structure.[9] It recounts the stages by which this ultimate communion has been pursued and achieved by God, and where its final consummation lies. To employ a central Pauline motif, through Christ human persons come to enjoy by adoption the triune familial life that Christ the Son enjoys by nature. Since the grace that comes through Christ overcomes human finitude and sin, it entails both enablement and restoration. It involves enablement because enjoyment of trinitarian communion is "natural" only for uncreated persons; created persons can enjoy it only by grace. Thus, human life in grace is life lived at a new level, one enabled by the triune God for the sake of communion in the trinitarian life. The grace of Christ involves restoration as well. No sinner can begin to enjoy ultimate communion without reconciliation and conversion in continual conformity to the cross.

But if this communion is personal, it must also be interpersonal. It affords nothing less than human engagement and communication with the triune God in knowledge and love. Faith, hope and charity

9. This discussion depends at many points on Thomas Aquinas's theology of grace; see especially *Summa theologiae* I, q. 43, a. 3; q. 62; q. 93; q. 95; I-II, qq.109–114; q. 62; II-II, qq. 1–46; III, q. 8; qq. 46–49; qq. 53–57; qq. 60–62. See also "Some Aspects of the Church Understood as Communion," *Origins* 22 (June 25, 1992): 108–12; J.-M. R. Tillard, OP, *Church of Churches. The Ecclesiology of Communion* (Collegeville, MN: Liturgical Press, 1992), and *Chair de l'Eglise, Chair du Christ: Aux Sources de l'Ecclesiologie de Communion* (Paris: Cerf, 1992).

are properly "theological" virtues because they permit precisely this level of engagement with God. The life of faith, hope and love in grace is the life of ultimate communion begun here on earth.

Those raised up with Christ and in Christ are joined to each other by the Spirit. No human community can have the depth of the communion of those called in Christ to share the life of the Spirit in the Church. No sinful community can have the reconciliation that overcomes obstructive human pride, factionalism, and selfishness. Through the sacramental and liturgical life of the Church, Christ's grace remains a permanent source of vitality and renewal for the community that is, in a true sense, his body. In this way, ultimate communion becomes the foundation of authentic human community. Part of the Church's mission in the world is to summon all human persons to share in this communion and to resist the social and political constraints that obstruct its cultivation. The Church thus has a story to tell not only to its members but to the whole human race. It is a story whose divinely assured happy ending will come only when the entire human race is united in communion with the triune God.

In the perspective of the culture of grace, then, all of the activities of the Catholic community—including its teaching activities—can be understood only when seen as directed toward fostering ultimate communion. It is in this context that a properly theological account of the role of magisterium can be advanced.

FAITH AND TRUTH

Since "faith comes from what is heard" (Rom 10:17), the teaching and learning activities of the Catholic community are essential to the cultivation of ultimate communion. Together with hope and love, faith is an element in the personal engagement and intercommunication with the triune God which the life of grace makes possible for human persons. The teaching activities of the community—with the Magisterium occupying a unique place among them—contribute to engendering and sustaining faith.

In revelation through scripture and tradition, the Catholic community as a whole has received the gift of God's truth, viz., the truth that is God himself who thus initiates ultimate communion with human persons. The church is—in Walter Kasper's felicitous phrase—"the place of truth."[10] To hear the truth, to learn it, to teach it, to believe it: these are basic activities in the Church.

As the recipient of the gift of First Truth, the community is bound to commend this truth to its members and to proclaim it to persons outside its ambit. In other words, a teaching role belongs to the whole community as such both with respect to its own members and with respect to the wider world. "We believe and so we speak" (2 Cor 4:13). Christian instruction occurs at many levels, beginning with that provided by the family and the local community who are the first teachers of the faith. Parents, pastors, catechists, and religious teachers furnish initial instruction in the Christian faith for children and adult new members of the community. Preachers, lecturers, and popular authors provide Christian instruction in a variety of media and forums. Theologians and other scholarly specialists perform a distinctive instructional service for the community through their dedication to a life of study, reflection, and authorship. Finally, the pope and the bishops—both together and singly—exercise their apostolic office through authoritative teaching of different degrees of solemnity. Authentic teaching and learning thus continue throughout the community on a variety of occasions and at several levels.[11]

This structure of teaching and learning illumines something of the unique role played by the Magisterium within the teaching activities of the community. For in this structure is embodied a central feature of the mystery of the truth present in the Church: this truth is a gift, not an acquisition whose discovery and possession can be claimed as a human or even an ecclesial accomplishment.

10. Walter Kasper, "The Church as the Place of Truth," in *Theology and Church* (New York: Crossroad, 1989), 129–47.

11. See Ladislas Orsy, SJ, *The Church: Learning and Teaching* (Wilmington, DE: Michael Glazier, 1987).

Revelation is itself a grace. Hence, there is a real sense in which no follower of Christ can assume the role of teacher: with respect to the divine truth, there is only one Teacher, and everyone else is a learner. This structure of human receptivity in the face of the superabundant grace of God is fundamental to every aspect of Christian communal and individual existence. It has an important place in the teaching and learning activities of the community as well. Openness to authoritative teaching on the part of members of the Catholic community replicates the structure of receptivity that characterizes human dispositions in the face of divine gifts. Just as the apostles received the gift of truth from Christ, so do bishops accept it from the apostles, the community from the bishops, pupils from their teachers, congregations from their pastors, children from their parents, and so on. The teaching and learning activities of the community thus reflect the radical receptivity with which all persons in the Church accept the word of the Divine Teacher and place their faith in him as First Truth.

It is the gift of God's truth that establishes the reality of ultimate communion in the Church. Yet the teaching activities of the community play a part in commending this truth. What is more, according to Catholic doctrine, the teaching of the pope and bishops—the official Magisterium, properly speaking—plays a decisive role.

"Faith comes from what is heard, and what is heard comes by the preaching of Christ" (Rom 10:17). Encompassed within the grace of ultimate communion, the learning that transpires in the community remains personal and interpersonal. Acceptance of the word of the Divine Teacher is a personal acceptance of the triune God. The faith that it engenders and sustains is a theological virtue: God as First Truth is its primary and immediate object.[12] The teaching activities

---

12. This paragraph adopts a Thomistic position on much-debated topics within Catholic theology, viz., the formal object of faith and the role of Church teaching in the genesis and act of faith. See Thomas Aquinas, *Summa theologiae* II-II, q. 1, aa. 1 & 10. For a general orientation to the debate and for a compressed argument for the Thomistic view, see Thomas C. O'Brien, Appendices 2 and 3, in Thomas Aquinas, *Summa theologiae*, Blackfriars edition (New York: McGraw-Hill, and London: Eyre & Spottiswoode,

of the community play an important part in the genesis of faith. But in the act of faith itself, it is God himself who is attained. Because of faith in God, the individual believer accepts all that the community teaches about him. The act of faith is "essentially an act of union."[13] What the Church proposes in its teaching is acknowledged as the contents that must be believed on the basis of the interior grace of faith that accepts God himself as First Truth. But, if through faith in God the believer assents to truths about him as these are expressed by the community, then the community exercises a crucial role, especially when it engages its official teaching authority. How can what is distinctive about this role be specified?

DOCTRINES

For the most part, the teaching and learning activities of the Catholic community have the objective of shaping the lives of its members with a view to the present and future enjoyment of ultimate communion with the triune God and with other human persons in ever-deepening charity. Through these teaching activities, the community seeks to cultivate the intellectual and moral dispositions appropriate to this enjoyment, to enhance understanding and appreciation of its profound meaning, and to commend it to non-members. In the course of teaching about these matters, the community will inevitably be engaged in proposing its doctrines. The ensemble

1974), Vol. 31, pp. 186–204. On II-II, q. 1, a. 10, see Yves M.-J. Congar, OP, "St. Thomas and the Infallibility of the Papal Magisterium," *The Thomist* 38 (1974): 81–105. Extensive discussion with references to the scholastic controversy can be found in Reginald Garrigou-Lagrange, OP, *De Revelatione*, Vol. 1, (Rome: F. Ferrari, 1929), 458–514, and, with less detail, in his *The Theological Virtues, Vol. 1: Faith* (St. Louis: B. Herder, 1965), 51–84, 154–55. For a brief discussion of some of this material, see Rene Latourelle, *Theology of Revelation* (New York: Alba House, 1966), 181–85. In "The Teaching Office of the Church," *Theological Investigations* XII (London: Darton, Longman & Todd, 1974), 24, Karl Rahner makes the crucial point succinctly when he says that, ultimately, the Catholic Christian "believes in the authority of the teaching office because he already believes in God."

13. Joseph Ratzinger, *Principles of Catholic Theology* (San Francisco: Ignatius Press, 1987), 329.

of Catholic doctrines encompasses the entire range of beliefs and practices that serve to shape life in a distinctively Catholic Christian pattern. Such doctrines answer questions about what must be believed, which courses of action should be pursued and which shunned, which interior dispositions must be cultivated and which avoided, and so on, in order to enjoy the life of ultimate communion to the full. Much of the teaching activity of the community, including the authoritative teaching of the Magisterium, is concerned with questions of this kind.

But another range of questions can arise. These are concerned not with what must be believed and undertaken in order to grow in the life of grace and charity, but with how it can be known reliably that such things should be believed and undertaken. It is with questions of this second type that the Magisterium has been especially concerned. Indeed, as we shall observe, the doctrine of the Magisterium can be construed as itself a partial answer to questions of this second form.

William A. Christian, Sr., has suggested that, in response to these two sorts of question, the teaching activities of religious communities can be understood to generate doctrines of two broad types: "primary doctrines," and "governing doctrines."[14] According to Christian, primary doctrines respond to the first set of questions. Thus, in its primary doctrines, a religious community commends the beliefs and practices that constitute its distinctive pattern of life.

Governing doctrines, on the other hand, respond to questions of the second type, such as the following: Is this really a doctrine of our community? Do we have procedures for deciding? Is this doctrine more important than other doctrines? Does what we teach about this matter mesh with what we teach on other topics? How do our doctrines relate to new information or new discoveries in science or history, or to new techniques in medicine and research? What is the bearing of our doctrines on issues which they do not explicitly address

14. William A. Christian, Sr., *Doctrines of Religious Communities: A Philosophical Study* (New Haven, CT: Yale University Press, 1987), Chapter 1.

or did not even envisage? Is it appropriate to develop understandings that seem implicit in our doctrines? Should we count these new understandings as doctrines? Who in the community is authorized to say one way or the other? These and similar questions relate to issues of the authenticity, ranking, consistency, derivation, and scope of a community's doctrines. In developing answers to questions of this type, a community generates and expresses what Christian calls "doctrines about doctrines" or, more simply, governing doctrines.

The history of the Catholic community and of other Christian communities has afforded many occasions for developing and invoking governing doctrines. Particularly germane to our topic is the fact that questions of the authenticity of its primary doctrines have been pressed upon the Catholic community almost without interruption for the past two hundred years. Thus, for example, more systematic attention has been given to the doctrine of revelation by both theologians and official Church bodies during this period than in all the previous centuries taken together. Largely in response to the challenge of modern philosophers and historians, the community has been compelled to articulate as official doctrines its operative but often largely implicit teachings about the sources of the truth of its primary doctrines.[15] Throughout this period, the community has gradually formulated a range of governing doctrines concerning the authenticity of its doctrines: to show that its primary doctrines (and governing doctrines as well) authentically express what is contained in scripture and tradition, that scripture and tradition themselves constitute the single source of revelation, that revelation involves in a real sense a divine communication mediated through prophets and apostles, that the scriptural record of this revelation is inspired, that the liturgical and doctrinal tradition embodies communally authorized readings of the scripture, and that the Church under the bishop of Rome is divinely guided in its formulation of primary doctrines about faith and morals.

15. See George A. Lindbeck, *The Nature of Doctrine* (Philadelphia: Westminster, 1984), 74, for the distinction between official and operative doctrines.

MAGISTERIUM

The now almost restricted use of the term "magisterium" as a designation for the official teaching authority of the Church is a relatively
recent development.[16] In scholastic usage, the term was more likely to have referred to the teaching authority of university faculties
of theology than to that of the pope and the bishops. This semantic
fact should not be taken to imply that the pope and bishops came
for the first time to be recognized as authoritative teachers in the
community only in the nineteenth century. On the contrary, historians have shown conclusively that their role as authoritative teachers
was recognized from the earliest Christian times.[17] As successors to
the apostles in their leadership of the Church, the pope and bishops
were seen to exercise this official teaching role particularly when as-
sembled in council or synod, or when deciding on some disputed
point of doctrine. Precisely in exercising this role, they relied heav-
ily on the assistance and counsel of the distinguished theological
faculties of the Christian world. The theologians and doctors were
themselves the subject of a governing doctrine: consensus among
the doctors was an important criterion to be invoked in judging the
authenticity of new doctrinal or theological proposals. For much of
the period from the medieval emergence of university theology until the end of the eighteenth century this situation prevailed with
minor variations throughout the Catholic world.[18]

16. Yves M.-J. Congar, OP, "A Semantic History of the Term 'Magisterium,'" in *Readings in Moral Theology 3: The Magisterium and Theology*, ed. Charles E. Curran and Richard A. McCormick, SJ (Ramsey, NJ: Paulist Press, 1982), 297–313.

17. In *Infallible? An Inquiry* (Garden City, NY: Doubleday, 1972), Hans Küng argued that theologians rather than bishops are the inheritors of the special teaching role
exercised by the prophets and teachers of the New Testament. Francis A. Sullivan, SJ,
convincingly refutes this contention in *Magisterium: Teaching Authority in the Catholic
Church* (Mahwah, NJ: Paulist Press, 1983), 35–51.

18. For this and the following paragraph, see Avery Dulles, SJ, "The Magisterium in
History: Theological Considerations," in *A Church to Believe In* (New York: Crossroad,
1982), 103–17. For the New Testament, see Joseph A. Fitzmyer, "The Office of Teaching
in the Christian Church According to the New Testament," in *Teaching Authority and
Infallibility in the Church*, ed. Paul C. Empie, T. Austin Murphy, and Joseph A. Burgess

The French Revolution, the Napoleonic Wars, and the rise of European state nationalism brought an abrupt end to this situation at the beginning of the nineteenth century. The ensuing secularization of the universities, the decline of the religious orders, and the collapse of the theological faculties contributed to the creation of what might be called a "magisterial" vacuum in the Church at a moment when it faced a range of critical intellectual challenges. As a result, beginning at least with the pontificate of Gregory XVI, the papal teaching office—the "Magisterium"—came into new prominence among the teaching activities of the Church and became, within a few decades, the focus of the conciliar definition of infallibility.

It is important to see this evolution within the context of the growing need for a clearer articulation of the community's governing doctrines. In circumstances in which the authenticity of Christian doctrines was a matter of persistent controversy, it was natural, as we have seen, that doctrinal developments addressing this issue should take place along several fronts at once: the nature of revelation, the interpretation of scripture, the authority of tradition, and the scope of the Church's teaching office. Each of these topics was central to the agenda of Vatican Council I and, in varying degrees, remains at the center of current debate. From the vantage point of the end of the twentieth century, it seems clear that the definition of papal infallibility at Vatican I was but an early stage in the Church's continuing endeavor to articulate a consistent set of governing doctrines in the face of modern challenges. Viewed in this context, the nineteenth-century emphasis on the Magisterium will appear, not

---

(Minneapolis: Augsburg, 1978), 186–212. For this and subsequent periods, see Eugene LaVerdiere, "The Teaching Authority of the Church: Origins in the Early New Testament Period"; John E. Lynch, "The Magistery and Theologians from the Apostolic Fathers to the Gregorian Reform"; Yves Congar, "Theologians and the Magisterium in the West: From the Gregorian Reform to the Council of Trent"; Michael D. Place, "Theologians and Magisterium from the Council of Trent to the First Vatican Council"; and T. Howland Sanks, "Co-operation, Co-optation and Condemnation: Theologians and the Magisterium 1870–1978," in *Chicago Studies* 17 (1978): 172–263. For a general perspective, see Patrick Granfield, *The Limits of the Papacy: Authority and Autonomy in the Church* (New York: Crossroad, 1987).

as an unwarranted inflation of papal power at the expense of other teaching authorities in the Church, but as a necessary aspect of a developing articulation of the community's governing doctrines, consistent with its primary doctrines.

In the Constitutions on Divine Revelation and on the Church, Vatican Council II attained a new level in this developing articulation. While reaffirming the central teachings of Vatican I, these constitutions located the teaching office of the Church in the broad context of the community's governing doctrines and of its teaching activities as it continues Christ's prophetic role. This new stage is strikingly reflected in the new Code of Canon Law (promulgated in 1983). In contrast to the previous code, in which references to the teaching office were distributed throughout the canons, the new code provides a unified and systematic treatment of the teaching activities of the community in an explicit endeavor to implement the directions indicated by Vatican II. The teaching responsibilities of all members of the Church are considered in turn after the discussion of the Magisterium.[19]

The modern doctrine of the Magisterium is thus in major part a product of ongoing developments in the Catholic community's articulation of its governing doctrines. In this doctrine, the community has given official formulation to its confidence that, by God's grace, it will be preserved from error and maintained in the truth when it proposes to its members and to the wide world the primary doctrines by which it seeks to foster the life of ultimate communion. Among the teaching activities of the community, only that exercised authoritatively by the pope and the bishops is understood to be divinely guaranteed in precisely this way. As successors of the apostles, only the pope and the bishops have the authority to determine

19. In his commentary on the Code of Canon Law, Book III: Teaching Office of the Church, James A. Coriden makes this point; see *The Code of Canon Law: A Text and Commentary*, ed. James A. Coriden, Thomas J. Green, and Donald E. Heintschel (Mahwah, NJ: Paulist Press, 1985), 545–89. See also Karl Rahner, "Theology and the Church's Teaching Authority after the Council," *Theological Investigations* IX (London: Darton, Longman & Todd, 1972), 83–100.

in a definitive way the authenticity of what is proposed for belief and practice in the Church. In essence, this determination consists in affirming that what is proposed accords with the revelation in scripture and tradition by which the Church itself is constituted and to which it must be obedient. This grace-given power extends to the determination of other matters addressed by governing doctrines: whether a particular proposal is consistent with other things that the community holds, whether one doctrine has priority over others, whether a proposed doctrinal formulation represents a legitimate development of the tradition, and so on. If, through faith in God, the believer assents to truths about God as these are expressed by the Church, then the Church engages its teaching activities in a distinctive mode when it seeks to determine the truth about First Truth.

DISSENT

If ultimate communion, and hence unity of faith, are the principal objectives which the Catholic community pursues in its teaching activities, then surely dissent from the common teaching is likely to be seen as a serious threat to communion. And, in some cases, it has proven to be so. But in the perspective of this paper, dissent can be viewed as a providential occasion for continued development in the Catholic community's governing doctrines. It is a fact that in the decades following Vatican Council II, the chief impetus for ongoing development of the theology of the Magisterium has come from the challenge posed for the Church by dissent from its teachings. Indeed, much of the literature upon which this paper has drawn is the product of the debate ensuing the promulgation of the encyclical, *Humanae Vitae*, in 1968. Dissent from the teaching of this encyclical provoked a major crisis in Catholic allegiance to the Magisterium.[20] While the strain on

20. See Joseph A. Komonchak, "*Humanae Vitae* and its Reception: Ecclesiological Reflections," *Theological Studies* 39 (1978): 221–57; and Avery Dulles, SJ, "*Humanae Vitae* and the Crisis of Dissent," unpublished address at the Twelfth Bishops' Workshop, Dallas, Texas, reported by the Catholic News Service, March 11, 1993. For a positive assessment of the encyclical and its impact, see Janet Smith, *Humanae Vitae: A Generation*

the visible communion of the Church has been considerable, the controversy surrounding dissent has had a beneficial outcome in stimu-
lating historical research and theological reflection on a wide range of
issues bearing on the nature of the Magisterium.

The debate has accelerated developments on several fronts. Perhaps the most significant outcome has been a thoroughgoing recon-
ception of the relation of theologians and the Magisterium. Historical studies have demonstrated the central "magisterial" role played
by Catholic theological faculties prior to the nineteenth century.
The Catholic community has struggled to reappropriate the doctrinal bases of collaboration between theologians and the Magisterium, and to formalize such collaboration in the vastly altered ecclesial
and academic contexts of contemporary societies. A central feature
of this reappropriation has been a renewed awareness of the creative
role of the theologian in contributing to the understanding and formulation of the Christian faith. The Magisterium itself has sought to
articulate an "ecclesial role" for theologians within the frame of an
ecclesiology of communion.[21]

In a related development, a much-debated issue concerns the

Later (Washington, DC: The Catholic University of America Press, 1991). See also Joseph. Komonchak; "Issues Behind the Curran Case," _Commonweal_ (January 30, 1987):
43–47.

21. For this paragraph, see Glenn W. Olsen, "The Theologian and the Magisterium:
The Ancient and Medieval Background of a Contemporary Controversy," _Communio:
International Catholic Review_ 7 (1980): 292–319; Yves M.-J. Congar, OP, "A Brief Histo-
ry of the Forms of Magisterium and Its Relations with Scholars," in _Readings in Moral
Theology_ 3, 314–31; Avery Dulles, SJ, "The Two Magisteria: An Interim Reflection," in _A
Church to Believe In_ (New York: Crossroad, 1982), 118–32. In _Imagination and Authority:
Theological Authorship in the Modern Tradition_ (Minneapolis: Fortress Press, 1991), John
E. Thiel has shown the importance of the shift in conceptions of theological authorship
from the classical to the modern periods. Congregation for the Doctrine of the Faith,
"Instruction on the Ecclesial Role of the Theologian," _Origins_ 20 (July 5,1990): 117–26,
and "Social Communications and the Doctrine of the Faith," _Origins_ 22 (June 18, 1992):
92–96; Francis A. Sullivan, SJ, "The Theologian's Ecclesial Vocation and the 1990 CDF
Instruction," _Theological Studies_ 52 (1991): 51–68; _Cooperation between Theologians and the
Ecclesiastical Magisterium_, ed. Leo J. O'Donovan, SJ (Washington, DC: Canon Law So-
ciety of America, 1982); Cardinal Joseph Ratzinger, "The Church and the Theologian,"
Origins 15 (May 8, 1986): 761–70; National Conference of Catholic Bishops, "Doctrinal
Responsibilities," _Origins_ 19 (June 29, 1989): 97–109.

force to be accorded to magisterial teaching in theological inquiry. Here, again, the community has been able to draw upon traditions of reflection in which classical and scholastic theologians sought to rank the authority of the different levels of sources bearing on theological inquiry. Discussion of this issue has advanced Catholic understanding of the community's governing doctrines and may provoke further developments in the official (as distinct from simply operative) formulations of such doctrines, particularly in refining the distinctions between different levels of magisterial teaching. This discussion is driven by controversy about the appropriateness and extent of a theologian's disagreement with magisterial teaching. It is in connection with this controversy that theologians and official teaching bodies in the Church have experimented with provisional formulations of the levels of magisterium (especially the difference between ordinary and extraordinary exercise of the teaching office), the nature of the teaching office of diocesan bishops and their national conferences, and the degree of acceptance (faith, assent, "obsequium") that are due to the distinct levels of magisterial teaching. Increasingly, theologians have recognized the relevance of theoretical studies on the nature of authority for intra-Christian reflection concerning the relation of the exercise of religious authority in the realm of religious knowledge. Church officials and concerned theologians have argued that, while privately expressed disagreement with Church teaching may be appropriate and even necessary, in certain circumstances, for ongoing development of official doctrine, public dissent undermines the Church's communion. Others have questioned the viability of the distinction between public and private dissent, given the nature of modern communication. There is a marked trend toward reserving the term "dissent" for public dissent that takes activist and politicized forms. In this context, official initiatives have involved the institutionalization of specific controls (canonical mission, profession of faith, oath of fidelity) by which the community can stipulate the ecclesial role of the theologian.[22]

22. For the bearing of the magisterium on theological inquiry, see J. A. Di Noia,

Debate on these issues has been extremely lively and promises to yield a more highly refined articulation of the community's governing doctrines as they bear on the teaching activities of the Magisterium. Part of the beneficial fallout has been a revived ecumenical discussion of issues of teaching authority.[23] There is no reason in principle why a debate that has been so productive should harm the visible communion of the Catholic Church, so long as it is characterized by restraint and charity on all sides.

CONCLUSION

The culture of grace represents the transformation of human life and society such that persons in grace can enjoy communion with the Persons of the Trinity and a transformed communion with each other. The governing doctrines of the Catholic community seek to preserve the unity of faith that in part constitutes the created, yet

OP, "Authority, Dissent and the Nature of Theological Thinking," *The Thomist* 52 (1988): 185–207; Avery Dulles, SJ, *The Craft of Theology* (New York: Crossroad, 1992), chapters 7, 10, and 11; Aidan Nichols, OP, *The Shape of Theology* (Collegeville, MN: Liturgical Press, 1991), chapter 18. See also Avery Dulles, SJ, "The Teaching Authority of Bishops' Conferences," in *The Reshaping of Catholicism* (San Francisco: Harper & Row, 1988), 207–26; National Conference of Catholic Bishops, "The Teaching Ministry of the Diocesan Bishop," *Origins* 21 (January 2, 1992): 743–92; Ladislas Orsy, SJ, *The Profession of Faith and the Oath of Fidelity* (Wilmington, DE: Michael Glazier, 1990). For studies of the nature of authority with direct bearing on the role of authority in religious knowledge, see Joseph M. Bochenski, OP, *Autorität, Freiheit, Glaube* (München: Philosophia Verlag, 1988), and *The Logic of Religion* (New York: New York University Press, 1965); Yves Simon, *A General Theory of Authority* (Notre Dame, IN: University of Notre Dame Press, 1962, 1980), especially chapter 3; Richard T. DeGeorge, *The Nature and Limits of Authority* (Lawrence: The University Press of Kansas, 1985). For a theological appropriation, see Joseph Komonchak, "Authority and Magisterium," in *Vatican Authority and American Catholic Dissent*, ed. William W. May (New York: Crossroad, 1987), 103–14.

23. For some current Protestant perspectives on teaching authority, see the papers by John B. Cobb, Jr., David C. Steinmetz, George Lindbeck, Carl Braaten, and Joseph C. Hough, Jr., in "Teaching Offices of the Church and Theological Education," *Theological Education* 19 (1983): 33–99. See also extensive discussion of these issues in an ecumenical perspective in *Teaching Authority and Infallibility in the Church*. For a historical perspective, see G. R. Evans, *Problems of Authority in the Reformation Debates* (Cambridge: Cambridge University Press, 1992). For a Catholic view of some aspects of the discussion, see Avery Dulles, SJ, "Moderate Infallibilism: An Ecumenical Approach," in *A Church to Believe In* (New York: Crossroad, 1982), 133–48.

supernatural, basis for this communion. The communion itself has nothing less than the triune God as its focus. Since natural structures of human social interaction are taken up into a new order of supernatural existence, every purely social account of the ecclesial community will be partial and limited. The culture of grace is essential to the understanding of the forms of the social structure embodied in the Catholic communion.

But the culture of grace and the culture of management are not strict alternatives. Functional explanation can have a role in understanding the structure and interaction involved in the necessarily social forms of the Church's visible communion—provided such explanation does not supplant, as John Milbank has convincingly shown it can, a properly theological account of ecclesial structures. Theological appropriation of the results of non-theological inquiries, like sociology of religion and sociology of knowledge, must be guided by relevant theological principles. Some of these principles have been sketched in this paper.

There are two points, among the many that might be mentioned, where theologically principled appropriation of social and functional explanation can enhance the Catholic community's understanding of itself.

The actual administration of a complex international organization inevitably requires rational management procedures and bureaucratic structures. As much as it may strive to cultivate the conditions for ultimate communion, the Church's international administration remains subject to the possibilities and limitations that affect all social structures. The need for continual reform of curial administration has been recognized and acted upon in the Church in recent decades.[24] There is no reason to think that these reform ef-

24. Reform of the Curia has proceeded in two stages since Vatican Council II. See the apostolic constitutions of Paul VI, *Regimini Ecclesiae universae, Acta Apostolicae Sedis* 59 (1967): 885–928, and John Paul II, *Pastor Bonus, Acta Apostolicae Sedis* 80 (1988): 841–912, articles 48–55 on the Congregation for the Doctrine of the Faith. [ed. note, to these two one can now add Pope Francis's Apostolic Constitution *Praedicate Evangelium* (March 19, 2022).] For discussion of this reform see the two articles by James Provost:

forts would not benefit from the kind of analysis of social interaction that has improved the functioning of other organizations, provided that reform is not reductionistically conceived only in these terms.

As it enters its third millennium, the Catholic Church has emerged clearly as a vast worldwide communion. Sociology of knowledge can contribute to its endeavor both to maintain unity of faith and at the same time to foster cultural and theological diversity across the many local, ethnic and national boundaries that score its worldwide communion. Leaving aside its pretensions to offer a complete explanation of religious phenomena, sociology of knowledge helps to illumine the interconnections between cultural forms and ideational structures, and thus the particular nature of the challenge to maintain communal identity in the midst of both secularizing and localizing pressures. In this perspective, the centralization of Church administration, the highly visible papal ministry, and the multiplication of ecclesiastical documents are not in themselves developments to be lamented (as they tend sometimes to be). Such developments do not suppress diversity but encourage it. The more the Church exercises a leadership role in maintaining the unity of the communion in faith, the more cultural and theological diversity will seem not threatening to but natural in a worldwide communion of such immense breadth. The identification and invocation of parameters has the effect of assuring that diversity will not undermine communion. In the present circumstances, the Magisterium can be seen to have a crucial role precisely at this point.

The emerging role of the Magisterium in the nineteenth and

"Reform of the Roman Curia," in *Synod 1985: An Evaluation*, Giuseppe Alberigo and James Provost, eds., *Concilium* 188 (Edinburgh: T&T Clark, 1986), 26–36, and *"Pastor Bonus:* Reflections on the Reorganization of the Roman Curia," *The Jurist* 48 (1988): 499–535. On the need for these reforms, see Hans Urs von Balthasar, *The Office of Peter and the Structure of the Church* (San Francisco: Ignatius Press, 1986). For discussion of the Congregation for the Doctrine of the Faith, see Jerome Hamer, "In the Service of the Magisterium: The Evolution of a Congregation," *The Jurist* 37 (1977): 340–57, and, in a more critical vein, Giuseppe Alberigo, "The Authority of the Church in the Documents of Vatican I and Vatican II," *Authority in the Church,* 119–45. For an important historical analysis of the actual workings of the Holy Office as distinct from the mythologizing of the inquisition, see Edward Peters, *Inquisition* (New York: The Free Press, 1988).

twentieth centuries should be seen as a pastoral response to the particular sorts of problems created for the Church by a range of modern intellectual, social and political revolutions. It may perhaps be regarded as providential that, as it enters the twenty-first century, the Catholic community has in place a strong conception of a teaching authority charged with the task of preserving the communion which has a unified faith as its basis. Social explanation can help to illumine the complexities of this situation, but not independently of faith in the overarching divine purposes at work in bringing humankind into the joy of ultimate communion.

CHAPTER 3

———————:———————

Theological Method and the
Magisterium of the Church

Is it possible to say anything new on the topic of the Magisterium and theology? The topic has been subjected to such intense study in the years since the publication of *Humanae Vitae* (1968) that one would seem to be compelled to do no more than summarize and repeat what has already been said by others.

Much of the recent discussion has been preoccupied with the problem of theological dissent regarding the Church's teaching on sexual morality. Here I will have very little to say about public dissent as such—except to note at the outset that the generalized tension between the Magisterium and theologians typical of recent decades is both unprecedented and anomalous. The normal situation is that Catholic theologians would acknowledge the authority of the Magisterium for their work. It is a mistake to allow the condition of public dissent to frame or dominate any account of the relationship between theology and the Magisterium.

When the problem of dissent is bracketed, at least for the purposes of discussion, it turns out that there may indeed be something

Originally published as "*Metodo teologico e magistero della chiesa*," in *PATH* (Pontificia Accademia Theologica) 3 (2004): 57–68. This English translation, "Theological Method and the Magisterium of the Church," appeared in *Dominicana* 64 (2011): 51–61.

new to say on our topic. If it is true that the doctrine of the Magisterium as we know it today was articulated in contention with modernity, then it may be expected that new developments in understanding the Magisterium and theology will emerge on the frontiers where modern preoccupations with the principle of autonomous reason are in retreat in the face of the recovery of the communal and traditional contexts of all rational activity that is characteristic of current philosophy. I believe this to be the case and I shall try to sketch what appear to me to be the most significant elements in the new situation for a deepened understanding of the relationship between the Magisterium and theology.

THE RULES OF THE GAME

Perhaps the simplest way for me to characterize the new situation is to offer a rather mundane analogy. Imagine a theological symposium underway on a beautiful spring afternoon. Imagine further that the participants decide to decamp to the college playing fields in order to have a game of softball. (Perhaps some of them could do little more than watch from the sidelines!) Suppose that after the captains and teams have been selected, someone asks about the rules to be followed in the game. Perhaps he says, "In Cincinnati, where I grew up, we played this way." But then someone else objects, "No, in Boston we play the game this way." And I say, "Well, in the Bronx, we play this way." And so on. The point of this simple analogy is that a debate about the rules of the game may consume all the time allowed for the game itself. It may turn out, in other words, that their disagreement about the rules of the game would prevent the symposium participants from actually playing the game itself, while agreement about and acceptance of some set of rules would make the game of softball possible on the afternoon in question.

Naturally, for perceptive readers, this analogy will bring the name of Wittgenstein to mind. But there is no need to invoke or defend the entire apparatus of Wittgenstein's philosophy of forms of life and language games to note in the analogy of our hypothetical softball game a deep and important truth about human activities. The rules, far from being a constraint, create the space in which a particular communal and social activity can proceed. To be sure, the rules impose limits. But these limits define possibilities like softball and baseball, soccer and rugby, or chess and bridge, to mention just a few of the more mundane human activities enabled by particular sets of rules. In this view of the matter, the rules are significant because they make the game possible. A disagreement about the rules, as we know from experience, brings the game to a halt, whereas the presumption of an agreement about the rules on the part of all the players is a necessary condition for the game to proceed.

This suggestive analogy goes part of the way in explaining why, in my view, it is a mistake to allow discussion of the doctrine of the Magisterium to be dominated and shaped by publicly dissenting theologians. Dissent about the *authority* with which a doctrine is taught (like a disagreement about the rules of a game) distracts our attention from the far more important issue of the *truth* of what is being taught (playing the game itself). Thus, for example, with regard to the Church's teaching about the immortality of artificial contraception, dissenting theologians force us to defend the infallibility of the ordinary magisterium, as represented by the teaching of *Humanae Vitae*, instead of focusing on the real issue of the Catholic teaching on sexuality. Or, to cite the example of the reservation of Holy Orders to men, we find ourselves enmeshed in controversies about the authority of *Ordinatio Sacerdotalis* rather than in the more important task of developing the theology of the natural signification of the maleness of the priest who represents both the victim and the one who offers sacrifice. When I worked as the executive director of the doctrinal office of the United States episcopal conference, the first question that journalists inevitably posed with regard to new magisterial documents like *Veritatis Splendor* and *Evangelium*

Vitae was "Is it infallible?" My answer was: "The far more important question is: is it *true*?"

The tendency to give questions about the authority of religious doctrines priority over questions about their truth is characteristic not just of dissenting theologians. It has been typical of modernity itself and is matched in philosophy by the preoccupation with epistemology and methodology. A refreshing element in the new situation has been a refusal to allow the reliability of the foundations or sources of truth to distract attention from the more substantive issue of truth itself. This reordering of priorities helps us to understand and interpret the history of the formulation of the doctrine of the Magisterium as it has evolved since the nineteenth century.

For the most part, the Church's teaching is directed to the glory of God and to leading us to holiness—the present and future enjoyment of ultimate communion with the Blessed Trinity and with other persons in lives of ever-deepening charity. Through her teaching activities—through the family, through catechesis, through preaching, through the Magisterium, through theology—the Church seeks to cultivate the intellectual and moral dispositions necessary for this enjoyment, to enhance understanding of its profound meaning, and to commend it to others. The whole ensemble of Catholic doctrine—the *depositum fidei*—embraces all the teachings that together serve to shape and direct our lives toward holiness. As the *Catechism of the Catholic Church* demonstrates, such doctrines answer questions about what must be believed, how divine grace transforms us through the liturgy and the sacraments, which courses of action should be pursued and which shunned, which interior dispositions must be cultivated and which avoided, and so on, in order to enjoy the life of ultimate communion to the full. Much of the teaching activity of the Church, including the authoritative teaching of the Magisterium, is concerned with questions of this kind.

PRIMARY DOCTRINES AND
GOVERNING DOCTRINES

But another range of questions can arise. These are concerned not with what must be believed and undertaken in order to grow in the life of grace and charity, but rather how it can be known reliably that such things *should be* believed and undertaken. Recent philosophical analysis of the nature of religious doctrines helps us to distinguish these two types of questions, and as well us to understand how the modern preoccupation with the authority and sources of truth compelled the Church to articulate the largely implicit doctrine of the Magisterium over the course of past two centuries. The philosopher of religion, William A. Christian, has suggested (in his book *Doctrines of Religious Communities*) that, in response to the two different kinds of questions sketched above, the teaching activities of religious communities generate two types of doctrines: *primary doctrines* in which a religion commends the beliefs and practices that constitute its distinctive pattern of life, and *governing doctrines*, in which a community states the sources for its primary doctrines. According to Christian's analysis, governing doctrines respond to such questions as the following: Is this really a doctrine of our community? What procedures do we have for deciding? Is this doctrine more important than other doctrines? Is it consistent with them? Is it appropriate to develop understandings that seem implicit in our doctrines? Should these also be considered as doctrines? Who in the community is authorized to decide? In his study of different religious traditions like Christianity, Buddhism, Islam, and others, Christian explores these different types of questions which generate what he calls "doctrines about doctrines" or, more simply, governing doctrines.

The history of the Catholic Church has afforded many occasions for developing and invoking governing doctrines. Particularly germane to our topic is the fact that questions of the authenticity of its primary doctrines have been pressed upon the Church almost without interruption for the past two hundred years. Thus, for example, more explicit attention has been devoted by the Magisterium to the doctrine of revelation during this period than in all the previous centuries taken together. Throughout this period, the Church has gradually formulated a range of previously implicit governing doctrines to affirm that her primary doctrines authentically express what is contained in Scripture and Tradition, that Scripture and Tradition themselves constitute the single source of revelation, that revelation involves a real divine communication mediated by Christ, the prophets and apostles, that the scriptural record of this revelation is divinely inspired, that the liturgical and doctrinal tradition embodies communally authorized readings of the Scripture, and that the Church under the Successor of Peter is divinely guided in its formulation of primary doctrines of faith and morals.

The increasingly explicit formulations of the doctrine of the Magisterium over the past two centuries is part of the evolution that represented a response to the growing need for a clear articulation of the governing doctrines of the Catholic faith. In circumstances in which the authenticity of Catholic doctrines was a matter of persistent and unrelenting controversy, it was natural that doctrinal developments addressing this issue should take place along several fronts at once: the nature of revelation, the interpretation of Scripture, the authority of Tradition, and the scope of the Church's teaching office. Each of these topics was central to the agenda of Vatican Council I and, in varying degrees, has remained prominent. In the Constitutions on Divine Revelation and on the Church, Vatican Council II attained a new level in this developing articulation. While reaffirming the central teachings of Vatican I, these constitutions located the teaching office of the Church in the broad context of her governing doctrines which make explicit her conviction that the truth she possesses and transmits is itself a *gift* to be received in faith, hope and love.

From the vantage point of the beginning of the twenty-first century, it seems clear that the definition of papal infallibility at Vatican

I was but an early stage in the Church's continuing endeavor to articulate a consistent set of governing doctrines in the face of modern challenges. Viewed in this context, the nineteenth-century emphasis on the official Magisterium and the twentieth-century prominence of the papal Magisterium will appear, not as an unwarranted inflation of papal power at the expense of other teaching authorities in the Church, but as a necessary aspect of a developing articulation of her governing doctrines in response to the challenges posed by modernity's exaltation of autonomous reason. In the face of such a challenge, the Church must affirm her faith that human beings cannot create the truth but must receive it as a gift. Despite the continuing influence of modernistic cultural assumptions of religious individualism and autonomy, the atmosphere generated by more recent intellectual trends is somewhat more receptive to Catholic convictions about the communally and traditionally constituted sources of truth.

The fundamental strategy, as pursued by thinkers like Alasdair MacIntyre and others, is to recover a truth which was repressed in modernity: tradition is not an enemy of reason but a child of reason. Rational activities in all fields—from the natural sciences to philosophy, the arts, and the humanities—are not constrained or obstructed, but, on the contrary, enabled and directed by a wide range of traditions and by the communities that develop and transmit them. According to this view, rational inquiry is itself tradition- and community-dependent. Communities of scientific, philosophical, theological, and other kinds of scholars conserve and transform traditions of inquiry which cumulatively enlarge and deepen various bodies of knowledge, and at the same time they undertake to initiate and cultivate new generations of students to continue in their footsteps.

THE ECCLESIAL VOCATION OF THE THEOLOGIAN

This perspective is helpful for understanding the relationship between the Magisterium and theology. On this view, the Magisterium acts not to constrain but to enable theological inquiry to proceed.

With Scripture and Tradition, it functions among the very conditions for the possibility of theology. What must be surely regarded as among the most significant official documents on the relation of theology to the Magisterium recognizes and affirms this. Prepared by the Congregation for the Doctrine of the Faith, the document was entitled "The Ecclesial Vocation of the Theologian" and appeared in 1990.

Although the documents of the Second Vatican Council mentioned theology and theologians at various points—perhaps most notably in the Constitution on Divine Revelation (*Dei Verbum*, §23–24), the Constitution on the Church (*Lumen Gentium*, §23), and the Decree on Priestly Formation (*Optatam Totius*, §12, 14–16), the council did not make this theme the focus of an extended treatment. Given the impact that the council had on the work of theologians, this may come as something of a surprise. Reprising significant elements of the Catholic tradition, as articulated in conciliar and postconciliar teaching, the *Instruction* forcefully argues that the theologian's vocation is a properly ecclesial one and that the bonds of ecclesial communion implied by this relationship can be expressed juridically. As is well known, the *Instruction* takes up in turn the divine gift of truth, the vocation of the theologian, and the role of the Magisterium. Under its consideration the role of the Magisterium, the *Instruction* gives extended attention to the problem of theological dissent.

But what is particularly noteworthy is that the *Instruction* begins, not with the Magisterium, but with the gift of divine truth. Indeed, the *Instruction*'s Latin title is *Donum Veritatis*, "the gift of truth." Because theology is not simply an ancillary function of the Magisterium, we need to locate the theologian and the work of theology in the broader context of the life of Church, precisely as she is the locus of a truth which she did not generate but which she received as a gift. At the center of this truth is the person of Jesus Christ who reveals the divine desire to draw us into the communion of trinitarian love and, moreover, who enables us to enjoy this communion. The function of the Magisterium is to guard and teach this truth in its entirety which the Church received as a gift and is bound to hand on. For this reason, according to then-Cardinal Joseph Ratzinger, the *Instruction* "treats the ecclesial mission of the theologian not in a duality of Magisterium-theology, but rather in the framework of a triangular relationship defined by the people of God, bearer of the *sensus fidei*, the Magisterium, and theology."[1] In different ways, therefore, both the Magisterium and theology are servants of a prior truth, received in the Church as a gift.

Perhaps the most important contribution of the Instruction is to have secured in this way what Pope Benedict has called the "ecclesial identity of theology" and, correspondingly, the ecclesial vocation of the theologian. In the words of the *Instruction* itself: "Among the vocations awakened ... by the Spirit in the Church is that of the theologian.... [whose] role is to pursue in a particular way an ever deeper understanding of the Word of God found in the inspired Scriptures and handed on by the living Tradition of the Church ... [which he does] in communion with the Magisterium which has been charged with the responsibility of preserving the deposit of faith."[2] The theological vocation responds to the intrinsic dynamic of faith which "appeals to reason" and "beckons reason ... to come to understand what it has believed."[3] In this way, "theological science responds to the invitation of truth as it seeks to understand the faith."[4] But the theological vocation also responds to the dynamic of love, for "in the act of faith, man knows God's goodness and begins to love Him ... [and] is ever desirous of a better knowledge of the beloved."[5]

---

1. Cardinal Joseph Ratzinger, *The Nature and Mission of Theology: Essays to Orient Theology in Today's Debates* (San Francisco: Ignatius, 1995), 104–5.

2. Congregation for the Doctrine of the Faith, Instruction on the Ecclesial Vocation of the Theologian (*Donum Veritatis*), May 15, 1990, §6.

3. *Instruction*, §6.

4. *Instruction*, §6.

5. *Instruction*, §7.

THE ECCLESIALLY RECEIVED TRUTH

The gift of truth received in the Church thus establishes both the context for the vocation and mission of the theologian, and the framework for the actual practice of the discipline of theology. This ecclesially received truth, as articulated in the deposit of faith and handed on by the Magisterium, constitutes not an *extrinsic* authority that poses odious limits on an inquiry that would otherwise be free but an *intrinsic* source and measure that gives theology its identity and finality as an intellectual activity. Examined independently of the assent of faith and the mediation of the ecclesial community, the texts, institutions, rites and beliefs of the Catholic Church can be the focus of the humanistic, philosophical and social scientific inquiries that together constitute the field of religious studies. But Christian theology is a different kind of inquiry. Cut off from an embrace of the truth that provides its subject matter and indicates the methods appropriate to its study, theology as the Church has always understood it loses its specific character as a scientific inquiry of a certain type. Its precise scope is to seek the intelligibility of a truth received in faith by the theologian who is himself a member of the ecclesial community that is "the place of truth."[6]

The theologian is thus free to seek the truth within limits imposed, not by an intrusive external authority, but by the nature of his discipline as such. As the *Instruction* points out: "Freedom of research, which the academic community holds most precious, means an openness to accepting the truth that emerges at the end of an investigation in which no element has intruded that is foreign to the methodology corresponding to the object under study."[7] Theology cannot "deny its own foundations," to use the words of Cardinal Avery Dulles, for the acceptance of the authority of Scripture and doctrines in theology is "not a limitation but rather the charter of its

6. See Walter Kasper, *Theology and Church* (New York: Crossroad, 1989).
7. *Instruction on the Ecclesial Vocation of the Theologian*, §12.

existence and freedom to be itself."[8] The freedom of inquiry proper
to theology, is, according to the *Instruction*, the "hallmark of a rational discipline whose object is given by Revelation, handed on and
interpreted in the Church under the authority of the Magisterium,
and received by faith. These givens have the force of principles. To
eliminate them would mean to cease doing theology."[9] The principles of theology are derived from revelation and constitute the discipline as such. In accepting them, the theologian is simply being
true to the nature of his subject, and to his vocation as a scholar in
this field.

These elements of the *Instruction*'s account of theology and its
relation to the Magisterium are contested wherever what George
Lindbeck somewhere termed the "individualistic foundational rationalism" of modernity holds sway. But, as the *Instruction* demonstrates, the Church has a solid, well-substantiated, and historically
warranted rationale for its account of the nature of theology as an
intellectual discipline of a particular sort, and of the inner connection between this discipline and magisterial teaching. It is central to
the convictions of the Catholic Church, and indeed of the Christian tradition as such, to give priority to a theonomous rather than
to an autonomous rationality. While it is true that the basis for this
understanding is itself a properly theological one that is rooted in
fundamental Christian convictions about the gift of truth and its reception in the ecclesial community, as we have seen, in the light certain postmodern intellectual trends, the Church's claims about the
"situatedness" of theology are perfectly intelligible. The *Instruction*,
in effect, constitutes an extended argument for the community- and
tradition-dependent character of theology. Whatever other challenges it may pose, the present intellectual climate is, to a certain extent,
more favorable to the defense of the principle of theonomous rationality that is crucial for the Catholic understanding of theology.

8. Avery Dulles, *The Craft of Theology: From Symbol to System* (New York: Crossroad,
1992), 168.

9. *Instruction on the Ecclesial Vocation of the Theologian*, §12.

We may note that this conclusion is also supported by recent philosophical studies of the nature of authority. Although it is true that Catholic theology is notably dependent on the authority of the Magisterium, it would be a mistake to exaggerate the singularity of theology at this point. Authoritative criteria and professional bodies exist in almost all intellectual disciplines. Authorities function to maintain the quality and standards of many of these disciplines. According to a recent philosophical analysis of authority, "the acceptance of a certain degree of authority—which those subject to it regard as more or less legitimate, which they accept more or less easily, and which they challenge only exceptionally—is the normal state of affairs."[10] In this sense, the Catholic understanding of the relationship of theology to the Magisterium has formal parallels to other academic disciplines in which authorities serve to foster rather than undermine intellectual and scholarly integrity.

Recent philosophical developments, as *Fides et Ratio* demonstrates, are not an unmixed blessing. Perhaps the most significant danger of "postmodern" intellectual trends is that, in stressing the cultural and social contexts of truth, they lead to relativism about truth itself. This is a real danger, but to deal with it thoroughly would require another paper. Here my objective has been to show that certain elements in the new philosophical situation are helpful in understanding and defending the Catholic vision of the relationship between the Magisterium and theology.

10. Richard. T. De George, *The Nature and Limits of Authority* (Lawrence: University Press of Kansas, 1985), 1.

CHAPTER 4

The Authority of Scripture in Sacramental Theology
Some Methodological Observations

What authority does the Bible have in the Church? The simplest answer is "God's." Because he is its primary author, the Bible has God's
authority and the Church thus consults it in faith. However, the
Lord of heaven and earth did not produce the Bible *ex nihilo* and
give it to us. Instead, rather than remain silent and aloof, God employed human authors and "in many and various ways spoke of old
to our fathers by the prophets; but in these last days he has spoken
to us by a Son, whom he has appointed heir of all things, through
whom he also created the world" (Heb 1:1–2). The Bible is in fact
part of a larger undertaking of divine disclosure and condescen-
sion—an economy of salvation—in which human beings, through
grace and the theological virtues of faith, hope and love, are accustomed and adapted to communion with the persons of the blessed
Trinity and with one another in them.

The broad context of the entire economy of salvation provides
the only adequate framework within which to advance properly

Originally published in *Pro Ecclesia* 10 (2001): 329–45, with Bernard Mulcahy, OP,
as coauthor. Reprinted here with Fr. Mulcahy's permission and in accordance with the
republication policy of *Pro Ecclesia*.

theological answers to methodological questions about the authority of the Bible for theology. This is especially true of the peculiarly modern questions which have arisen in the aftermath of the application of historical-critical methods to biblical study, when it has seemed to some that the church cannot with confidence claim the Bible's authority for her central beliefs about the economy of salvation.

In the present paper, we seek to focus this vast topic by addressing a slender skein of methodological questions which run through the church's faith that the sacraments were instituted by Christ. Consideration of this crucial topic within sacramental theology keeps our methodological inquiry anchored in the concrete realities of the economy of salvation at the same time that it forces us to confront the formidable challenges which are posed for the Church's faith and theology by modern critical exegesis. The objective of this paper is to suggest how, in principle, the results of critical historical inquiries into the text of the Bible could be appropriated by theological exegesis without detriment to the Church's confidence in the scriptural warrant of her Christological and sacramental faith.

THE SACRAMENTAL ECONOMY: TRINITARIAN COMMUNION AND PASCHAL MYSTERY

In the *Catechism of the Catholic Church* and elsewhere, the expression "sacramental economy" has taken the place of the once common "sacramental order." What the term "economy" implies here, even more strongly than does "order," is that there is not only arrangement but transaction and transformation in the sacraments. The sacramental economy is a divine arrangement, designed for bodily human beings, by which grace is given by God in virtue of the passion, death, and resurrection of Christ. It is a divine provision which respects the structure of human nature as it is in the world—embodied, passionate, rational, but also fallen and prone to sin—and employs or deploys the natural significations of things, actions, and words to the divine end of bringing us progressively closer to the triune God and closer to one another in the triune God.

The belief that God is about the work of uniting us with himself in Christ by the action of the Holy Spirit is fundamental. We can hope to make no progress whatsoever in sacramental theology, ecclesiology, or in any other theological topic if we do not begin with the divine plan—dare we say, the divine desire—to bring creaturely persons into the communion of trinitarian life. We read in 2 Peter: "His divine power has granted to us all things that pertain to life and holiness, through the knowledge of him who called us to his own glory and excellence, by which he has granted to us his precious and very great promises, that through these you may become partakers of the divine nature" (2 Pt 1:3–4). There is no reason but this given in revelation for the existence of the world, or for our or any other created persons' being in it: God desires to share the communion of trinitarian life with created persons. So deep, in fact, is the intimacy being brought about between the divine persons and ourselves that one could say that none greater could possibly be achieved, even by God. What the Father has undertaken by bringing us into communion with himself in Christ and the Holy Spirit in baptism, and will consummate in the life to come, could not possibly be surpassed, since it is nothing less than our adoption and incorporation into the life of the divine persons themselves.

It follows from the fact that God intends this communion that he has a way of effecting it, since there is no merely wishful thinking on God's part. Hence, we must be prepared to affirm that there is a plan, a divine provision, through which this intimate union is to be effected. This plan, as we know, entails that, through Jesus Christ, we should both learn of God's intentions and actually enter into this communion with the Holy Trinity

Our communion with the triune God and with one another in him is realized in Christ himself: *I am the Way* (Jn 14:6). In practice, this communion occurs through our transformation in Christ, a change which is both an elevating and a healing grace. By ourselves, we are impeded from the company of God both by our creatureliness and by our sinfulness. Only by being made partakers of the divine nature through grace can creaturely persons come to enjoy the company of the uncreated persons. Only by having their sins forgiven through the power of Christ can sinful persons come to share the company of the all-holy God. Only when we *put on Christ* (Gal 3:27) do we find that we can be at home in the divine company. The Father looks out, as it were, at all those who are saved, and he sees Christ. As the English translation of one of the prefaces from the Roman Missal has it, "Father, you sent [your Son] as one like ourselves, though free from sin, that you might see and love in us what you see and love in Christ." God sees us as Christ because he changes us and conforms us to Christ, overcoming our sin and raising us toward the good that transcends our nature, namely, the trinitarian communion.

How does this transformation, our adoption into Christ the eternal Son, occur? In the Catholic perspective the sacraments are the main way in which our transformation is accomplished by Christ through the Holy Spirit in the Church. The sacraments, far from being magical ceremonies held in the Church's possession, are acts of Christ himself, acts in which physical signs and human agents are used by God to accomplish a divine purpose. That purpose, to put it boldly, is none other than the salvific work of Christ—the sacraments accomplish in us everything Christ wrought and purchased by his cross and resurrection. Because the sacraments are Christ's own, and only because they are his own, they effect our forgiveness, healing and transformation for the life of heavenly adoption.

It would be erroneous to suppose, as did certain late medieval nominalists, that the sacraments are human activities to which God occasionally attaches his own undertakings. Likewise, it would be wrong to think of the sacraments as mere outward tokens of secret interior gifts, let alone just celebrations of special moments in human life. Rather, the sacraments are acts in which Christ is present and active. While indeed symbolic, the sacraments bring about the very things they symbolize, so that the reality of any sacrament is *effectively* represented in the visible rite.

The sacraments—to borrow a phrase from Austin Farrer's account of instrumental causality—are deeds of "double agency." That is to say, they are actions in which two agents act concurrently. In the Baptism of an infant, for example, we believe that after the words, "I baptize you in the name of the Father and of the Son and of the Holy Spirit," and the immersion or pouring of water, the child is united to God. We would even say that now the infant is reborn in Christ and that God the Holy Spirit dwells in him. Granting this, it takes only a moment's reflection to see that causing such effects, including the indwelling of the Holy Spirit, is beyond the capacity of any mere human minister. So, while we could not claim personally to have caused God to act, we would nevertheless be bound to confess that God took up and concurred with our action. Hence the idea of instrumental causality or double agency: God, the principal agent, acts through the human minister of the sacrament to achieve divine purposes and effects. In no way does this mean that God is powerless to act without us. Rather, it means that God has graciously deigned to use us for his work, and that he instructed us to baptize and to enact the other sacraments for the sake of making real the good he intends to accomplish in us: nothing less than transformation in Christ and communion with the Father and with one another in the Holy Spirit.

Why God has chosen to require this human participation in his own action is something he has not told us, though we can perceive something of the fittingness of this disposition. For example, the sacramental rites are inherently communal, which is a blow to individualism and gives scope to love of neighbor. Or, again, the sacraments are found as objects and not only as our experiences, thus emphasizing the reality and divinity of grace. Or, we could say that the sacraments drive home the fact that God loves creatures, including lowly material ones. Nevertheless, the sacramental economy remains essentially mysterious to us—not because the sacraments themselves are entirely hidden, but because we have only an imperfect share in the divine wisdom which orders the economy of salvation from start to finish. What we do know is that God has freely and wisely tied certain crucial effects—indeed literally *crucial* effects, things realized in virtue of the cross of Christ—to the acts and words of human agents. While the effects of the sacraments transcend the capacities of human agency, God nevertheless takes our activity up into his own action and purpose to accomplish what only he can do.[1]

This claim merits our attention here because if the sacraments do accomplish effects beyond the power of human agents, then they cannot possibly have been established or instituted by anyone but God. No person, no community, not even the whole Church in the plenitude of her spiritual power, can invent a sacrament or radically alter the sacramental economy which is God's gift to us in Christ and the Holy Spirit. So, it follows that either the sacraments have been instituted by God himself or there are no sacraments at all. In fact, the Church can only believe that the sacraments accomplish the things they do if she believes that Christ instituted them, and that in them the same Christ who came in the flesh, who suffered, died, rose from the dead, and reigns now in the glory of the Father, is active and present every time they are celebrated and administered.[2] In the words of the *Catechism of the Catholic Church*, "'Seated at the right hand of the Father' and pouring out the Holy Spirit on his body which is the Church, Christ now acts through the sacraments he instituted to communicate his grace" (§1084), for, according to St. Leo the Great, "what was visible in our Savior has passed over into his mysteries" (§1115).

1. The review of certain basic elements of Catholic doctrine contained in the preceding paragraphs has been deeply influenced by the following works: St. Thomas Aquinas, *Summa theologiae* III, qq. 60–65; Johann Auer, *A General Doctrine of the Sacraments* (Washington, DC: The Catholic University of America Press, 1995); Colman O'Neill, *Meeting Christ in the Sacraments*, revised edition (New York: Alba House, 1990), and *Sacramental Realism* (Wilmington, DE: Michael Glazier, 1993).

2. See Auer, *A General Doctrine of the Sacraments*, 83–87.

THE DOMINICAL INSTITUTION OF THE SACRAMENTS:
FAITH, REVELATION, AND THE BIBLE

The Church's conviction that Christ instituted the sacraments and that he continues to be active in them is one that arises from faith and is rooted in an understanding of Scripture as read and interpreted in faith.[3]

The economy of salvation is a product, not of human providence, but of divine providence. God has ordered it in such a way that visible, created realities are embraced by his own divine action. But we know of the real, but invisible, activity of Christ in the sacraments only in faith. Our participation is enhanced, and indeed partly realized, by our knowing God and his salvific works. Since these objects of knowledge are not open to our direct scrutiny, we need the grace of faith to "see" the divine truth present before our eyes. The supreme and perfect revelation has taken place, of course, in the incarnate Word himself, our Lord Jesus Christ. Even this greatest revelation was not apparent to human sight: it was by the infusion of the grace of faith, and not only by plain vision, that Christ was known for who he was by those who saw him.

According to the Constitution on Divine Revelation *Dei Verbum* of the Second Vatican Council:

In his gracious goodness, God has seen to it that what he had revealed for the salvation of all nations would abide perpetually in its full integrity and be handed on to all generations. Therefore Christ the Lord in whom the full revelation of the supreme God is brought to completion (see I Corinthians 1:20, 3:13, 4:6), commissioned the Apostles to preach to all men the Gospel which is the source of all saving truth and moral teaching, and to impart to them heavenly gifts. This Gospel has been promised in former times through the prophets, and Christ himself has fulfilled it and promulgated it with his lips. This commission was faithfully fulfilled by the Apostles who, by their oral preaching, by example, and by observances handed on what they had received from the lips of Christ, from living with him,

---

3. See Romanus Cessario, *Christian Faith and the Theological Life* (Washington, DC: The Catholic University of America Press, 1996).

and from what he did, or what they had learned through the prompting of the Holy Spirit. The commission was fulfilled, too, by those Apostles and apostolic men who under the inspiration of the same Holy Spirit committed the message of salvation to writing.

But in order to keep the Gospel forever whole and alive within the church, the Apostles left bishops as their successors, "handing over" to them "the authority to teach in their own place." This sacred tradition, therefore, and sacred Scripture of both the Old and New Testaments are like a mirror in which the pilgrim church on earth looks at God, from whom she has received everything, until she is brought finally to see him as he is, face to face (see 1 Jn 3:2). (§7)

The Council went on to affirm that the Apostles handed on "everything which contributes toward the holiness of life and increase in faith of the people of God; and so the Church, in her teaching, life and worship, [by the help of the Holy Spirit] perpetuates and hands on to all generations all that she herself is, all that she believes" (§8).

In the Catholic view, Scripture and Tradition (which is preserved intact through the Holy Spirit's imparting the sure charism of truth to the episcopate) emerge from the same divine source and are inseparable. Scripture and Tradition are not two *parts* of a whole revelation, as though the inspired authors wrote in ignorance of the preached gospel, but rather are both faithful witnesses to the one revealed Word. Nevertheless, the Bible, relative to the continuing oral and practical Tradition, is fixed in a way that the latter is not: the text of the Bible is inspired and authored by God (even though he uses men as instruments), whereas preaching is authored by man (even when the truth preached is the truth of revelation). Thus, a particular instance of ordinary preaching may be imperfect, whereas Scripture is inerrant; and Scripture is itself unregulated by its interpreters, though every reader must interpret. If we call Scripture the *norma normans non normata* of Christian faith and practice, we mean that it is the rule or measure for authentic Christianity. This does not mean, however, that Catholics consider the Bible "self-interpreting" or revelatory on an entirely literal level. As the *Catechism of the Catholic Church* puts it, "the Christian faith is not a 'religion of the book.'

Christianity is the religion of the 'Word' of God, a word which is 'not a written and mute word, but the Word which is incarnate and living.' If the Scriptures are not to remain a dead letter, Christ, the eternal Word of the living God, must, through the Holy Spirit, 'open [our] minds to understand the Scriptures'" (§108).[4] The conviction that the meaning of the Bible for the Church, and thus its authority for doctrine, practice and theology, can only be grasped in faith under the guidance of the Holy Spirit was, and generally continues to be, shared by all Christian churches, their disagreements about many details of interpretation to the contrary notwithstanding.[5]

In the Catholic Church, this conviction is fundamental to the faith that the sacraments were instituted by Christ. The Church has taught that the claim of dominical institution can be sustained with reference to each of the seven sacraments. Johann Auer summarizes the matter nicely:

The institution by Christ is clear in Scripture for the sacraments of baptism (Mt 28:19), eucharist (Lk 22:19), and penance (Jn 20:23). For the other sacraments we possess at least a clear apostolic tradition, and such a tradition must be traced back to Christ himself inasmuch as the Apostles considered themselves to be no more than "servants of Christ and ministers of the mysteries of God" (1 Cor 4:1). Thus institution by Christ must be concluded for confirmation from Acts 8:17 and 19:6, for anointing of the sick from James 5:14ff, for priestly orders from 2 Timothy 1:6, and 2:2, and for marriage from Ephesians 5:25, and Matthew 19:3–9.[6]

In this paper, however, our concern is not with the complex issues that arise with respect to the dominical institution of each of the seven sacraments, but with the more general issue of the significance and biblical basis of the belief that the church can rely on the scriptural witness to the intentions and actions of Christ with regard

4. See Aidan Nichols, *The Shape of Catholic Theology* (Collegeville, MN: Liturgical Press, 1991), 99–180.

5. For discussion of this issue, see: *The Theological Interpretation of Scripture*, ed. Stephen E. Fowl (Cambridge: Blackwell, 1997), esp. essays by Henri de Lubac, David Steinmetz, George Lindbeck, and David Yeago; Robert M. Grant, with David Tracy, *A Short History of the Interpretation of the Bible*, 2nd ed. (Philadelphia: Fortress Press, 1975).

6. Auer, *A General Doctrine of the Sacraments*, 85.

to the sacramental economy as a whole. It is the appeal to scriptural authority for this general affirmation that has been challenged both explicitly and, by association with recurrent quests for the historical Jesus, implicitly as well by modern critical studies of the Bible.[7]

THE CHALLENGE OF
CRITICAL EXEGESIS TO CHRISTOLOGICAL FAITH
AND SACRAMENTAL THEOLOGY

With the rise of historical critical study of the Bible, the broad Christian consensus about the priority of a reading of Scripture guided by faith was challenged by what has come to be seen in hindsight as an alternative way of reading the Bible. If the Christian consensus can be described as an endeavor to read the Bible precisely as *Scripture*—i.e., as God's word heard and read in a community of faith, and glossed in an evolving tradition of doctrinal interpretation and theological and pastoral commentary—then critical exegesis is best described as the endeavor to read the Bible as *text*—i.e., as a literary product, considered independently of its status as the Church's Scripture, whose historical sources and diverse meanings are susceptible of study and interpretation according to the same scholarly methods as are applicable to other ancient texts.[8]

The impact of critical historical and literary readings of the Bible on all areas of the Church's life has been considerable. For the purposes of the present paper, we want to draw attention particularly to their impact on Christological affirmation and, by implication, on

7. For a recent example, Michael D. Whalen, "Instituted by Christ: The 'Third Quest' for the Historical Jesus and the Praxis of Christian Sacraments," *The Living Light* 33 (Fall 1996): 18–28.

8. Indispensable for understanding the emergence and impact of modern critical exegesis is Hans Frei, *The Eclipse of Biblical Narrative: A Study of Eighteenth and Nineteenth Century Hermeneutics* (New Haven, CT: Yale University Press, 1974). See also Hans Reventlow, *The Authority of the Bible and the Rise of the Modern World* (London: SCM Press, 1985); Klaus Scholder, *The Birth of Modern Critical Theology: Origins and Problems of Biblical Criticism in the Seventeenth Century* (Philadelphia: Trinity International Press, 1990).

Christian convictions about the dominical institution of the sacraments.

The doctrine that Jesus Christ, through his passion, death, and resurrection, accomplished the salvation of humankind is central to Christian life and belief. Classical theologians assumed the historical truth implicit in the doctrine, *viz.*, that Jesus of Nazareth was born, lived, and died in first-century Palestine. More precisely, they assumed Jesus' identity, words, actions, and dispositions for the Church to be reliably recounted in the New Testament. Given the sometimes-conflicting readings to which the Gospels are susceptible, these theologians were concerned to identify the rules communally operative in affirming the soteriological significance of the narratives about Christ. Their faith in the unity of God's salvific purposes led these theologians to strive to discern and exhibit the inner coherence, consistency, and complementarity of the narratives about Christ. These narratives are to be read, they insisted, in such a way as never to deny Christ's true bodiliness (against Docetism), his true and eternal divinity (against subordinationism and adoptionism), his true humanity (against Monophysitism and Monothelitism) and the unity of his personal identity (against Nestorianism). Early on, this complex set of rules, in important instances secured by conciliar formulations, came to embody an ecumenical consensus on the construal of the Gospel narratives about Jesus in the light of their use and significance in the prevailing liturgical, didactic, and pastoral practices of diverse Christian churches. The metaphysical and logical conceptualities in which this set of rules was originally framed continued to invite theological analysis and refinement throughout the subsequent history of Christology and soteriology.

Although there was little interest in establishing the historical truth of the Gospel narratives as such, nothing in the communally ruled reading of these narratives in principle excluded historical investigations of the events they recounted or presupposed. As it happened, however, when in the eighteenth and nineteenth centuries there emerged the means to pursue such investigations and an

active interest in doing so, it was for a variety of reasons commonplace to view this historical inquiry as an undertaking independent
of (though not necessarily opposed to) the communally-shaped
reading.

This has led to recurrent "quests" for the historical Jesus whose
object is, according to one practitioner, an historical reconstruction
of "the Jesus whom we can 'recover' and examine by using the scientific tools of modern historical research."[9] Scholars in this vein want
to pursue historical inquiry independently of the doctrinally-ruled
reading of the Gospels that evolved in the historic Christian mainstream.[10]

One reason they advance for investigating the historical Jesus
without reference to the Christian confession about him can be stated in strong and weak versions. According to the strong version,
which will not be considered here, the developed doctrinal tradition
has distorted (deliberately or otherwise) the historical truth about
Jesus of Nazareth. According to the weak version—which, because
more influential, does require our attention here—the doctrinal tradition obscures the historical truth about Jesus.

Some such view was widespread in the nineteenth-century
English and German theological circles in which the historical
claims embedded in Christological and soteriological beliefs were
for the first time systematically distinguished from their scriptural and doctrinal settings and subjected to independent investigation. It is perhaps no accident that this development coincided

9. John P. Meier, *A Marginal Jew: Rethinking the Historical Jesus* (Garden City, NY:
Doubleday, 1991), 25.

10. From the vast literature on this topic the following works might usefully be
consulted in order to chart the various phases of the quest for the historical Jesus: Albert Schweitzer, *The Quest for the Historical Jesus*, revised edition (New York: Macmillan
1968); James M. Robinson, *A New Quest for the Historical Jesus* (Philadelphia: Fortress,
1959); Ben Witherington III, *The Jesus Quest: The Third Search for the Jew of Nazareth*
(Downers Grove, IL: InterVarsity Press, 1994). [ed. note: for a Dominican perspective,
see also, Anthony Giambrone, OP, *A Quest for the Historical Christ: Scientia Christi and
the Modern Study of Jesus* (Washington, DC: The Catholic University of America Press,
2022).]

with growing acceptance of the Kantian critique of metaphysics. The ontologically-framed doctrinal formulae of the tradition were increasingly displaced in the articulation of faith in Christ or reinterpreted in moral, religious, and historical categories. In this intellectual environment, historical investigation provided the means for a recovery of the religious significance of Jesus now understood to have been obscured by centuries of doctrinal overlay. Indeed, since it was recognized that the Gospels were themselves not simply historical reports, but confessional accounts, the goal of investigation was increasingly seen as the historical reconstruction of a figure concealed not only by the veil of a metaphysically-shaped doctrinal tradition but also by Scripture as well.

Often scholars have not considered these philosophical and theological presuppositions of the quest for the historical Jesus, nor the degree to which they may continue to be operative in the now uncontested separation of the historical from the doctrinally-ruled reading of the Gospels.[11] They do not, for example, consider the anti-metaphysical bias of the questers, nor the implicit positivism and rationalism of their views of history, nor their failure to grasp the narrative character of the depiction basic to the Gospel genre.

The presupposition of the recurrent quests for the historical Jesus seems to be that inquiries in this vein—despite the acknowledged exiguity of their results and the lack of consensus among their practitioners—can provide the basis for a recovery of elements of the identity of Jesus and an insight into his intentions as a religious figure that are obscured by the doctrinal tradition. This presupposition challenges a range of Christian convictions concerning the reliability of the Bible as witness to the truth about Jesus Christ and the scriptural basis for the Church's Christological, soteriological, and sacramental doctrines.[12]

11. See Bruce D. Marshall, "Christology," in *The Blackwell Encyclopedia of Modern Christian Thought*, ed. Alister E. McGrath (Cambridge: Blackwell, 1993), 80–93.

12. For a trenchant critique of the recurrent quests for the historical Jesus, see Luke Timothy Johnson, *The Real Jesus* (San Francisco: Harper Collins, 1996). For discussion of the general issues of theology and biblical interpretation, see: *Reclaiming the Bible for*

But is this methodological presupposition necessary for exegesis? Suppose that one were to adopt the view that the doctrinal tradition, far from obscuring the historical truth about Jesus Christ and his dispositions for the church, in fact provides a privileged access to this truth.[13] Suppose, in other words, that exegetes were to view historical inquiries as integral to a properly theological inquiry rather than as propaedeutic to and even independent of such an inquiry. Precisely as faith seeking understanding, theology does not leave faith behind but draws its principles from faith, and thus from the doctrinal tradition. To put the matter in classical terms, faith and reason are interrelated levels of a single, unified theological inquiry, which recognizes in the Bible a crucial moment in the divine pedagogy leading human persons into communion with the persons of the blessed Trinity.[14] How, in general terms, might such an inquiry be conceived? How would it affect the central affirmations of Catholic sacramental theology?

---

the Church, ed. Carl E. Braaten and Robert W. Jenson (Grand Rapids, MI: Eerdmans, 1995); Brevard S. Childs, "Toward Recovering Theological Exegesis," Pro Ecclesia 6 (1997): 16–26; Joseph Ratzinger, Principles of Catholic Theology (San Francisco: Ignatius Press, 1987); Francis Watson, The Text and the Church: Biblical Interpretation in Theological Perspective (Grand Rapids, MI: Eerdmans, 1994). [ed. note, for a systematic exposition of Ratzinger's approach, see Aaron Pidel, SJ, The Inspiration and Truth of Scripture: Testing the Ratzinger Paradigm, Verbum Domini series (Washington, DC: The Catholic University of America Press, 2023). See also Gregory Vall, Ecclesial Exegesis: A Synthesis of Ancient and Modern Approaches to Scripture (Washington, DC: The Catholic University of America Press, 2022).]

13. See Hans Frei, The Identity of Jesus Christ (Philadelphia: Fortress, 1975); C. Stephen Evans, The Historical Christ and the Jesus of Faith: The Incarnational Narrative as History (Oxford: Clarendon Press, 1996); and William M. Thompson, The Struggle for Theology's Soul: Contesting Scripture in Christology (New York: Crossroad Herder, 1996).

14. See J. A. Di Noia, "Authority, Public Dissent and the Nature of Theological Thinking," The Thomist 52 (1988): 185–207, for a more complete account of the "nature and grace" of theology.

THEOLOGICAL EXEGESIS
(BIBLE AS SCRIPTURE) AND OTHER EXEGETICAL
INQUIRIES (BIBLE AS *TEXT*)

In order to make some headway in describing a properly theological exegesis, it is useful to turn to David Kelsey's analysis of the different kinds of inquiries identified by the term "exegesis." Kelsey distinguishes three species of exegesis in modern biblical studies which, for want of more precise nomenclature, he simply calls exegesis1, exegesis2 and exegesis3.[15]

Exegesis1 Kelsey identifies as essentially reconstructive. Adopting critical methods applicable to texts of all kinds—not just the Bible—its aim is to identify the events and sources *behind* the text under examination. The main emphasis of this kind of criticism is historical, and its practitioners are concerned with establishing, by the standards common among modern historians, what realities *probably* gave rise to the text being studied. The celebrated "quests" for the historical Jesus are perhaps the best and worst examples of this type of study.

Exegesis2 refers to what most people who employ the word "exegesis" today probably have in mind when they use it, namely, literary interpretation. The goal of exegesis2 is to establish what the text means *as written by its human author*. This includes establishing what its human author may have *meant* to convey to his contemporaries to whom he wrote. Again, the principles and scholarly standards employed in this art are not derived from faith but from secular disciplines. In taking the Bible as an object for exegesis2, scholars usually prescind from faith, from issues of the divine authorship of the text, and from its churchly uses and interpretations.

Together exegesis1 and exegesis2 yield literary and historical judgments about texts *without* reference to any status of privilege or claims to inspiration made for them by the Christian community.

---

15. David H. Kelsey, *The Uses of Scripture in Current Theology* (Philadelphia: Fortress, 1975), 198–201.

Ordinarily, these two kinds of exegesis enhance one another and influence the third type, exegesis3.

This last variety of interpretation is properly theological, and considers the text at hand not simply *as text* but precisely *as Scripture*. Exegesis3 is theological exegesis *per se*, inasmuch as it takes cognizance of the text as identified by its place, not only within the whole scriptural corpus, but within and according to patterns of interpretation which logically and imaginatively *precede* commentary on that text *as normative for the community*. Thus, exegesis3 examines texts inasmuch as they relate to faith, doctrine, theology, and any religious act of those who receive them as Scripture. Writes Kelsey,

> Neither [exegesis1 nor exegesis2] is a way in which the results of exegesis function normatively in doing theology; only exegesis3 can provide that. Only exegesis3 is a study of biblical texts as Scripture. But that means that it is study of Scripture done within the context of a certain construal of the text: studying it in regard to certain patterns which are taken to be authoritative, and not in regard to others, as filling certain kinds of functions in the life of the church, and not others, as having certain kinds of logical force, and not others.[16]

To admit this much is not to say that theological interpretation—exegesis3—is properly separable from historical or literary study. On the contrary, at least within those communions which consider themselves to be "under" Scripture's authority, exegesis2 (if not exegesis1) serves to ground and limit theology's historical and literary assertions about a given text and influences the theological interpreter's rational and imaginative construal of revelation as a whole. Yet whatever impact literary or historical studies may have on theological exegesis as such, it is not the case that they supply a hermeneutical context sufficient for the task of theology. The use of Scripture as a rule or authority requires (absolutely speaking) an interpretive horizon or principles or standard of discrimination by which the reader can sift and make sense of the texts at hand.

All Christian communities share a conviction that theological

16. Kelsey, 200.

exegesis must take as authoritative the trinitarian, Christological, and soteriological patterns discernible in the Scripture and, at least in part, formulated as doctrinal rules by the great ecumenical councils. In different Christian communities, the interpretive horizon or hermeneutical rule may take different forms. For example, one may infer a rule or canon from within Scripture itself, taking some passage or passages as normative for construing the meaning of others—one might see Martin Luther's emphasis on Romans as a choice of this kind. Or, again, one might take the Pietists' route and trust that God guides the Bible's devout readers. Or, one may have confidence in a particular interpretive tradition, like that reflected in the Talmud. In any case, exegesis1 and exegesis2 do not close the question of what Scriptural text means *qua* revelation—indeed, prescinding methodologically from all consideration of the text of Scripture *per se* (that is, as authored by and revelatory of God) has been the very act by which exegesis1 and exegesis2 have among Christians and Jews alike become disciplines distinct from exegesis3.

The pastors and teachers of the Catholic Church have tended to keep to consistently more specific use of the word "exegesis" than has the academic community. In formal Church documents on biblical interpretation the Pope and bishops have seemed to use the word consistently to refer only to what David Kelsey would call exegesis3, i.e., theological interpretation. This is, of course, not very surprising, since the Church's interest in Scripture arises wholly from its conviction that the Bible is the Word of God. According to the Dogmatic Constitution *Dei Filius* of Vatican Council I:

These [books of the Old and New Testaments] the Church holds sacred and canonical, not because she approved them by her authority after they had been composed by human industry alone, nor merely because they contain revelation without error; but because, composed with the Holy Spirit inspiring, they have God for their author, and were passed on as such to the Church. (§2)

The Church's pronouncements on biblical study and interpretation, beginning with Leo XIII's 1893 encyclical *Providentissimus Deus* and working up to the topic's most recent and forceful treatment in the 1994 *Catechism of the Catholic Church*, contain a two-fold demand and instruction that Catholic exegetes 1) use the best critical tools and methods available, and 2) interpret Scripture within the context of the Catholic faith.[17]

The first mandate requires no apology, since it seems obvious that our understanding of a text is improved by an appreciation of its author's culture, language, literary models, and so on. The second requirement, however, seems suspect. A look at the concrete rules proposed for such genuinely Catholic exegesis will not set many non-theological exegetes at ease. As explained in the *Catechism*, the hermeneutical criteria proposed by Vatican II are as follows (the quotations given in the italicized headings are from *Dei Verbum*, §12):

1. *Be especially attentive "to the content and unity of the whole Scripture."* Different as the books which comprise it may be, Scripture is a unity by reason of the unity of God's plan, of which Christ Jesus is the center and heart, open since his Passover. (§112)

2. *Read the Scripture "within the Living tradition of the whole Church."* According to the sayings of the Fathers, sacred Scripture is written principally in the Church's heart rather than in documents and records, for the Church carries in her Tradition the living memorial of God's Word, and it is the Holy Spirit who gives her the spiritual interpretation of the Scripture ("according to the spiritual meaning which the Spirit grants to the Church"). (§113)

3. *Be attentive to the analogy of faith.* By "analogy of faith" we mean the coherence of the truths of faith among themselves and within the whole plan of Revelation. (§114)

---

17. See *Official Catholic Teachings: Biblical Interpretation*, ed. James J. McGivern (Wilmington, DE: McGrath Publishing, 1978). See the statement of the Pontifical Biblical Commission, "The Interpretation of the Bible in the Church" (Washington, DC: United States Catholic Conference, 1990). [ed. note, also see Benedict XVI, Post-Synodal Apostolic Exhortation *Verbum Domini* (September 30, 2010).]

One must admit that these rules, the concrete demands of the requirement that Catholic exegetes interpret Scripture according to a deliberately Catholic, ecclesial hermeneutic, need to be defended not only in ecumenical discussion—where it will inevitably seem that the Church is stacking the exegetical deck—but before a considerable number of those Catholic Scripture scholars who are professionally occupied with interpreting the Bible without regard for its unity, divine authorship, or constant reference to Christ. The current essay is no place to offer a long apology for the Catholic position, which is certainly controverted in the modern academy, but perhaps the understandable fears of Catholic scholars will be allayed by the suggestions which follow.

THEOLOGICAL EXEGESIS AND
SACRAMENTAL THEOLOGY

It is not only possible to interpret the Bible, or parts of it, solely by methods which do not depend upon faith, but it is obviously done. And while it would be easy to adduce examples of frivolous, sensational, or ill-informed work in the field of non-theological exegesis, there remain thousands of rigorous and sober practitioners of this discipline. Is such scholarship—that is, the best non-theological interpretation of Scripture—inimical to theological exegesis? Or, as others have suggested, is it propaedeutic to the work of theology? Here, we want to suggest a third way of thinking about the discipline of modern, critical biblical studies and their relationship to Catholic doctrine and theology. But it is important first to note the weaknesses of the other alternatives.

Besides running counter to the expressed wisdom of the Church, flat opposition to modern critical exegesis effectively denies the reality of biblical inspiration—not by denying divine authorship, but by ignoring the nature of revelation. A book composed under the influence of the Holy Spirit is still a book, with a language, genre, historical setting, and other dimensions which cannot all be entirely accidental to the meaning of the text. It is plain to all but the most stubborn that a knowledge of the "humanity" of Scripture—everything from its vocabulary and grammar to its poetic devices and the circumstances of its composition—can be helpful for understanding the biblical texts *as Scripture.*

In the scholarly world, the more common view is that studies of parts of the Bible *as texts*—and not within the context of revelation and Christian doctrine as a whole—yield a body of knowledge independent of, and in some sense prior to, theological inquiry. However, this view also appears inadequate in that it fails to interpret the Bible as such. Moreover, such inquiries, unless correlated to theological exegesis, are liable to extend beyond their competence to questions of Christian doctrine—that is, to questions about God, Christ, salvation, sacraments, church order, and so on. They need not do this, of course, but very few people would pursue careers in non-theological exegesis if they could only study questions essentially irrelevant to the Bible as *Scripture* ("What does the Bible tell us about Antiochus Epiphanes?"). Because, in fact, most people who study the Bible are interested in it precisely because it is received by believers as divine revelation, the question we would like to address is not *whether* theological exegesis should use modern scholarly methods, but *how.*

Kelsey's analysis demonstrates that historical and literary inquiries have an integrity and purposes of their own and that exegetical studies of the Bible as *text* have a legitimacy independent of the theological uses to which their results may be put. But this implies that theological exegesis possesses its own integrity as an intellectual inquiry (or, as medieval theologians would have said, a science), with a distinctive set of principles which must guide its appropriation of the results of historical and literary studies.

Aquinas made an analogous point.[18] He did not contend that

18. For what follows, see St. Thomas Aquinas, *Summa theologiae* I, q. 1; *In Boethius de Trinitate,* q. 6, a. 3; William A. Wallace, *The Role of Demonstration in Moral Theology* (Washington DC: The Thomist Press, 1962), 39–43; J. A. Di Noia, "Thomas after Thomism:

the truth of revelation and the discipline of theology make other, natural human inquiries superfluous. Instead, he spoke of the subalternation or subordination of sciences—that is, of their interdependence and ordering among themselves. For example, we could say that music is subalternated to mathematics, since music depends on timing, intervals (of pitch), and other qualities which are measured by mathematics. This does not mean that doing calculus is more noble than playing the French horn, but only that musicians need arithmetic if they are to make headway in some of their own proper business, e.g., composing harmonies. To adopt an expression from Steven Toulmin, we could say that disciplines like mathematics are field-encompassing, in the sense that they embrace the fields which depend on them. This does not mean that one could reasonably demand that a musician answer questions about higher mathematics, nor that a mathematician must be able to play a music instrument. It does mean, however, that one discipline depends on the other in such a way that the lower draws its principles from the higher.

On Aquinas' account, the relationship between mathematics and music is analogous to that between Christian doctrine and theological exegesis in that, in each case, the second discipline is subalternated to the first. (Note that the relationship at issue is not between the *Bible* and doctrine, but between the disciplines of *biblical interpretation* and doctrine.) This description of theology and exegesis as discrete inquiries would not have made any sense, of course, before the emergence of critical exegesis which treats the Bible *as though* it could be validly read apart from the theological interests and principles which had guided all pre-modern rigorous interpretation. In fact, the emergence of the new fields of non-theological exegesis of biblical texts—that is, the study of the Bible as *text*—has caused almost inevitable confusion for two reasons. First, the new fields of studying the Bible simply as a set of texts, and not as Scripture, have not, for believers, replaced theological exegesis. Second,

Aquinas and the Future of Theology," in *The Future of Thomism*, ed. Deal W. Hudson and Dennis W. Moran (Notre Dame, IN: University of Notre Dame Press, 1992), 231–45.

this confusion has been compounded by the fact that a great many practitioners of non-theological exegesis are themselves believers who, quite legitimately, prescind from the truth of revelation in their study of the texts which happen to be biblical but which are studied with historical or literary interests in view.

The impact on theology has not been a happy one. On one hand, some scholars specializing in non-theological exegesis have spoken as though their studies examined the Bible as *Scripture*, which they do not. Similarly, theologians have mistaken non-theological exegesis for scriptural interpretation properly so called. The result of mistakes of these kinds has been a deep, thick, and widespread confusion from which we cannot yet be said to have recovered. Believers have put themselves in the untenable position of saying that our best access to the meaning of Scripture is afforded not by the study of the Bible as *Scripture* but by studies which treat the Bible as something other than what Christians believe it to be. In fact, it is theological interpretation—with attention to the meaning intended not only by the sacred human authors but by God—which enjoys a privileged access to the text, precisely in virtue of its reliance upon that virtue of faith by which we believe the main subject of all Scripture inasmuch as it is divinely authored, namely, Christ our God.

Turning to Christology and sacramental theology, it follows that a doctrinally-principled inquiry about what can be known through historical study about the actual facts of the life of Jesus would be pursued with the context of a Christologically- and soteriologically-ruled reading of the Bible. Nothing in the tradition excludes the application of historical methods to the theological study and explication of the Christian faith. If such methods were applied in ways that were continuous with the fundamental presuppositions of the so-called "pre-critical" doctrinal and theological traditions, a doctrinally-ruled reading of the Gospels would be understood to have evolved under the guidance of the Holy Spirit, precisely to insure that the full significance of the living Christ and of his dispositions for the church would be known, proclaimed and confessed.

Since a complete account of the events narrated in the Gospels must include a reference to the divine agency and intentions at work in them, it is only in the light of faith that the events of Christ's life, his teaching, actions, and injunctions, can be understood in their historical reality as such. It is a mistake to suppose that a religious and theological interpretation of these events can be developed only after their historical reality is established. The Christian tradition understands religious and theological factors to be intrinsic to and inseparable from the meaning of these events in themselves. On this understanding of things, theological exegesis can demonstrate the scriptural basis for the Christological and sacramental faith of the church.

At the present time, sacramental theology—perhaps only less urgently than Christology itself—stands in need of deliverance from the confusion that has arisen for theology since the advent of modern biblical criticism. The distinctions presented in this discussion are meant to contribute to a rethinking of the authority of Scripture for theology which acknowledges the integrity of non-theological forms of exegesis without conflating these with properly theological exegesis. It is vitally important for theologians to recognize, for instance, that in considering the doctrine and practice of the sacraments theological resolution cannot be produced simply by non-theological inquiries about the texts of Scripture, not because such studies tell us nothing about the Bible at all, but because what the sacraments are (divine actions uniting us to the triune God through the actions of human agents and material signs) can only be known by faith.

CHAPTER 5

The Ecclesial Vocation of the Theologian in Catholic Higher Education

It should be admitted at the outset that the cosy juxtaposition of terms in my title, as much as they might reflect an ideal state of relations, do not fully correspond to the reality of the situation in which we find ourselves today.

THEOLOGY, THEOLOGIANS, AND CATHOLIC HIGHER EDUCATION: SOME DISPUTED QUESTIONS

For one thing, that the vocation of theologians is a properly ecclesial one has been and continues to be doubted, disputed or denied. Even if it is conceded that the theological profession entails a calling of some kind, it is supposed that this would be primarily an academic or intellectual vocation, involving overriding allegiances, not to a church or denomination, but to one's scholarly guild and the larger academic community. The code of free inquiry upheld by these communities is thought to exclude in principle the intrusion of non-scholarly considerations (such as creedal

Originally published in *Called to Holiness and Communion: Vatican II on the Church*, ed. Steven C. Boguslawski, OP, and Robert L. Fastiggi (Scranton, PA: University of Scranton Press, 2009), 321–39.

or dogmatic ones) and even more so the interference of representatives of non-academic communities (such as bishops or the Holy
See) in the pursuit of the theologian's specific intellectual vocation.
In this perspective, if the possibility of an ecclesial vocation were to
be granted at all, then it would presumably have to be defined and
expressed in ways that did not contradict the supervening obligations of a strictly academic or intellectual vocation.

Furthermore, that the theologian has a place in higher education is a proposition that has not been self-evident at any time in the
past hundred years and that remains in doubt among Catholic and
non-Catholic educators alike. The issue here concerns not theologians qua theologians but the field of theology itself. It may come as
something of a surprise—especially to Catholics thinking of the historic importance of theological faculties in the great universities of
western Europe—that theology found its place in American higher
education only relatively late, with difficulty, and at a moment coin-
ciding with the ascendancy of religious studies. With or without an
ecclesial vocation, the theologian's place in Catholic higher education at the present can hardly be said to be a secure one.

Finally, that institutions of higher learning could maintain recognizable—not to say institutional—bonds to the Catholic Church
and still be true to their mission as modern research institutions has
been and continues to be questioned by many, both within the Catholic Church and beyond it. Behind this doubt stretches a long history of which the period since the publication of *Ex Corde Ecclesiae*
is but the most recent phase. The view that church affiliation and
academic integrity might be incompatible with one another has led
many Catholic and Protestant institutions of higher learning over
past century to weaken or dissolve the affiliations that bound them
to their founding ecclesial communities. The pressure to pursue this
course has perhaps been felt more acutely by Catholic higher education because the polity of the Catholic Church, in contrast to that of
most other churches and ecclesial communities, is perceived to allow for a more direct involvement in the life of the Catholic campus.

In the years since *Ex Corde Ecclesia,* it has perhaps become clearer that the issue here is not just the maintenance of a Catholic identity but also participation in Catholic communion. Disagreements about how to track the relationships between the Catholic college or university and the Catholic Church influence perceptions of the theologian's vocation, as well as judgments about his or her place in Catholic higher education.

It is clear then that, far from announcing the exposition of truths concerning which there is an undisturbed consensus in Catholic higher education in the United States, my title in effect introduces a set of disputed questions about which there are widespread and persistent doubts even within Catholic circles. In the form of powerful cultural assumptions, these doubts have influenced the actual shape of Catholic higher education in this country.

CATHOLIC HIGHER EDUCATION AND THE ECCLESIOLOGY OF COMMUNION

The Church's teaching authorities, while cognizant of these doubts, cannot be said to share them.

Consider higher education first. The Second Vatican Council reaffirmed the traditional Catholic view of the possibility and character of Church sponsorship of colleges and universities (in *Gravissimum Educationis*). Following upon and implementing the conciliar teaching were two companion documents: *Sapientia Christiana* (1979), concerning the governance of ecclesiastically accredited institutions, and *Ex Corde Ecclesiae* (1990), concerning all other Catholic institutions of higher learning. These apostolic constitutions laid out the different ways that ecclesial communion is embodied by Catholic institutions of these diverse types. The publication of *Sapientia Christiana* initiated a period during which American ecclesiastical faculties brought their own statutes into line with the new legislation, while in 2000 the United States Conference of Catholic Bishops' application of *Ex Corde Ecclesiae* received official recognition by the Holy

See.[1] What is more, within postconciliar teaching, theology and education have been regularly addressed by Pope John Paul II in his many discourses and encyclicals.

In the terms of the overall theme of this symposium, the call to holiness and communion is central to understanding the confidence—one could as well say the absence of doubts—with which the Church advances her vision of Catholic higher education and the place of theology within it. The ecclesiology of communion is of fundamental importance in sustaining this confidence and in articulating this vision.

The gift of truth that we have received from Christ is this: to know that no one has ever wanted anything more than God wants to share the communion of his life with us. What Christ taught us and what we proclaim to the world is that the triune God invites all human persons to participate in the communion of the Father, Son, and Holy Spirit, and with one another in them. Holiness is nothing less than the transformed capacity to enjoy this communion, and ecclesial communion is at root nothing less than trinitarian communion.

This basic truth of Catholic faith unfolds in an ensemble of other truths about creation, incarnation, redemption, and sanctification. The central truths of the Christian faith find their deepest meaning in the reality of trinitarian communion. Everything created exists so that the Blessed Trinity could realize this plan of love. Through the Incarnation and the Paschal Mystery, Christ enables creaturely persons to enter into the life of the uncreated Persons. In the Church, the Holy Spirit unites all those transformed in Christ and draws them into the communion of trinitarian love. Ecclesial communion is nothing less than the beginning of our participation in the life of the Blessed Trinity.

Pope John Paul II has repeatedly described this communion as a "participated theonomy" that draws us into the communion of trinitarian love in such a way that our full humanity is fulfilled and

1. United States Conference of Catholic Bishops, *Ex Corde Ecclesiae: An Application to the United States*, *Origins* 30 (2000): 68–75.

at the same time transcended. This theme, frequently reiterated in the Holy Father's great encyclicals, is fundamental for developing a properly Catholic understanding of the place of education and scholarship in human personal, social, and cultural life. In Christian faith, the human reality is not suppressed but is fully realized. To embrace the First Truth and the Absolute Good who is God is not to accept constraints on human reason and desire, but to free them for their divinely willed destiny.

The Church's teaching and legislation regarding Catholic higher education are unintelligible apart from the ecclesiology of communion.

It is clear that a wide range of teaching activities is required if the Church is to be able to communicate the gift of truth she has received from Christ.[2] The institutional expression of these teaching activities has taken many different forms throughout Christian history. In the field of higher education the evidence for continuing and vigorous Catholic presence is indisputable. Far from experiencing any doubts about this possibility, the Church assumes as her rightful role the establishment of colleges and universities, and the maintenance of appropriate relations with them.

From a theological perspective, the genius of Catholic jurisprudence in this area arises from its underlying Christian humanism. As personal and social beings, the Christian faithful possess an inherent dignity and autonomy that must be respected if ecclesial communion is to be realized. The reality of communion presupposes the reality of persons in communion and, in an ordered community like the Catholic Church, the reality of institutions in communion. It would be self-contradictory to invoke the ecclesiology of communion as grounds for infringing upon the autonomy rightly enjoyed by persons and institutions, and thus juridically protected, in the Catholic Church. The very notion of being in communion presupposes

2. J. A. Di Noia, "Communion and Magisterium: Teaching Authority and the Culture of Grace," *Modern Theology* 9 (1993): 403–18. [ed. note—see chapter 2 of this volume.]

the integrity and autonomy, if also the interdependence, of the participants in ecclesial communion. The concrete expression of a series of relationships by its very nature affirms the proper autonomy and distinctive competencies of the persons and institutions enjoying ecclesial communion.

Although the grace of ecclesial communion is in the deepest sense an invisible reality, it is not an abstraction. Catholic tradition insists that it must take visible form in concrete communities and in their social and institutional structures. In the aftermath of the Second Vatican Council, the Church has invited Catholic colleges and universities to internalize the renewed ecclesiology of communion in the structures of their institutions, and in different ways depending on whether they are ecclesiastically accredited or not.

The historical record in the United States supports the conclusion that, given the political and cultural pressures favoring increasing secularization over the past hundred years and into the foreseeable future, the Catholic identity of currently Catholic institutions of higher learning is not likely to be sustainable without concrete juridical bonds between these institutions and the Church. Naturally, in developing its teaching and legislation in this area, the Holy See does not have only the situation in the United States in view. But the practical implications of an ecclesiology of communion, formulated with the whole Catholic Church in view, nonetheless have particular urgency in a situation where "the disengagement of colleges and universities from their Christian churches" has become endemic. In his indispensable book on this topic, *The Dying of the Light: The Disengagement of Colleges and Universities from Their Christian Churches*, Father James Burtchaell documented with considerable detail the informal arrangements by which hundreds of sincere and well-meaning faculty, administrators, and church leaders of countless once church-related colleges and universities believed that they would be able to ensure the Lutheran, Presbyterian, Methodist, Anglican, and other denominational identities of their institutions.[3]

3. James T. Burtchaell, *The Dying of the Light: The Disengagement of Colleges and Universities from Their Christian Churches* (Grand Rapids, MI: Eerdmans, 1998). On these

Without the adoption of juridical provisions, and relying solely on the good will and sense of commitment of Catholic educators and bishops—as was strongly suggested by some—few of the currently Catholic institutions of higher learning in the U. S. are likely to remain distinctively and recognizably Catholic. Even with the adoption of something like clearly stated juridical provisions of the USCCB Application, it may be that the secularizing trends will turn out to have been irreversible in some of the two hundred or more Catholic institutions of higher learning in the U. S.

Recent studies, including those by Father Burtchaell, Philip Gleason, John McGreevy, Philip Hamburger, and others, have made it possible to identify with greater precision the cultural and political forces operative in the relatively swift transformation that has occurred in Catholic higher education in the U. S. since the 1960s.[4] Significant anti-Catholic cultural assumptions, which in part contributed to shaping public policy towards education, gave prevalence to the notion that church affiliation, most especially in the Catholic ambit, inevitably compromised the academic excellence, research capacity, and institutional autonomy of institutions enmeshed in such relationships. In addition, it was widely held that, because of their submissiveness to church authority, Catholics could never fully internalize the valued American traits of individual autonomy, and freedom of thought and expression, that would make for good citizens of the republic. In so far as they were not actively anti-religious, these forces favored the development of a broadly enlightened form of religiosity, free of ties to particular churches or denominations, and of the dogmatic and institutional commitments entailed by these ties. The impact of these cultural and political forces was

themes, see also David J. O'Brien, *From the Heart of the American University* (Maryknoll, NY: Orbis Books, 1994), and George Mardsen, *The Soul of the American University* (New York: Oxford University Press, 1994).

4. Philip Gleason, *Contending with Modernity: Catholic Higher Education in the Twentieth Century* (New York: Oxford University Press, 1995); Philip Hamburger, *Separation of Church and State* (Cambridge, MA: Harvard University Press, 2002); Philip Jenkins, *The New Anti-Catholicism* (New York: Oxford University Press, 2003); John T. McGreevy, *Catholicism and American Freedom* (New York: Norton, 2003).

aggravated after the Second Vatican Council, not only by the collapse of a distinctively Catholic culture, but also by the uncritical embrace of the secular culture (mistakenly thought to be warranted by the Council's constitution, *Gaudium et Spes*).[5] Catholic educators (and others) failed to recognize that the ambient culture, whose values they sought to embody institutionally, was not religiously neutral but often encoded with actively dechristianizing assumptions.

The call to holiness and communion, reaffirmed by the Second Vatican Council and vigorously reasserted in the pontificate of Pope John Paul II, offers an opportunity for Catholic Church-related institutions of higher education in the U. S. to recover their distinctively Catholic identity and to embody it in clearly expressed communal bonds with the Church. With a tradition of academic excellence and freedom of inquiry stretching back to the medieval universities, Catholic higher education should courageously address the range of anti-Catholic and, increasingly, anti-Christian prejudices that seek to exclude Catholics and other Christians from participation in public life and from influence on public policy. According to the Second Vatican Council, Catholic universities aim to ensure that the Christian outlook should acquire "a public, stable and universal influence in the whole process of the promotion of higher culture" (*Gravissimum Educationis*, §10). As was true in the past, Catholic colleges and universities in the U. S. have an important contribution to make to the christianization of American culture. George Lindbeck, the distinguished Lutheran theologian and astute observer of the Catholic scene, has written: "The waning of cultural Christianity may not be a good thing for societies. Traditionally Christian lands, when stripped of their historic faith, become unworkable and demonic....

5. On American Catholic culture in the twentieth century, see Philip Gleason, *Keeping the Faith* (Notre Dame, IN: University of Notre Dame Press, 1987), and William M. Halsey, *Survival of American Innocence* (Notre Dame, IN: University of Notre Dame Press, 1980). On the impact of *Gaudium et Spes*, see Tracy Rowland, *Culture and the Thomist Tradition* (London: Routledge, 2003). For a general view of Christianity and culture, see Kathryn Tanner, *Theories of Culture: A New Agenda for Theology* (Minneapolis: Fortress Press, 1997).

Christianization of culture can be in some situations the church's major contribution to feeding the poor, clothing the hungry and liberating the imprisoned."[6] Catholic institutions of higher learning can play a central role in helping the Church, as well as other Christian communities, to monitor the impact of mass culture on the communication of the faith and the expression of Catholic and Christian life in Western postmodern societies.

THE PLACE OF THEOLOGY IN CATHOLIC HIGHER EDUCATION

In addition to articulating a comprehensive vision of Catholic higher education, both conciliar and post-conciliar teaching consistently assigned a central role to theology and its cognate disciplines in Catholic higher education. Following upon *Gravissimum Educationis* of the Second Vatican Council, the twin post-conciliar apostolic constitutions on higher education each assume that theology will find a place in the Catholic colleges and universities. As might be expected in a document that contains norms for ecclesiastical faculties and seminaries, *Sapientia Christiana* provides a complete picture of the curriculum of theology and its associated disciplines. But *Ex Corde Ecclesiae* is no less explicit on the matter, even if it concedes that in certain situations nothing more than a chair of theology will be possible (*Ex Corde Ecclesiae*, §19). Both documents affirm that the primary focus of theology is to investigate and explain the doctrines of the Catholic faith as drawn from revelation. It is assumed that this study will be pursued in a spirit of true freedom of inquiry, employing appropriate methods, and acknowledging the derived character of the knowledge sought and thus its dependence on divine revelation. Significantly, both documents ascribe important integrating functions to theology within the overall programs of

6. George A. Lindbeck, *The Church in A Postliberal Age*, ed. James J. Buckley (Grand Rapids, MI: Eerdmans, 2002), 7. See also Aidan Nichols, *Christendom Awake: On Reenergizing Church and Culture* (Grand Rapids, MI: Eerdmans, 1999).

Catholic colleges and universities, a traditional emphasis in the rationales for theology in almost all church-related higher education.

Studying these documents within the framework of Catholic history in western Europe, one might well expect the legitimacy of theology's place in the curriculum of higher education to be self-evident. Indeed, as Cardinal Avery Dulles has noted, it is unrealistic not to include theology in the university curriculum since "the Church and the Catholic people legitimately expect that some universities will provide an intellectual environment in which the meaning and implications of the faith can be studied in relation to the whole realm of human knowledge."[7]

Nonetheless, for a variety of reasons, which are lately being subjected to more systematic study, the study of religion and theology did not enjoy an unchallenged place in the evolution of church-related, and indeed public, higher education in the U. S. Two brilliant books—D. G. Hart's on the history of Protestant rationales for the study of theology and religion and Philip Gleason's on the history of Catholic higher education in the twentieth century—give the topic the attention it deserves and at the same time provide fascinating reading for anyone interested in understanding the current situation of the study and teaching of religion and theology in American higher education.[8]

Hart and Gleason show that in the United States throughout much of the nineteenth century both Catholic and Protestant educators tended to view theology as a discipline that belonged in the seminary, not in the college or university. In church-affiliated Catholic and Protestant colleges, religious instruction was more likely to be seen as catechetical and moral formation than as properly theological inquiry. Later, with the emergence of the modern research university, Protestant educators struggled to legitimate teaching and research in the Christian religion while at the same time downplaying

7. Avery Dulles, *The Craft of Theology* (New York: Crossroad, 1992), 172.

8. Gleason, *Contending with Modernity*, and D. G. Hart, *The University Gets Religion: Religious Studies in American Higher Education* (Baltimore: Johns Hopkins University, 1999), with extensive bibliography.

the particular denominational entailments such teaching and research might otherwise involve. Catholic higher education in early twentieth century America tended to give a central role to religiously colored philosophical studies rather than to theology itself. Between the 1920s and the 1950s, neoscholastic philosophy played an influential role in curricular integration in Catholic colleges and universities and in the provision of the self-understanding that gave Catholic culture its shape. During this period, theology properly so-called only gradually began to find a place in Catholic higher education, though kerygmatic, liturgical, and Thomistic approaches remained in contention as Catholic educators strove to identify the kind of teaching that would be appropriate for undergraduates. Inevitably, both Protestant and Catholic curricula were influenced by the teaching of theology as conducted in their seminaries. For different but related reasons, neither Protestant nor Catholic university theology enjoyed the undiluted respect of the broader academic community. With the erosion of the hold of neo-orthodoxy in Protestant theology and the collapse of the neoscholastic synthesis in Catholic higher education, the 1960s were a time of crisis for both Catholic and Protestant theological and religious educators. The 1960s set in motion powerful cultural and educational trends that eventuated in the widespread (albeit unstable) prevalence of religious studies in Catholic, Protestant, and public higher education.[9]

In Catholic higher education, the displacement of theology by religious studies poses significant challenges. Frank Schubert's important study of this shift covers the crucial period 1955–1985 and demonstrates the steady move away from courses engaging in appropriation of the Catholic tradition toward courses in the history, anthropology,

9. See Patrick W. Carey and Earl Muller, eds., *Theological Education in the Catholic Tradition: Contemporary Challenges*, (New York: Crossroad, 1998); Patrick Carey, "College Theology in Historical Perspective," in *American Catholic Traditions: Resources for Renewal*, ed. Sandra Mize and William Portier (Maryknoll, NY: Orbis Books, 1996), 242–71; Susan M. Mountin, "A Study of Undergraduate Roman Catholic Theology Education, 1952–1976," Ph.D. diss., Marquette University, 1994; Pamela C. Young, "Theological Education in American Catholic Higher Education, 1939–1973," Ph.D. diss., Marquette University, 1995.

and sociology of religion.[10] While admitting areas of overlap between theology and religious studies, most scholars acknowledge the fundamental difference in perspective represented by the approaches to religious realities in these diverse fields. Whereas theology takes the claim to truth made by the sources of Christian revelation as its framework, the field(s) of religious studies systematically bracket the claims to truth made for contending religious traditions. For theology, revelation provides the principles for inquiry, and the truth of Christian doctrines is the basic assumption for this inquiry. For religious studies, the world's religions present a richly diverse set of texts, institutions, rites, and other phenomena, which are studied employing a range of humanistic and social scientific methodologies.

In Catholic colleges and universities where this shift is complete and likewise unchallenged, it is difficult for theology to maintain its integrity and finality as *fides quaerens intellectum*. Apart from any other secularizing pressures that might be operative, in the midst of predominantly religious studies departments, theology itself can easily yield to the methods and perspectives of the study of religion. As we shall see shortly, the transformation of theology into a branch of religious studies makes it nearly unintelligible to claim for theologians any properly ecclesial vocation or even connection with the believing community.

THE ECCLESIAL VOCATION OF THE THEOLOGIAN

What must be surely regarded as among the most significant official documents on the place of the theologian in the Church appeared in 1990. It was prepared by the Congregation for the Doctrine of the Faith and was confidently entitled *The Ecclesial Vocation of the Theologian*.

Although the documents of the Second Vatican Council

10. Frank D. Schubert, *A Sociological Study of Secularization Trends in the American Catholic University* (Lewiston, ME: Edwin Mellen Press, 1990).

mentioned theology and theologians at various points—perhaps most notably in the Constitution on Divine Revelation (*Dei Verbum,* §23–24), the Constitution on the Church (*Lumen Gentium,* §23), and the Decree on Priestly Formation (*Optatam Totius,* §12, 14–16), the council did not make this theme the focus of an extended treatment.[11] Given the impact that the council had on the work of theologians, this may come as something of a surprise—all the more so perhaps, since, as Cardinal Ratzinger has noted, it was "the great blossoming of theology between the world wars which made the Second Vatican Council possible."[12] After the conclusion of the council the continuing contribution of theologians was institutionalized in a remarkable way when Pope Paul VI established the International Theological Commission in 1969.[13]

The CDF *Instruction* reflects the Church's renewed consciousness of the centrality of the role of the theologian in her life. Reprising significant elements of the Catholic tradition, as articulated in conciliar and post-conciliar teaching, the *Instruction* forcefully argues that the theologian's vocation is a properly ecclesial one and, as in the case of Catholic colleges and universities, that the bonds of ecclesial communion implied by this relationship can be expressed juridically. In the terms of the overall theme of this symposium, the CDF *Instruction* may be taken as a robust reminder that the call to holiness and communion comes to theologians at least in part through the mediation of their ecclesial vocation precisely as theologians.[14]

At the start of his splendid book, *The Shape of Theology,* Father

11. For a helpful discussion of conciliar teaching regarding theology, see Anthony J. Figueiredo, *The Magisterium-Theology Relationship: Contemporary Theological Conceptions in the Light of Universal Church Teaching* (Rome: Gregorian University Press, 2001), 211–37; for the historical background and setting, 167–237; for the relations between bishops and theologians in the United States, 287–342.

12. Joseph Ratzinger, *Nature and Mission of Theology* (San Francisco: Ignatius Press, 1995), 66. See also Karl H. Neufeld, "In the Service of the Council: Bishops and Theologians at the Second Vatican Council," in *Vatican Council II: Assessments and Perspectives,* Vol. II, ed. René Latourelle (New York: Crossroad, 1988), 74–105.

13. Michael Sharkey, ed. *International Theological Commission: Texts and Documents 1969–1985* (San Francisco: Ignatius Press, 1989).

14. For postconciliar teaching on theology, see Figueiredo, *The Magisterium-Theology Relationship,* 239–86.

Aidan Nichols asks the question: "What sort of person must I be in order to become a theologian?"—to which we might well add, "and in order to continue being one."[15] This, in effect, is the arresting question posed by the CDF document. In addressing this question, the *Instruction* takes up in turn the divine gift of truth, the vocation of the theologian, and the role of the magisterium. Under its consideration the role of the magisterium, the *Instruction* gives extended attention to the problem of theological dissent.[16]

But what is particularly noteworthy, in Cardinal Ratzinger's view, is that the *Instruction* begins, not with the magisterium, but with the gift of divine truth. Indeed, the *Instruction's* Latin title is *Donum Veritatis*, "the gift of truth." Because theology is not simply an "ancillary function" of the magisterium, we need to locate the theologian and the work of theology in the broader context of the life of Church, precisely as she is the locus of a truth that she did not generate but that she received as a gift. At the center of this truth is the person of Jesus Christ who reveals the divine desire to draw us into the communion of trinitarian love and, moreover, who enables us to enjoy this communion. The function of the magisterium is to guard and teach this truth in its entirety that the Church received as a gift and is bound to hand on. For this reason, according to Cardinal Ratzinger, the *Instruction* "treats the ecclesial mission of the theologian not in a duality of magisterium-theology, but rather in the framework of a triangular relationship defined by the people of God, bearer of the *sensus fidei*, the magisterium, and theology."[17] In different ways, therefore, both the magisterium and theology are servants of a prior truth, received in the Church as a gift.[18]

15. Aidan Nichols, *The Shape of Theology* (Collegeville, MN: Liturgical Press, 1991), 13.

16. This discussion of dissent is perhaps the most complete to be found in any official Catholic document. For the setting of this discussion, see Figueiredo, *The Magisterium-Theology Relationship*, 232–33; 254–60. It could be noted here that, for a Catholic theologian, the situation of being in dissent from Catholic doctrine is essentially an anamolous one and should not be allowed to frame the treatment of the ecclesial vocation of the theologian.

17. Ratzinger, *Nature and Mission of Theology*, 104–5.

18. See Di Noia, "Communion and Magisterium."

Perhaps the most important contribution of the *Instruction* is to have secured in this way what Cardinal Ratzinger calls the "ecclesial identity of theology"[19] and, correspondingly, the ecclesial vocation of the theologian. In the words of the *Instruction* itself: "Among the vocations awakened ... by the Spirit in the Church is that of the theologian ... [whose] role is to pursue in a particular way an ever deeper understanding of the Word of God found in the inspired Scriptures and handed on by the living Tradition of the Church ... [which he does] in communion with the Magisterium which has been charged with the responsibility of preserving the deposit of faith" (*Instruction*, §6) The theological vocation responds to the intrinsic dynamic of faith that "appeals to reason" and "beckons reason ... to come to understand what it has believed" (§6). In this way, "theological science responds to the invitation of truth as it seeks to understand the faith" (§6). But the theological vocation also responds to the dynamic of love, for "in the act of faith, man knows God's goodness and begins to love Him ... [and] is ever desirous of a better knowledge of the beloved" (§7).

The gift of truth received in the Church thus establishes both the context for the vocation and mission of the theologian, and the framework for the actual practice of the discipline of theology. This ecclesially received truth, as articulated in the deposit of faith and handed on by the magisterium, constitutes not an *extrinsic* authority that poses odious limits on an inquiry that would otherwise be free but an *intrinsic* source and measure that gives theology its identity and finality as an intellectual activity. Hence, as Cardinal Ratzinger asks, "Is theology for which the Church is no longer meaningful really a theology in the proper sense of the word?"[20] Examined independently of the assent of faith and the mediation of the ecclesial community, the texts, institutions, rites, and beliefs of the Catholic Church can be the focus of the humanistic, philosophical, and social

19. Ratzinger, *Nature and Mission of Theology*, 105.
20. Joseph Ratzinger, *Principles of Catholic Theology* (San Francisco: Ignatius Press, 1987), 323.

scientific inquiries that together constitute the field of religious studies. But Christian theology is a different kind of inquiry. Cut off from
an embrace of the truth that provides its subject matter and indicates
the methods appropriate to its study, theology as the Church has always understood it loses its specific character as a scientific inquiry
of a certain type.[21] Its precise scope is to seek the intelligibility of a
truth received in faith by the theologian who is himself a member of
the ecclesial community that is, as Cardinal Walter Kasper has said,
"the place of truth."[22]

The theologian is thus free to seek the truth within limits imposed, not by an intrusive external authority, but by the nature of
his discipline as such. As the *Instruction* points out: "Freedom of research, which the academic community holds most precious, means
an openness to accepting the truth that emerges at the end of an investigation in which no element has intruded that is foreign to the
methodology corresponding to the object under study" (§12). Theology cannot "deny its own foundations," to use the words of Cardinal Dulles; the acceptance of the authority of Scripture and doctrines in theology is "not a limitation but rather the charter of its
existence and freedom to be itself."[23] The freedom of inquiry proper
to theology, is, according to the CDF *Instruction*, the "hallmark of a
rational discipline whose object is given by Revelation, handed on
and interpreted in the Church under the authority of the Magisterium, and received by faith. These givens have the force of principles.
To eliminate them would mean to cease doing theology" (§12). The
principles of theology, as we noted earlier, are derived from revelation, and constitute the discipline as such. In accepting them, the
theologian is simply being true to the nature of his subject, and to
his vocation as a scholar in this field.

These elements of the *Instruction's* account of the theological

21. See J. A. Di Noia, "Authority, Dissent and the Nature of Theological Thinking,"
The Thomist 52 (1988): 185–207. [Reprinted in revised form in this volume as Chapter
One.]
22. Walter Kasper, *Theology and Church* (New York: Crossroad, 1989), 129–47.
23. Dulles, *The Craft of Theology*, 168.

vocation are ferociously contested in today's academy, largely on the basis of what Lindbeck has called the "individualistic foundational rationalism" that shapes the deepest cultural assumptions of modernity.[24] But the Church has a solid, well-substantiated, and historically warranted rationale for its account of the nature of theology as an intellectual discipline of a particular sort, and of the responsibilities of its practitioners. In the present circumstances, we need to make this case without apology. It is central to the convictions of the Catholic Church, and indeed of the Christian tradition as such, to give priority to a theonomous rather than to an autonomous rationality. It so happens that certain postmodern intellectual trends have begun to advance what Alasdair MacIntyre calls the traditioned character of all rational inquiry[25] and Lindbeck calls the socially and linguistically constituted character of belief. This intellectual climate is, to a certain extent, more favorable to the defense of the principle of theonomous rationality that is crucial for the Catholic understanding of theology. But it must be recognized that the basis for this understanding is itself a properly theological one that is rooted in fundamental Christian convictions about the gift of truth and its reception in the ecclesial community.[26]

The Church embodies her understanding of the nature of theology and of the ecclesial vocation of the theologian by according to both the discipline and its practitioners a role in Catholic higher education according to the principles of the ecclesiology of communion that we considered earlier.

According to *Ex Corde Ecclesiae* and *Sapientia Christiana*, the standard theological disciplines include: sacred Scripture, dogmatic

---

24. Lindbeck, *The Church in A Postliberal Age*, 7.

25. Alasdair MacIntyre, *Three Rival Versions of Moral Theology* (Notre Dame, IN: University of Notre Dame Press, 1990). See especially the essays by Jean Porter, Stephen P. Turner, and Terry Pinkard in *Alasdair MacIntyre*, ed. Mark C. Murphy (Cambridge: Cambridge University Press, 2003).

26. See Lindbeck's *The Nature of Doctrine* (Philadelphia: Westminster, 1984). For an excellent overview, see Bernhard A. Eckerstorfer, "The One Church in the Postmodern World: Hermeneutics, Key Concepts and Perspectives in the Work of George Lindbeck," *Pro Ecclesia* 13 (2004): 399–423.

theology, moral theology, pastoral theology, canon law, liturgy, and church history. Those teaching these disciplines are invited to make a profession of faith and oath of fidelity in order to express the derived character of these disciplines and the ecclesial space they inhabit. These formulas in effect allow the scholar to express a promise to respect the principles of his or her field as well as the personal communion of the theologian with the Church. Viewed in this light, theological disciplines and their practitioners are in a situation analogous to other disciplines and to scholars in other fields that are supervised by professional societies, by peer review, and by a whole range of certifying and accrediting bodies who maintain the standards within these fields and the credibility that they rightly enjoy among the general public.

In addition, the Church offers a canonical mission to theologians teaching in ecclesiastical faculties, and a *mandatum* to those teaching in all other institutions of higher learning. Although both the canonical mission and the *mandatum* have provoked controversy, the necessity of the canonical mission is perhaps better understood within the context of ecclesiastically accredited faculties. Here, I will confine my remarks to the *mandatum*.[27]

The nature of the *mandatum* referred to in *Ex Corde Ecclesiae* is best understood in the light of the Second Vatican Council's decree on the laity: "Thus, making various dispositions of the apostolate according to the circumstances, the hierarchy enjoins some particular form of it more closely with its own apostolic function. Yet the proper nature and distinctiveness of each apostolate must be preserved, and the laity must not be deprived of the possibility of acting on their own accord. In various church documents this procedure of the hierarchy is call a mandate" (*Apostolicam Actuositatem*, §24). While the *mandatum* has a different juridical character from the canonical mission of professors teaching in ecclesiastical faculties as required by *Sapientia Christiana*, both express in a concrete way the ecclesial

---

27. For helpful discussions of the canonical mission and the *mandatum*, see Figueiredo, *The Magisterium-Theology Relationship*, 185–87; 253–54; 374–80.

identity of the theologian. According to canonist Father Reginald Whitt, the above-mentioned mandate "refers to those apostolic activities that remain activities proper to the laity in virtue of their baptism yet joined closely to the apostolic ministry of the bishop." A Catholic professor of theology in a Catholic university is thus considered "as one of the faithful engaged in the higher education apostolate entitled and required to obtain endorsement from the competent hierarch."[28]

In requiring the *mandatum* (and, for that matter, the canonical mission), the Church acknowledges that the Catholic theologian pursues his or her inquiries under the light of revelation as contained in Scripture and tradition and proclaimed by the magisterium. In seeking the *mandatum*, the individual theologian gives a concrete expression to the relationship of ecclesial communion that exists between the Church and the Catholic teacher of a theological discipline in a Catholic institution of higher learning. The acceptance of the *mandatum* does not make the pursuit and recognition of truth a matter of obedience to authority: as we have seen, it is not that the doctrines of the faith are true because the magisterium teaches them, but that the magisterium teaches them because they are true. It is the Catholic conviction that the truths of faith point ultimately to nothing less than the First Truth itself, whose inner intelligibility constantly draws the inquiring mind to himself. The acceptance of the *mandatum* by a theologian is simply the public affirmation and social expression of this fundamental Catholic conviction.

We have considered the ecclesial vocation of the theologian in Catholic higher education in a symposium devoted to the teaching of the Second Vatican Council and the legacy of Pope John Paul II. We began with a series of doubts, but we end on a note of confidence. Surely, if the example of the Holy Father teaches us nothing else, it should teach us confidence in the inherent attractiveness of the Christian faith, and, in particular, the Catholic vision of

---

28. D. R. Whitt, "'What We Have Here is a Failure to Communicate': The Mind of the Legislator in *Ex Corde Ecclesiae*," *Journal of College and University Law* 25 (1999): 790.

higher education and of the vocation of the theologian. While the assumptions of the ambient culture will not always be friendly to it, this vision nonetheless deserves to be presented fully and without compromise. Indeed, because the call to holiness and communion originates not with us but with Christ, our hearers deserve from us a confident and unapologetic invitation to share a vision of human life that finds its consummation in the divine life of trinitarian communion. Nothing less will do.

CHAPTER 6

The Dominican Charism in Catholic Higher Education

Providence College on the Eve of Its Second Century

INTRODUCTION: RELIGIOUSLY SPONSORED HIGHER EDUCATION IN THE U.S.

There are about four thousand institutions of higher learning in the United States. A great number of these colleges and universities began their existence under the auspices of various Christian churches and communities. Yale and Harvard, Davidson and Emory, Wake Forest and Gettysburg, Brown, George Washington, and Vassar—these and countless other schools started out variously as Congregationalist, Presbyterian, Methodist, Baptist, Lutheran, or Evangelical institutions. But, as is well known, many of these schools "no longer have a serious, valued or functioning relationship with their religious sponsors of the past."[1]

When it was founded in 1917, Providence College was the hundred and third Catholic college to be founded in the United States

Address delivered at the Academic Convocation at Providence College, October 1, 2005.

1. James T. Burtchaell, *The Dying of the Light: The Disengagement of Colleges and Universities from Their Christian Churches* (Grand Rapids, MI: Eerdmans, 1998), xi.

since the establishment of the first—Georgetown University—in 1789. Today, in 2005, the College is just twelve years away from celebrating its hundredth anniversary, and has just inaugurated the president, its twelfth, who will, in all likelihood, usher it into its second century.

To my mind—and I am sure to yours—it is unthinkable that Providence College would not continue into the foreseeable future as a Catholic and Dominican institution of higher learning. We want this future to be an assured one: how could something as wonderful and blessed as this College has been *not* go on like this forever?

I have been invited to reflect with you about the Catholic *and* Dominican future of the College. I am well aware that in doing so I am joining a conversation that has been underway here for nearly twenty years. Just lately, your new president, Fr. Shanley, established an office for mission and ministry at the vice-presidential level of the College's administration. My own brief remarks this morning are intended as a modest contribution to your own reflection on these critically important issues, particularly in two areas: the inseparability of the Dominican and Catholic elements in the College's historic identity, and the need for deliberate measures to ensure this Dominican and Catholic identity in the future.

In his indispensable book on religiously sponsored higher education in the U.S., *The Dying of the Light*, Father James Burtchaell demonstrated that the disengagement of many of previously religiously affiliated schools from their founding communities rarely resulted from policies deliberately chosen to achieve disaffiliation. On the contrary, this estrangement between colleges and churches was effected by men and women who appeared to want the opposite.

The history of religiously sponsored higher education in the United States, as well as currently powerful secularizing trends in all sectors of our society, strongly suggest that the Catholic and Dominican future of Providence College will be assured only by deliberate and consistent policy decisions taken in the present by the faculty and the administration, the students and families, and the Board of

Trustees, the diocese of Providence and the Dominican friars of the Province of St. Joseph. I shall argue here that among the concrete measures that need to be taken in the present should be this one: to strengthen the Dominican identity of the College as the key to securing and fostering its Catholic identity.

DOMINICAN IDENTITY AND THE
DOMINICAN CHARISM

According to a 1994 joint statement of the Congregation for Catholic Education and the Pontifical Councils for the Laity and for Culture: "Religious orders and congregations bring a specific presence to the universities. By the wealth and diversity of their charism—especially their educational charism—they contribute to the formation of Christian teachers and students."[2]

Many of the more than two hundred Catholic colleges and universities in the U.S. were founded by religious communities of men and women. In these schools, "the universal ideals of Catholic higher education were embodied in the diversity of distinctive *cultures* represented by the religious communities who sponsor" them.[3] Thus, paraphrasing a remark made by Cardinal Anthony Bevilacqua a few years ago at De Sales University, when we speak of the Catholic and Dominican identity of Providence College, we mean to say, not that being a Dominican college is something in addition to being a Catholic college, but that *being a Dominican college is a way of being a Catholic college.*

The Catholic identity of Providence College is uniquely configured in its Dominican identity. What this means is that the Dominican charism has given shape to the characteristically Catholic

2. Congregation for Catholic Education, Pontifical Council for Culture, and Pontifical Council for the Laity, "The Presence of the Church in the University and in University Culture" (22 May 1994), Part II, section 1 (https://www.vatican.va/roman_curia/pontifical_councils/cultr/documents/rc_pc_cultr_doc_22051994_presence_en.html).

3. Anthony Bevilacqua, "Diversity among Catholic Universities" *Origins* 29 (2000): 476.

institutional and cultural reality of the College over its nearly ninety years of existence.

In the Catholic tradition, the term "charism" is generally used to refer to a gift of grace, bestowed by the Holy Spirit, that equips the recipient for a particular communal service. Applied to the founding charisms of particular religious communities like the Dominicans, Franciscans, and Jesuits, the term refers to a special gift of the Holy Spirit, given to the founders of these communities—St. Dominic, St. Francis, St. Ignatius, and others. This charism they then sought to embody in the distinctive forms of Christian life that they established in order to lead others to a fuller Christian life and to serve the Church in various ministries of evangelization, education, and the like. Religious institutes—as the various orders and congregations are called—are organized forms of consecrated life, recognized and approved by the Church, in which the fullness of the following of Christ can be found and pursued. Hence, the importance of fidelity to the founding charism and subsequent religious heritage of the religious community. In the words of Pope John Paul II: "It is precisely in this fidelity to the inspiration of the founders and foundresses ... that the essential elements of the consecrated life can be more readily discerned and more fervently put into practice."[4]

The Dominican charism captures all the essential elements of the Christian life, but configured according to the characteristic grace, vision, genius, and example of St. Dominic.[5] Ecclesiastical approval of the Constitutions of the Order is not simply a canonical formality, but a certification that the form of life to which the Dominican charism has given rise encompasses the way of the Gospel in its entirety. A form of life found in its institutional and communal embodiments, it is also a tradition of practical wisdom to whose tutelage one commends one's life and destiny. One's personal identity, one's own life, one's ways of thinking and acting, come to be shaped

4. Pope John Paul II, Post-Synodal Apostolic Exhortation *Vita Consecrata* (1996), §36.
5. See Guy Bedouelle, *St. Dominic: Grace of the Word* (San Francisco: Ignatius Press, 1987).

by the distinctive form of life to which the Dominican charism has given rise.

This is the reason why formation in a community is so crucial to becoming a Dominican, and why membership in a community—whether in a priory, a convent, or a Third Order chapter —is normally considered to be indispensable to persevering as a Dominican. In the setting of particular communal relationships and commitments, the individual friar, nun, sister, or lay Dominican undertakes the essential practices by which his or her Dominican identity is cultivated: pondering the word of God in the Scriptures, daily celebration of the Eucharist and the Liturgy of the Hours, attunement to the Paschal Mystery as it unfolds in the liturgical year, study, silence, recollection and meditation, and so on—all for the sake of preaching and the salvation of souls. There is a necessarily outward or apostolic thrust in the Dominican charism. No wonder that Dominicans have cheerfully embraced the mottos *contemplata et aliis tradere* ("to share with others the fruits of contemplation") and *laudare, benedicere, praedicare* ("to praise, to bless, to preach") as handy descriptions of what they're about.

The distinctive charism of a religious community is a *spiritual* reality, but it is not an *invisible* reality. The Dominican charism, like other religious charisms, is embodied in the life and teachings of its founder, in its rule and constitutions, in its characteristic embrace of the evangelical counsels of poverty, chastity, and obedience, in its institutions and apostolates, in its characteristic garb and observances, and, perhaps above all, in the exemplary lives of its saintly members. Alongside the Benedictine, Carmelite, Jesuit, and certain other great Catholic religious traditions, the Dominican charism has given rise to its own distinctive *spirituality* characterized notably (though not solely) by love of study and contemplation, a passion to know the truth and to share it with others, an abiding dedication to the preaching of the divine mercy, a profound Eucharistic piety, and, finally, deep devotion to the passion of Christ and to the Blessed Virgin Mary.[6]

6. See William A. Hinnebusch, *Dominican Spirituality: Principles and Practice* (Washington, DC: Thomist Press, 1965); Kent Emery and Joseph P. Wawrykow, eds.,

But it's a lot easier to *recognize* the Dominican charism than it is to *define* it. As a student brother in Dover, Massachusetts, years ago, I can remember endless conversations—after celebrating the feast of St. Francis with the Franciscans at their friary in Rye, New Hampshire, for example—about what makes Dominicans different from Franciscans. As we discovered in those conversations, and as many of you have undoubtedly discovered as well: it's something easier to recognize than to define. The religious charism is not an abstract essence: rather, it is a particular spiritual gift which both shapes and is shaped by its recipient, and at the same time gives rise to particular institutional and social forms as others are drawn to embrace it and be transformed by it over the course of time.[7]

In recent years the concepts of culture and identity have been applied to understanding the characteristic institutional, communal, and social forms in which religious charisms have come to be embodied.[8] Within this framework, the ways of life of particular religious orders and communities are seen as distinctive cultures—Benedictine monasticism, Dominican life, and so on—that shape the personal identities of their members and influence the ambient cultures.

This is not the place to enter into a discussion of the fascinating theoretical issues entailed in the use of the concepts of culture and identity in this context.[9] It is interesting to note that the concept of identity first came to prominence in the 1950s in the work of Erik H.

Christ among the Medieval Dominicans (Notre Dame, IN: University of Notre Dame Press, 1998).

7. See Benedict M. Ashley, *The Dominicans* (Collegeville, MN: Liturgical Press, 1990).

8. Cf. Francis M. Mannion, "Monasticism and Modern Culture," *American Benedictine Review* 44 (1993): 3–21, 125–42, 290–307; Aidan Nichols, *Dominican Gallery: Portrait of a Culture* (Leominster: Gracewing, 1997).

9. See the following articles in the *International Encyclopedia of the Social and Behavioral Sciences* (Amsterdam: Elsevier, 2001): D. Abrams, "Social Identity, Psychology of," pp. 14306–9; A. Bilgrami, "Identity and Identification: Philosophical Aspects," pp. 7148–54; D. F. Eickelman, "Transnational Religious Identities (Islam, Catholicism, and Judaism): Cultural Concerns," pp. 15862–66; R. Hardin, "Identity: Social," pp. 7166–70; T. M. Luhrmann, "Identity in Anthropology," pp. 7154–59.

Erikson and his followers concerning personal identity and the challenges of what he called the "identity crisis" in psychosocial development. Especially since the last quarter of the twentieth century, the concept has been widely utilized in the social sciences to study a variety of social and collective identities.[10]

Loosened somewhat from its conceptual home in the social sciences, the notion of identity has entered popular usage as a way for social groups of all types to specify the ensemble of features that together constitute what they consider to be the distinctive character of their group. It is in this more generalized sense that the concept of identity has entered the world of Catholic discourse, especially to aid reflection on the range of challenges to maintaining the specifically Catholic character of health care organizations, educational institutions, and social welfare services operating under Church auspices. Recent talk about "identity" in these contexts has almost always implied a "crisis of identity" (remember Erikson?), arising from either internal factors (e.g., self-doubt, declining membership in the sponsoring religious communities), or external factors (e.g., governmental regulation, secularizing ideologies), or from some combination of these. Nonetheless, for our purposes and independently of any perceived "identity crisis," the concept is useful to highlight the embodied and socially transforming character of the Dominican charism and its central role as the bearer of the Catholic identity of Providence College.

THE DOMINICAN CHARISM AT
PROVIDENCE COLLEGE

Along with their apostolic zeal and professional competence, the nine friars who started teaching at Providence College in 1919 brought their Dominican charism and its distinctive form of Catholic culture with them. Over the next eighty years, this Dominican

10. D. A. Snow, "Collective Identity and Expressive Forms," *International Encyclopedia of the Social and Behavioral Sciences*, pp. 2212–19.

Catholic culture molded the College in countless ways and contributed to making it the splendid place it is today.

It is significant that the friars were almost immediately joined by lay collaborators in the College's educational apostolate. In speaking about the impact of the distinctive religious charisms of the founding communities of many of the Catholic colleges and universities in the country, Cardinal Bevilacqua made these telling comments: "The inherent attractiveness of their religious charisms, combined with their competence, dedication and zeal, quickly drew to them lay collaborators who either joined them as teachers and coworkers in these apostolic endeavors, or contributed material support for the institutions of higher learning which they established." Thus, the charisms of these religious families embraced teachers and other coworkers, students and their parents, friends and benefactors, and the local churches and surrounding communities, drawing them "into a deeper experience of their faith through the medium of the distinctive, yet fully Catholic, religious cultures of these institutions of higher learning."[11] This happened in many Catholic colleges and universities sponsored by religious communities throughout United States, and it certainly has happened here at Providence College.

Where is the Dominican Catholic identity of the College located? What elements are essential to maintaining and fostering it? These are not easy questions to answer. The Catholic and Dominican identity of the College is embedded in an interlocking web of structures, policies, curricula, understandings, historical memory, shared narratives, relationships, virtues, comportment, ways of praying, and ways of dressing. Its transforming influence spreads out into the diocese and the local community here in Rhode Island, and, to some extent, even to the wider national community. Yet it remains here in the very stones of the place. The Catholic and Dominican identity of the College is at once readily recognizable and stubbornly indefinable, palpable and seemingly durable, and yet also fragile because tied to an ensemble of shifting structural factors and personal commitments.

11. Bevilacqua, "Diversity among Catholic Universities," 476.

When I first arrived here as a student in 1961 and then returned in 1970 for three blissful years on the theology faculty and campus ministry team, the question of the Catholic and Dominican identity of the College simply didn't arise. It was everywhere taken for granted—from the maintenance department to the president's office, and in the wide world beyond. But, for a variety of reasons (many of them common to other U.S. Catholic colleges and universities founded by religious communities), the Catholic and Dominican identity of Providence College can no longer be taken for granted—not because this identity is directly threatened but because the decision to maintain and develop it depends more critically than in the past on deliberately embraced policies and commitments. It has only been in the aftermath the Second Vatican Council, and especially in the lively discussion provoked by *Ex Corde Ecclesiae*, that we have come to see this so clearly.

EX CORDE ECCLESIAE AND CATHOLIC IDENTITY IN HIGHER EDUCATION

The Council had reaffirmed the traditional Catholic view of the possibility and character of Church sponsorship of colleges and universities (in *Gravissimum Educationis*). Following upon and implementing the conciliar teaching were two companion documents: *Sapientia Christiana* in 1979, concerning the governance of ecclesiastically accredited institutions, and, in 1990, *Ex Corde Ecclesiae*, concerning all other Catholic institutions of higher learning. In one sense, these documents were little more than a bit of canonical housekeeping. But because they articulate the different ways for ecclesial communion to be embodied by Catholic institutions of diverse types, they proved to be far more timely and far-reaching in their impact here in the U.S. than might have been expected. Our attention is focused here chiefly on *Ex Corde Ecclesiae* and in its *Application* in the U.S. by our Episcopal Conference.

In the final decades of the twentieth century, it had become clear that, given the political and cultural pressures favoring increasing secularization over the past hundred years and into the foreseeable future, the Catholic identity of currently Catholic institutions of higher learning would not be likely to be sustainable without concrete bonds between these institutions and the Church. Although we cannot rehearse their results here, recent studies have made it possible to identify with greater precision the cultural and political forces operative in the relatively swift transformation that has already occurred in Catholic higher education in the U.S. since the 1960s.[12]

Naturally, in developing its teaching and legislation in this area, the Church did not have only the situation in the United States in view. But the practical implications of an ecclesiology of communion, formulated with the whole Catholic Church in view, nonetheless had particular urgency in a situation where the disengagement of colleges and universities from their Christian churches had become endemic.

We have before us the record of the failure of countless informal arrangements by which sincere and well-meaning faculty, administrators and church leaders of once church-related colleges and universities believed that they would be able to ensure the Lutheran, Presbyterian, Methodist, Congregationalist, and other denominational identities of their institutions.[13] Without the adoption of concrete provisions, and relying solely on the good will and sense of commitment of Catholic educators and bishops, few of the currently Catholic institutions of higher learning in the U.S. are likely to remain distinctively and recognizably Catholic. Even with the adoption of something like clearly stated juridical provisions of the USCCB *Application of Ex Corde Ecclesiae for the United States*, it may be that the secularizing trends will turn out to have been irreversible in some of the two hundred or more Catholic institutions of higher learning in the U.S.

Simply expressed, the fundamental concern of *Ex Corde Ecclesiae*

12. See Philip Gleason, *Contending with Modernity: Catholic Higher Education in the Twentieth Century* (New York: Oxford University Press, 1995).

13. See James T. Burtchaell, *The Dying of the Light*; George M. Mardsen, *The Soul of the American University* (New York: Oxford University Press, 1994).

was to ensure the present and future Catholic identity of the colleges and universities founded and sponsored by the Catholic Church throughout the world. In the U.S., in the discussions both of its early drafts in the 1980s and then of the formulation of the national norms for its application here, *Ex Corde Ecclesiae* came as a wake-up call for Catholic higher education.[14]

THE CATHOLIC AND DOMINICAN FUTURE
OF PROVIDENCE COLLEGE

Central to both *Ex Corde Ecclesiae* and its *Application* for the U.S. is the requirement that Catholic colleges and universities internalize the renewed ecclesiology of communion in the structures of their institutions.

Catholic identity will not be sustainable over the long haul without clearly expressed communal bonds with the universal and local Church. Drawing upon *Ex Corde Ecclesiae*, the *Application* summarizes the four characteristics that are essential for Catholic identity and that need to be expressed in concrete provisions guiding the life of the university community: (1) Christian inspiration in individuals and the university community; (2) reflection and research on human knowledge in the light of Catholic faith; (3) fidelity to the Christian message in conformity with the Magisterium of the Church; (4) institutional commitment to the service of others. The *Application* proceeds to supply a series of norms to help to ensure the Catholic identity of colleges and universities operating under Church auspices in the U.S.

The *Application* invites us to consider the concrete measures that will secure the Catholic identity of the schools in our charge through the prism of these schools' founding religious charisms: "Catholic universities cherish their Catholic tradition and in many cases the special charisms of the religious communities that founded them. In

14. See J. A. Di Noia, "Ecclesiology of Communion and Catholic Higher Education," *Origins* 29 (1999): 268–72.

the United States, they enjoyed the freedom to incorporate these religious values into their academic mission. The principles of *Ex Corde Ecclesiae* afford them an opportunity to re-examine their origin and renew their way of living out this precious heritage" (Section VII).

This text supports the cumulative argument I have been advancing today: in the present cultural and ecclesial context, the continual recovery of the founding charism of the Dominican Order is crucial to maintaining the essential characteristics of the Catholic identity of Providence College. This argument depends in part on a theological understanding of the nature of religious charisms, especially in major traditions of consecrated life such as the Benedictines, the Dominicans, and the Jesuits. It also draws upon on the application of the concepts of culture and identity to the communities and institutions that express and embody these religious charisms. In addition, my argument has been influenced by a reading of the history of religiously sponsored higher education in the U.S. and by observing how Catholic health care and social service organizations have confronted a range of challenges to their Catholic identity in recent decades. All of this leads me to say, with some confidence, that the Catholic future of Providence College depends to a significant degree on its Dominican future.

If I am right about this, then the Catholic identity and mission of Providence College are not likely to prove sustainable in the long term apart from a community of persons dedicated to fostering the relationships that express ecclesial communion in its particular Dominican embodiment.

Throughout the history of the Catholic Church, the Catholic identity and mission of our educational, health care, and social service institutions have depended on the commitment and dedication of communities formed in Christ and united in ecclesial communion by their particular religious charisms. Their educational, healing, and charitable services arose out of the explicitly religious motivation of communities founded to advance a particular mission in these areas and to undertake these services as corporate apostolates of their institutes. The issue of the "Catholic identity" of the institutions dedicated to the provision of these services in the U.S. has in part arisen as the outcome of the decline in membership in the sponsoring religious communities of these institutions. In response to this development, Catholic health care, for example, has made an effort to introduce "formation programs" for the members of their boards, for their administrators and staff, and even for the constituencies they serve so that these people can internalize a sound Catholic vision as well as the particular charisms of the founding communities (e.g., Sisters of Mercy or the Daughters of Charity). These efforts are farsighted and exemplary.

Both *Ex Corde Ecclesiae* and the U.S. *Application* envisage similar efforts on the part of Catholic higher education. The *Application* contains provisions to ensure a critical mass of Catholic professionals on the boards and faculties of our institutions of higher learning. Even more important is the establishment of programs for the Catholic formation of these dedicated persons.

It is not my place to say what sorts of measures Providence College will find appropriate to cultivate the kind of community upon whom its Dominican and Catholic future will continue crucially to depend. Allow me to suggest just a few elements of the vision that will have to be shared by these persons if the College is to enjoy a vital Catholic and Dominican future.

By profession and instinct, Dominicans grasp the importance of broadly shared convictions about the distinctive message of the Catholic Christian faith, especially at a moment when rival religious and quasi-religious alternatives compete for attention and allegiance. In short, Dominicans understand that it cannot be taken for granted that people know what it means for a person or a college to be Catholic. The distinctive Catholic vision of human existence and of the academic life needs to be articulated, discussed, and shared by the College community, even while non-Catholic faculty, staff, and students are welcomed and treasured.

Furthermore, both *Ex Corde Ecclesiae* and the USCCB application document frame the distinctive character of the Catholic faith in terms of an ecclesiology of communion that is itself a distinctive element in Dominican theology and spirituality. What Christ taught us and what we proclaim to the world is that the triune God invites all human persons to participate in the communion of the Father, Son, and Holy Spirit, and with one another in them. God desires this and, as I sometimes say, no one has ever desired anything more, and nothing makes sense apart from it. Holiness is the transformed capacity to enjoy this communion, and ecclesial communion is at root nothing less than trinitarian communion. This basic truth of Catholic faith unfolds in an ensemble of other truths about creation, incarnation, redemption, and sanctification. The central truths of the Christian faith find their deepest meaning in the reality of trinitarian communion. Everything created exists so that the Blessed Trinity could realize this plan of love. Through the Incarnation and the Paschal Mystery, Christ enables creaturely persons to enter into the life of the uncreated Persons. In the Church, the Holy Spirit unites all those transformed in Christ and draws them into the communion of trinitarian love. Ecclesial communion is nothing less than the beginning of our participation in the life of the Blessed Trinity.

A reflective, unapologetic, and forthright articulation of this distinctive vision of human existence and academic life has always been central to the Dominican culture of Providence College.

What is more, in the Catholic tradition, particularly as it has been shaped over the centuries by Dominican thinkers, it is understood that to view one's life and one's vocation in the light of this invitation to trinitarian communion does not constrain human reason and freedom but opens them out to their widest conceivable fulfillments. It has been an especially important contribution of Dominicans like Albert the Great and Thomas Aquinas to show that intellectual inquiries pursued within the framework of this vision nonetheless possess an integrity and finality of their own.[15] To

---

15. See Alasdair MacIntyre, *Three Rival Versions of Moral Theology* (Notre Dame, IN: University of Notre Dame Press, 1990).

say that the triune God is the ultimate end of human thinking and striving is not to exclude other interests and ends, but to order them to the all-encompassing end of interpersonally shared communion. Applied to intellectual life, this insight in many ways constituted the charter for Catholic higher education and the authentic freedom of those who pursue it.

In addition, Providence College has been and should continue to be a place where students can imbibe an authentic Christian humanism that affirms the intrinsic link between what human beings are and what they can hope to become. Created in the image of God, human beings are meant to grow into the image of Christ. As they become increasingly conformed to the perfect man, Jesus Christ, the fullness of their humanity is realized. There "a finality built into human nature as such, and, although its realization is possible only with the assistance of divine grace, this realization is in a real sense continuous with the tendencies and aspirations of human nature."[16] Deeply characteristic of the vision central to Dominican identity is a wholly refreshing optimism about this possibility.

Dominicans understand that, apart from the sanctification of desire, the possibility of such a realization will be sharply curtailed. The cultural circumstances created by the late twentieth-century sexual revolution are uncannily similar to the thirteenth-century situation in which the Dominican Order emerged. Like thirteenth-century Albigensianism, the ideology of the sexual revolution—with its fateful separation of sexuality and procreation—drives a wedge between the realms of spirit and matter, between mind and body. People have been led to believe that the human body can be instrumentalized for the satisfaction of any type of sexual desire as long as the mind retains its lofty—Albigensians would say "pure"—intentions. Dominicans understand that this is an idea with lethal consequences for the body and for the soul. For one thing, pace postmodern Albigensianism, what you do with your body can hurt your soul—lofty

16. J. A. Di Noia, OP, "Imago Dei—Imago Christi: The Theological Foundations of Christian Humanism," *Nova et Vetera* 2 (2004): 270.

intentions to the contrary notwithstanding. But, far more seriously, from the perspective of an authentic Christian humanism, the divorce of physical and spiritual desire and fulfillment short-circuits the natural tendency of desire to seek the divine Good through the enjoyment of created goods like sexual pleasure in marriage. Without the sanctification of desire, through the virtues of chastity and temperance, there can be no true human fulfillment and certainly no attainment of wisdom.

I am painfully aware of how much more has to be said about the richness of the characteristically Dominican embodiment of Catholic faith and life, and its realization here at Providence College. Dominicans and their collaborators will surely want to help their students and associates not only how to think and study, but also how to love, how to pray, how to value—and indeed to adore—Christ present in the blessed Eucharist, how to integrate traditional Catholic devotion into their personal piety, how to cherish the holiness of their bodies, how to take responsibility for the poor, the underprivileged, and vulnerable members of society, how to live for God above all else.

Throughout its history, the College has demonstrated an astonishing ability to attract board members, faculty and staff, benefactors and friends, who are deeply convinced of and profoundly committed to the Dominican and Catholic identity of the College. Undoubtedly, the new Vice President for Mission and Ministry, as well as the newly established Institute for Dominican Studies, will have central roles to play in the formation of a community of persons fully committed to the Catholic and Dominican identity of Providence College—a complex cultural and social reality which perhaps more than anything else depends on the dedication and commitment of people who have been formed and transformed by it.

The history of religiously sponsored higher education in the United States demonstrates that, if the Catholic and Dominican future of the College is to be an assured one, it will only be because of decisions and policies embraced in the present. In *Ex Corde Ecclesiae* and the *Application of Ex Corde Ecclesiae for the United States,* the Church has provided some effective tools for thinking about what these decisions and policies should be. Everyone who holds the future of Providence College in their hands should ponder how deeply entwined is the Dominican and Catholic identity of this remarkable institution which finds itself today with a new young president contemplating the second glorious century of its existence.

CHAPTER 7

Discere et Docere

The Identity and Mission of the Dominican House of Studies in the 21st Century

INTRODUCTION: LEARNING AND TEACHING IN THE DOMINICAN ORDER

When he was asked once to state what rule he professed, Blessed Jordan, the successor of St. Dominic at the head of the Dominican Order, declared: "Nothing beyond the rule of the Friars Preachers, which is to live virtuously, to learn, and to teach" (*Lives of the Brethren,* Pt. IV, Ch. 31). To live virtuously, to learn and to teach (*honeste vivere, discere et docere*)—for Blessed Jordan, it was a phrase that summed up the whole Dominican vocation. For us today, as we celebrate the dedication of this new academic center and theological library, Blessed Jordan's simple phrase can serve as a compact description of the mission of the Dominican House of Studies: *learning and teaching in the setting of a life of prayer.*

It will hardly be news to you—though it bears repeating—that the centrality of learning and teaching in the Dominican charism derives directly from St. Dominic himself.[1] Blessed Jordan's succinct

---

Originally published in *The Thomist* 73 (2009): 111–27.

1. See Guy Bedouelle, OP, *St. Dominic: Grace of the Word* (San Francisco: Ignatius Press, 1987).

formula expressed what he had learned from St. Dominic, whose experience with the Catharist heresy in southern France convinced him of the absolute necessity of a solid intellectual formation for his new band of preaching friars.

The link between study and the apostolic aims of the Order was thus clear from the very beginning. The primitive constitutions state: "Our study must aim principally at this, that we might be useful to the souls of others."[2] Blessed Jordan makes this point vividly when, in his encyclical letter of May 1233, he complains that brethren who are uninterested in study, "apart from neglecting their own benefit and depressing their teachers, ... deprive many people of a chance of salvation, when they could have helped them on their way to eternal life if only they had studied properly, instead of being careless about it."[3] The *Lives of the Brethren* recount the story of a certain friar in the early days of the Order who, because he neglected study for the sake of long prayers and works of asceticism, was accused by the brethren "of making himself useless to the Order by not studying."[4] With his usual clarity, Blessed Humbert of Romans, the fifth master general, sums it up nicely: "Study is not the purpose of the Order, but it is of the greatest necessity for the aims we have mentioned, namely, preaching and working for the salvation of souls, for without study we can achieve neither."[5]

The centrality of study for the apostolic aims of the Order meant that learning and teaching could not be left to chance. Successive general chapters created the organization and structures that would provide a solid institutional basis—unique at the time—for studies in the Order. They were organized in such a way that every priory took on the responsibility of structured learning and teaching in a system that was capped by the establishment of *studia generalia*, first

2. James A. Weisheipl, OP, *The Place of Study in the Ideal of St. Dominic* (River Forest, IL: Dominican House of Studies, 1960), 11.

3. Simon Tugwell, OP, ed., *Early Dominicans* (New York: Paulist Press, 1982), 123–24.

4. Weisheipl, *The Place of Study in the Ideal of St. Dominic*, 13.

5. Weisheipl, *The Place of Study in the Ideal of St. Dominic*, 5.

in Paris, and subsequently at Oxford, Cologne, Montpellier, and Bologna.[6]

It is only within the framework of this long tradition that the identity and mission of a *studium generale* like the Dominican House of Studies can be properly understood. The study of philosophy and theology in the Dominican Order—albeit having an integrity and finality of its own—is nonetheless intended to form friars who will be "useful to the souls of others."

LEARNING AND TEACHING IN THE PROVINCE
OF ST. JOSEPH: 1805–1905

Exactly one hundred years before the establishment of the Dominican House of Studies, the Province of St. Joseph itself was founded by Maryland native Edward Dominic Fenwick and two English friars. Fenwick had received his formation and education from the English friars living in exile in Belgium since the English Reformation. Remember that, generally speaking, the early 1800s were a catastrophic moment for religious orders in Europe's Catholic countries, where they were the victims of the aggressively secularist policies of Napoleon and Emperor Joseph of Austria.

Bishop John Carroll sent Fenwick and his companions to Kentucky—at that time the largest Catholic population center in the eastern United States apart from Maryland itself. And so it happened that, for much of our first hundred years, we were a missionary and preaching province, founding and caring for churches in Ohio and Tennessee where the first bishops were Dominicans. There were few resources available for the establishment of priories that could support the full range of traditional Dominican life, much less the regular structures enjoined for philosophical and theological studies in the Order.

Naturally, we mustn't think that the province had been bereft of

6. See William A. Hinnebusch, OP, *The History of the Dominican Order (Volume 2): Intellectual and Cultural Life to 1500* (New York: Alba House, 1973), 37–82.

learning and teaching during these first hundred years. In fact, the first *studium generale* of the Dominican Order in the United States was founded in 1834 at St. Joseph's Priory in Somerset, Ohio. But maintaining the characteristically Dominican program of studies had proven difficult—despite the efforts of the great Italian Dominican, Eugenio Giacinto Pozzo, who, upon his arrival in 1841, was appointed the first regent of studies in the Province of St. Joseph. "Never, before Pozzo, had [the province] known the meaning of Dominican intellectual training."[7] Under his influence, the historic intermediate provincial chapter of 1845 enjoined a two-year course of philosophy according to Thomistic principles, and a five-year course of theology to be taught from the text of the *Summa Theologiae* of St. Thomas, supplemented by the commentary of the Belgian Dominican, Charles René Billuart. The capitular fathers were well aware that their ordinations would not fulfill all the requirements of the Order's legislation for a Dominican *studium*, but it was the best they could do given the small number of students as well as the paucity of qualified faculty.

The latter difficulty plagued the province's program of studies throughout much of the nineteenth century. For various reasons, provincials were unwilling to send qualified friars to study in Rome, despite the persistent requests of the master general, Father Vincent Jandel (1850–72). The turning point occurred during the 1881 visitation of the Master General, Father José Maria Larroca (1879–91). He ordered that Brothers Lawrence Francis Kearney and Daniel Joseph Kennedy be sent to Louvain to receive a solid Thomistic training from the Belgian Dominicans. Larroca's initiative prompted a more consistent program for the preparation of qualified friars for service as professors of philosophy and theology—essential for the establishment of the intellectual life and theological formation characteristic of a mature Dominican province.

In effect, the seeds of the present Dominican House of Studies

7. Reginald M. Coffey, OP, *The American Dominicans: A History of St. Joseph's Province* (New York: St. Martin De Porres Guild, 1969), 222.

were planted by Father Larroca. Their experience with the Belgian Dominicans provided the vision and inspiration for Kearney and Kennedy who, upon their return to America, were determined to provide a properly Dominican form for learning and teaching in the province with the establishment of a *studium generale*.

THE FOUNDATION OF THE DOMINICAN HOUSE OF STUDIES (1902–1907)

Not until his second term as provincial was Father Kearney able to execute this plan. The decision to erect a new *studium generale* in Washington, D.C. was taken on 2 January 1902 and Father Richard Jerome Meaney was placed in charge of the project. Having taken up residence at St. Dominic's across town, Father Meaney rode his Rambler bicycle to the (then) Bunker Hill Road building site every morning to supervise the work.

We owe to Father Meaney the existence of a detailed account of the progress of the construction from the development of the initial plans, through the groundbreaking ceremony on 23 April 1903 and the laying of the cornerstone on 16 August of the same year, to the blessing of the new building on 20 August 1905 and, finally, to the dedication of the chapel on 4 February 1907.

At the solemn dedication of the chapel on that Sunday morning, Meaney tells us, James Cardinal Gibbons presided, along with the Apostolic Delegate, Archbishop Diomede Falconio (auspiciously, it was felt, a Franciscan), while Father Kearney preached the sermon. Kearney was finally able to give voice to his joy at the fulfillment of his cherished dream and his gratitude to the friends of the Dominican Order for their bountiful generosity whom he thanked when he said in conclusion: "[T]his chapel today dedicated and this building raised to the honor and glory of God, is the monument of the poor whom we have served long, silently and faithfully."[8] A festive dinner

8. *Dominican Year Book*, "The Dominican House of Studies at Washington" (Somerset, OH: The Rosary Press, 1908), 71.

followed the Solemn Mass and, according to Father Meaney, "the refectory was well filled, everything white and clean, the snowy white habits of the Dominicans contrasting with the brown of the Franciscans and the black of the seculars and purple scattered through it all; and happiness shining in every countenance."[9]

The learning and teaching of philosophy and theology according to Thomistic principles in the Province of St. Joseph was finally established on a solid institutional basis in a true *studium generale* that could meet all the requirements of Dominican legislation. As Father Kearney declared in his sermon at the dedication of the chapel: "Here the sons of Dominic will be trained in piety and learning, walking in the spirit of their vocation, going forth to meet the needs of the Church in America as priestly scholars, as faithful religious, as zealous missionaries."[10]

Moreover, the province had fulfilled the traditional Dominican expectation that a *studium generale* be located in the vicinity of a major university. Cardinal Gibbons—who had since 1890 urged the Dominicans to establish their *studium* at The Catholic University of America in Washington—happily presided at all of the founding events of the new Dominican House of Studies. For their part, the friars were delighted that, while maintaining its independence as a *studium generale,* the Dominican House of Studies would enjoy a wide range of mutually beneficial exchange and collaboration with The Catholic University of America.

In the hundred years since its foundation, the Dominican House of Studies has fulfilled and even surpassed the expectations and the dreams of its founders. It has turned out to be a distinguished center of learning and teaching in the Order and beyond. The intellectual formation received by the friars at the Dominican House of Studies led to such widely diverse initiatives as the foundation of Providence College, the Theology for the Layman movement, and the

9. Richard J. Meaney, OP, *Account of the Construction of the Dominican House of Studies* (manuscript, 1934), 245.
10. *Dominican Year Book,* 71.

establishment of Blackfriars Theater.[11] The parishes and parish missions conducted by the Dominican friars became famous for the quality of preaching and pastoral care that they provided. Dominicans holding distinguished professorships at Catholic University and teaching at Catholic colleges throughout the nation insisted on a high level of theological teaching based on Aquinas's *Summa Theologiae* as opposed to the more catechetical approach of the so-called kerygmatic theology.[12] These teachers also contributed to the cultivation of a potent Catholic intellectual culture in the U.S.[13]

But during this time there were also developments that reshaped the identity of the Dominican House of Studies and redefined its mission without altering its fundamental character as a *studium generale*. It is of immense importance to understand the significance of these developments for the new century.

DEVELOPMENTS AFFECTING THE IDENTITY AND MISSION OF DHS

A critical moment in the continuing evolution of the Dominican House of Studies occurred with the relatively calm assimilation of the renewal measures promulgated by the Second Vatican Council. This development was due, at least in part, to the fact that during and after the years of the council the faculty and senior friars in the DHS community and in the province construed the conciliar teachings as being in essential continuity, rather than a disruption or break (to use Pope Benedict's language), with previous Catholic teaching and the tradition. Although there were difficulties, perhaps especially during the 1970s, the Council was generally not

11. See John Vidmar, OP, *Fr. Fenwick's "Little Dominican Province"* (New York: Dominican Province of St. Joseph, 2005).

12. See J. A. Di Noia, OP, "Communion and the Ecclesial Vocation of the Theologian in Catholic Higher Education," in *Called to Holiness and Communion: Vatican II on the Church*, ed. Steven Boguslawski, OP, and Robert Fastiggi (Scranton, PA: University of Scranton Press, 2009), 321–38.

13. See Philip Gleason, *Keeping the Faith: American Catholicism, Past and Present* (Notre Dame, IN: University of Notre Dame Press, 1987).

experienced as a revolution. Without the destructive turmoil that had beset some other Catholic institutions and communities, the fundamental patterns of the Dominican religious and liturgical life of the priory, as well as those of formation and theological education in the Thomistic tradition, while undergoing necessary adjustments, continued more or less undisturbed.

Two postconciliar trends did affect the Dominican House of Studies very early on. Cooperation among theological schools and consolidation of Catholic seminaries came to be seen as desirable and were widely encouraged. Driven by both ecumenical and educational concerns, the national trend toward cooperation among Catholic and non-Catholic theological schools led here in Washington in 1967 to the foundation of the Washington Theological Consortium, of which the Dominican House of Studies was a founding member and always an active participant. The consolidation of Catholic seminaries in Washington proceeded at a rapid pace and led the Franciscans, the Carmelites, the Augustinians, and other religious communities with formation houses in Brookland to join together in 1969 in the creation of the Washington Theological Union as an independent theological school with a unified curriculum. In order to maintain the prized civil or ecclesiastical accreditation their schools already enjoyed, the Dominicans, the Oblates of Mary Immaculate, and the Oblates of St. Francis De Sales declined to join the WTC (or Coalition, as it was then called) and instead, in 1970, established the Cluster of Independent Theological Schools.

That the priory and academic community experienced the Second Vatican Council as a time of renewal in fundamental continuity with the great Catholic tradition was a tremendous grace—attributable, in the view of many of us, to nothing less than the protection and intercession of Our Lady. This grace laid the foundation for the revival and renewal of the Dominican House of Studies of which we are the happy, if somewhat amazed, witnesses today.

Throughout this period, the Dominican House of Studies retained its independence and identity—along with a strong conviction that, in the philosophy and theology of St. Thomas, it possessed a distinctive intellectual tradition that served well as the framework for teaching and learning within as well as for engagement with other traditions beyond its ambit. It was drawn into new relationships that profoundly affected its self-understanding and day-to-day operations. The Dominican House of Studies has emerged from this process with a durable set of interlocking identities that have secured its independence and thus ensured its capacity to sustain and transmit its distinctive intellectual tradition.

The *studium generale* at DHS emerged from this period as, at one and the same time, a seminary, an ecclesiastical faculty, and a theological school. Its fundamental character as a *studium generale* (according to current Dominican legislation, a "center of institutional studies") is maintained by observance of the legislation that regulates studies in the Order and in the province (as formulated in the *Ratio Studiorum*). As a seminary, DHS must also abide by the *Program of Priestly Formation* of the United States Conference of Catholic Bishops. The *Program of Priestly Formation* incorporates a vast amount of magisterial and episcopal teaching as it bears on the intellectual, pastoral, and spiritual preparation of young men for the Catholic priesthood.

In its wider ecclesial identity, DHS is also governed by the provisions of the apostolic constitution *Sapientia Christiana* (1979) since, on 15 November 1941, the *studium generale* here was erected as the Pontifical Faculty of the Immaculate Conception—at the time, only the second such faculty in the United States after The Catholic University of America. From that date, DHS has operated by virtue of the authority granted to it by the Holy See according to standards that govern ecclesiastical faculties of theology in the Catholic Church and is thus empowered to offer basic and advanced programs of theological learning leading to the conferral of degrees recognized throughout the universal church and the international academic community.

In addition, over the course of the twenty-five years after 1970, the Dominican House of Studies has won civil accreditation from the Association of Theological Schools and Middle States Association, first as part of the Cluster of Independent Theological Schools and now, since the closing in 1996 of Oblate College and De Sales Hall, as a freestanding faculty of theology. Hence, the programs of study and degrees granted are recognized by all other institutions of higher education in the United States and elsewhere.

These interlocking identities—while they naturally create some headaches for the school's hardworking administrators—have secured the independence and distinctive intellectual tradition of the Dominican House of Studies, and at the same time immeasurably enlarged the scope for its pursuit of the mission to promote learning and teaching "useful to the souls of others."

ST. THOMAS AQUINAS AND THE DISTINCTIVE INTELLECTUAL HERITAGE AT DHS

The interlocking identities and new institutional affiliations, along with the setting of a stable conventual and liturgical life, have enlarged the public profile of the Dominican House of Studies and prompted a considerable expansion and diversification of the student body. In addition, the Washington location of DHS affords an unprecedented scope for the exercise of the intellectual apostolate of the Order. The Dominican faculty of the relatively enclosed *studium* of earlier generations could not itself reach such a wide audience as is afforded by the "free market" of ideas created and sustained by these new institutional affiliations and identities. Current circumstances permit a previously unanticipated realization of precisely those Dominican ideals that inspired the transfer of the *studium generale* from Somerset, Ohio, to Washington, D.C.

When the *studium* was still in Somerset, the Province of St. Joseph recognized that the study of the philosophy and theology of St. Thomas are fundamental elements of the Dominican intellectual heritage. Throughout its history, the Thomistic tradition has been significantly, though not exclusively, associated with the Dominican Order. Indeed, since the end of the thirteenth century, the Dominican Order has built its institutional learning and teaching around the works of St. Thomas Aquinas.[14] There are many reasons for this, not the least of which is that this tradition is a natural outgrowth of the Dominican charism with its optimism about the rationality and fundamental goodness of the created order, its conviction about the centrality of divine grace and mercy, its realism about the peril of the human condition apart from the redemptive sacrifice of Christ, its appreciation of the inner intelligibility of divine revelation, and its resistance to all purely moralistic accounts of the Christian life. The Dominican House of Studies has been able to sustain and develop this Thomistic vision over the years.

The climate of pluralism in which DHS finds itself flourishing today has so far favored the articulation of this distinctive Dominican theological tradition and has also stimulated the growth of interest and enrollments in DHS/PFIC programs. An important factor in the attractiveness of the DHS course offerings will continue to be the vibrancy and relevance of their presentation of the theology of St. Thomas.

Students who are drawn to the study of Aquinas and who appreciate his contemporary relevance want the kind of education that DHS programs provide. Perhaps ironically, the growth of pluralism in Catholic theological education, although initially unfavorable to the study of Aquinas and Thomism,[15] now seems indirectly to stimulate interest in this theological and philosophical tradition. The climate of pluralism tends to foster the vitality of distinctive traditions and to permit them to stand (or fall) on their own merits.[16] In this climate, the presentation of Aquinas exhibits a direct relevance to

14. See Benedict Ashley, OP, *The Dominicans* (Collegeville, MN: Liturgical Press, 1990).

15. See J. A. Di Noia, OP, "American Theology at Century's End," *The Thomist* 54 (1990): 507–11.

16. See Alasdair MacIntyre, *Three Rival Versions of Moral Inquiry* (Notre Dame, IN: University of Notre Dame Press, 1990).

theological and philosophical debates in a way that attracts many students, Catholic and Protestant alike.

The potential of this modest flowering of Thomism should not be underestimated. In effect, this magnificent new academic center and theological library wing is a testimony to our confidence that this is indeed the case. Small beginnings have marked the start of similar movements in the history of the Order. Although Catholic circles have been slow to catch on, the interest in Aquinas manifest here is matched by a definite revival of his thought throughout the English-speaking world. This development has provided members of the DHS/PFIC faculty with numerous conversation partners in faculties and professional societies throughout the nation and beyond.

The recognition that the potential exists here for a distinctive contribution to the pressing theological, philosophical, and pastoral issues of our time has led the province to envisage the establishment of a Thomistic institute here at the Dominican House of Studies. Although still in its planning stages, the institute would presumably encourage historical and textual studies of St. Thomas and Thomism with a view to promoting the constructive engagement of this distinctive intellectual tradition with other traditions in such a way as to deepen understanding of the great philosophical and theological questions as they are posed in our time. Precisely this kind of study of Aquinas and the Thomistic tradition draws a growing number of young scholars into a movement that has been called by some the "new Thomism." Building on nineteenth and twentieth century historical research inspired by the Thomistic revival fostered by Pope Leo XIII, this "new Thomism" seeks to bring Aquinas and the Thomistic tradition into dialogue with contemporary philosophical and theological positions.

It is of critical importance to notice that, while these purposes flow from a deeply apostolic motivation in the Dominican spirit, they have an integrity and finality of their own. To view one's life and one's vocation in the light of the invitation to trinitarian communion—as Catholics do—does not constrain human reason and freedom but opens them out to their widest conceivable fulfillments. It has been an especially important contribution of Dominicans like Albertus Magnus and Thomas Aquinas to show that intellectual inquiries pursued within the framework of this vision nonetheless enjoy their own scope. To say that the triune God is the ultimate end of human thinking and striving is not to exclude other interests and ends, but to order them to the all-encompassing end of interpersonally shared communion. Applied to intellectual life, this insight in many ways constituted the charter for "speculative" philosophy and theology, as well as the authentic freedom of those who pursue this study.

THE THOMISTIC SYNTHESIS AS BASIS FOR THEOLOGICAL EDUCATION AT DHS

It remains true nonetheless that, as we have seen, Dominican "study must aim principally at this, that we might be useful to the souls of others." It is the experience and conviction of the Order that the study of Aquinas—especially his *Summa Theologiae*—provides not just an object of specialized study, but also the basis for theological education itself. It promotes an overall vision of the Catholic faith that, unmatched as it is for its intelligibility, comprehensiveness, and integration, precisely makes the study of philosophy and theology useful to the souls of others.

This approach to the sacred sciences sustains a robust theological realism through which the student learns that theology is not just about discourse, or narratives, or texts—and certainly not about the structures of consciousness, but about the living God and the realities of His saving work.[17] These features of Aquinas's synthesis foster in the student a true theological *habitus*—a way of thinking

17. See J. A. Di Noia, OP, "The Practice of Catholic Theology," in *Blackwell Companion to Catholicism*, ed. James J. Buckley and F. C. Bauerschmidt (Cambridge: Blackwell Publishing, 2007), 238–50.

about the Catholic faith in its entirety and in its inner intelligibility. Insisting that the theological virtue of faith involves a participation in the divine knowledge itself,[18] Aquinas invites the student to adopt what might be called a God's-eye-view not only of the created order and the economy of salvation but also of everyday life, of the course of human history, and of all human inquiries, including the physical, social, and philosophical disciplines. With Aquinas as guide, the student gains a working knowledge of how faith and reason interact in achieving understanding of the truths of revelation, and thus how a theological perspective can encompass the perspectives of other disciplines—especially metaphysics—without suppressing them. In a time when fragmentation is everywhere the bane of theological education, the Thomistic synthesis presupposes and cultivates the integration of scriptural, historical, philosophical, theological, and pastoral studies, on the part of both teachers and students at the Dominican House of Studies.

For Aquinas, the fundamental structure of the economy of salvation is a trinitarian one. Just as the Father loves the Son and from this love springs the Holy Spirit, so, in reverse order, we are transformed by the Holy Spirit in the image of the Son and thus come to be loved by the Father who sees and loves in us what He sees and loves in Christ. Thus, the overarching Thomistic theme of adoptive filiation—participation in the communion of divine life through conformity to Jesus Christ—permits a profound integration between the mysteries of our faith and the demands of the moral life. There is a deeply Christian humanism at work here that affirms the intrinsic link between what human beings are and what they can hope to become. Created in the image of God, human beings are meant to grow into the image of Christ. As they become increasingly conformed to the perfect man, Jesus Christ, the fullness of their humanity is realized. There is "a finality built into human nature as such, and, although its realization is possible only with the assistance of divine

18. See Romanus Cessario, OP, *Christian Faith and the Theological Life* (Washington, DC: The Catholic University of America Press, 1996).

grace, this realization is in a real sense continuous with the tendencies and aspirations of human nature."[19] A Christian anthropology—itself tied to trinitarian theology, Christology, and soteriology—thus furnishes the basis for moral theology.

Overall, the Thomistic approach to theology gives students the ability to reason through the intellectual difficulties and questions that people have and that can create barriers to their Christian life.[20] Here the paradigm is St. Dominic himself who argued through the night with a Catharist innkeeper in order to persuade him to abandon his errors. This approach presupposes in the student a readiness to seek through study an understanding of the sorts of questions that typically arise today, to take the questions seriously, and to guide inquirers to the truths of faith that will respond to these questions. A person trained in the Thomistic approach to theology will not prematurely cry "It's a mystery!" in response to the questions people raise. Remember Blessed Jordan's complaint about friars who "could have helped [others] on their way to eternal life if only they had studied properly, instead of being careless about it." Sometimes the response "It's a mystery!" is just a cover for theological ignorance on the part of people who should know better. The kind of study that makes itself useful to others is untiring in its pursuit of an understanding of the underlying cultural presuppositions—sometimes involving deep confusions—that block acceptance of the message of the gospel.

It is of considerable interest, in this connection, that some of these cultural presuppositions are in a sense already familiar to us in their nominalist sources. Recent authors have sought to identify the pre-Enlightenment roots of modernity in nominalist theses, particularly those concerning the primacy of the divine will and omnipotence as well as the non-universality of human nature.[21] Among

19. J. A. Di Noia, OP, "Imago Dei—Imago Christi: The Theological Foundations of Christian Humanism," *Nova et Vetera* 2 (2004): 270.

20. See J. A. Di Noia, OP, "Clearing Away the Barriers: Preaching to Young Adults Today," (Carl Peter Lecture, North American College), *Origins* 38 (2009): 490–94.

21. See, for example, Louis Dupré, *Religion and the Rise of Modern Culture* (South

these cultural presuppositions, the most intractable obstacles to the acceptance and understanding of the Christian faith have arisen from typically modern views with nominalist roots, especially concerning the alleged meaninglessness and unpredictability of the universe (especially with respect to evolutionary processes), the lack of fit between human flourishing and eternal beatitude,[22] the arbitrariness of the moral law,[23] the opacity as opposed to luminosity of divine action in the economy of salvation,[24] the erosion of metaphysics in philosophy and theology,[25] and the eclipse of the category of "mediation" in speaking of the role of Christ, the Church and the sacraments. It is an interesting historical question why the legacy of nominalism proved more durable than its forceful Thomistic opponents. But the fact remains that characteristically nominalist theses, even when only implicitly, have remained influential at key points in Catholic systematic and moral theology, at the same time that they framed the agenda for western thinkers beginning with Descartes.

Other cultural presuppositions—loosely or not at all ascribable to nominalist influence—can also create barriers to the understanding and acceptance of the Catholic faith. One thinks of the prevailing subjectivism that locates all talk about God in the structures of consciousness. Connected with this is the view that, through consciousness itself, all persons have access to the transcendent realm and can give expression to their experience of the divine in the equally valid forms of sacred literature, institutions, and ways of life that we find

---

Bend, IN: Notre Dame University Press, 2008); Michael Allen Gillespie, *The Theological Origins of Modernity* (Chicago: University of Chicago Press, 2008); Charles Taylor, *A Secular Age* (Cambridge, MA: Harvard University Press, 2007).

22. See Anthony Levi, *Renaissance and Reformation: The Intellectual Genesis* (New Haven, CT: Yale University Press, 2002).

23. See Servais Pinckaers, OP, *Sources of Christian Ethics* (Washington, DC: The Catholic University of America Press, 1995); Terence Irwin, *The Development of Ethics: A Historical and Critical Study*, Volume 1 (New York: Oxford University Press, 2007) especially 434–652 on Aquinas, 653–700 on Scotus, and 701–24 on Ockham.

24. See J. A. Di Noia, OP, "Communion and Magisterium: Teaching Authority and the Culture of Grace," *Modern Theology* 9 (1993): 403–18.

25. See Benedict Ashley, OP, *The Way Toward Wisdom: Introduction to Metaphysics* (Notre Dame, IN: University of Notre Dame Press, 2006).

arrayed in the world religions.[26] In the climate created by this pluralism, it becomes increasingly difficult to affirm the unique role of Jesus Christ and the Church in salvation.

A formidable obstacle to Catholic moral teaching is posed by the fateful separation of procreation and sexuality that goes by the name of "the sexual revolution." Thus separated from one another, reproduction (as it is termed) and sexuality have each evolved a whole menu of possibilities that are claimed by their proponents as offering perfectly legitimate alternatives for the achievement of self-authenticity—alternatives, alas, that cannot make the persons who embrace them authentically happy.

The effort to grasp the impact of these cultural presuppositions involves tireless reading and study. I am reminded of a recommendation from the primitive constitutions in force during Blessed Jordan's tenure as master general: "The brethren ought to be so intent on study that by day and by night, at home or on a journey, they read or meditate on something, and endeavor to commit to memory whatever they can."[27] There is a great deal of work to be done here. To propose the truth often requires of us that we be able to understand and to clear up the errors that stand in the way of its acceptance. The study of St. Thomas—who was famous for his ability to frame the arguments of his opponents more effectively than they could themselves—provides a useful training ground for the kind of work that is needed today for preachers and teachers of the faith.

For these and for many other reasons, Dominicans have come to be persuaded of the enormous pastoral efficacy of the study of philosophy and theology with Thomas Aquinas as master and guide. It is to provide a place for this study that the Dominican House of Studies exists

Allow me to conclude on a more personal note. I was happy and honored to have been invited by Father Izzo and Father Boguslawski

---

26. See J. A. Di Noia, OP, "Religion and the Religions," in *The Cambridge Companion to Karl Barth*, ed. John Webster (Cambridge: Cambridge University Press, 2000), 243–57.

27. Weisheipl, *The Place of Study in the Ideal of St. Dominic*, 6.

to address you today as you dedicate this academic center and theological library. It represents for many of us, of an earlier generation, a dream come true—a dream that we had perhaps before the time for it was ripe, but whose time, as I have tried to show in this paper, has certainly come now. May the Immaculate Virgin Mary, the patroness who has never failed us, preserve all of you who, as it happens, will have the job to construct the future of *honeste vivere, discere et docere*—living virtuously, learning and teaching at the Dominican House of Studies in this new century.

PART II

Responding to
Modernity and Postmodernity
by *Ressourcement*

CHAPTER 8

---·---

Taking the Cure at Yale

From Aquinas to Rahner and Back (by Way of Wittgenstein and Barth)

INTERPRETATION AND IMPLEMENTATION OF
THE SECOND VATICAN COUNCIL

When I moved into St. Mary's Priory in New Haven in the fall of 1974 to begin graduate studies, the Second Vatican Council had concluded just about ten years before. George Lindbeck—the man with whom I was to work on the theology of religions and interreligious dialogue—had been among the Delegated Observers at the Council (1962–64) and had already written a book about his experience and the implications of the Council for the future of Catholic theology.[1] He was fascinated by the fact that my time of formation in the Dominican Order had coincided with the years of the Council and its somewhat tumultuous immediate aftermath.

It would not be until years later that I would become more reflective about the impact of the Council on our formation communities and on the province generally. At the time of my conversations with

Paper presented at the Thomistic Institute at the Dominican House of Studies in Washington, DC, April 8, 2017.

1. George A. Lindbeck, *The Future of Roman Catholic Theology* (Philadelphia: Fortress Press, 1970).

Lindbeck, I recalled my formation years as largely peaceful ones. Considering my experience in the light of the fragmentation that he had seen elsewhere in the postconciliar Church, Lindbeck marveled at the comparative tranquility of the situation I described, and eventually he found a way to interpret it for me.

Part of what I learned from him in those conversations, I later formulated in a talk I gave here in 2009 on the occasion of the dedication of the new academic wing and the new theological library at the Dominican House of Studies.[2] Lindbeck had helped me to see the importance, for the DHS and the province of St. Joseph, of

the relatively calm assimilation of the renewal measures promulgated by the Second Vatican Council. This development was due, at least in part, to the fact that during and after the years of the council the faculty and senior friars in the DHS community and in the province construed the conciliar teachings as being in essential continuity, rather than a disruption or break (to use Pope Benedict's language), with previous Catholic teaching and the tradition. Although there were difficulties, perhaps especially during the 1970s, the council was generally not experienced as a revolution. Without the destructive turmoil that had beset some other Catholic institutions and communities, the fundamental patterns of the Dominican religious and liturgical life of the priory, as well as those of formation and theological education in the Thomistic tradition, while undergoing necessary adjustments, continued more or less undisturbed.

When, in his momentous Christmas discourse to the Curia on 22 December 2005, I heard Pope Benedict contrast the hermeneutic of discontinuity and rupture with the hermeneutic of reform and continuity in the interpretation and implementation of the Second Vatican Council, I naturally thought of George Lindbeck who had, over thirty years before, first introduced me to these categories for understanding the postconciliar period.

2. Reprinted in this volume as Chapter Seven, "*Discere et Docere:* The Identity and Mission of the Dominican House of Studies in the 21st Century."

RESSOURCEMENT AND AGGIORNAMENTO

What I had absorbed in my conversations with Lindbeck about the impact of Vatican II in our province of Dominican friars was just one element in his analysis of the state of late twentieth-century theology. For me—and probably for others as well—the immense interpretive power of this analysis only emerged gradually as I began to teach theology after leaving Yale (in 1980).

Lindbeck notably framed his analysis of the state of American theology in terms of a perceptive account of the aftermath of the Second Vatican Council. According to this analysis, although united in their appeal to the authority of Vatican II, rival American Catholic theological positions were divided by two opposed readings of the nature of the conciliar response to modernity and its implications for the theological agenda. According to one reading, the Council was understood to commend a strong reaffirmation of Catholic Christian identity, taking the broadest view of its historic traditions, yet open to the cultural and religious pluralism characteristic of our times. But, in the eyes of a numerous and influential group of American theologians, such a reading reversed the true priorities of the Council. It was not restoration, but modernization, dialogue, and social commitment that Vatican II chiefly sought to cultivate in the contemporary Church. To a large extent, the state of theology in the U. S. (and elsewhere as well) reflected the predominance of the second interpretation of the Council.

As the conciliar documents reveal, both programs—*ressourcement* and *aggiornamento*, as they came to be called—were addressed at the Council. But which of them had priority? The documents themselves did not provide an explicit answer to this question. Lindbeck would persuasively argue that if one gives priority to *ressourcement*, then one will read the conciliar documents in the light of the Constitutions on Divine Revelation and the Church (*Dei Verbum* and *Lumen Gentium*). But, if *aggiornamento* has priority, then the Constitution on the Church in the Modern World (*Gaudium et*

Spes) is seen as providing the interpretative key for the rest of the documents.[3] In an effort aimed at what Aidan Nichols called *reaccentramento*, the Extraordinary Synod of 1985, under the leadership of Pope St. John Paul II and then Cardinal Ratzinger, sought to resolve this question by balancing tradition-mindedness with modernization. But it was a sign of the ascendancy of *aggiornamento* in the American Catholic reception of the Council that such recentering efforts were routinely decried by late twentieth-century theologians as retrogressive and anti-conciliar.

This disagreement about the nature of the Council's response to modernity needed to be set within the context of broad trends in twentieth-century theology. Throughout most of the earlier part of the century, Catholic theologians saw the program of modernization (*aggiornamento*) as possessing an important but subordinate value in comparison with that of the program of *ressourcement*.

It is well known that *ressourcement* furnished a powerful impetus for theological work in both Catholic and Protestant circles throughout the first half of the twentieth century, and even more so in the period between World War II and the opening of Vatican II. The impulse arose not from historical or antiquarian interests but from a determination to reaffirm Catholic Christian identity by means of a creative reappropriation of its principal formative sources. In part, and especially in its late 19th century phase, *ressourcement* involved the recovery of medieval and scholastic sources. But, gradually and more broadly, attention shifted to Scripture, liturgy, and the Fathers of the Church.

It became increasingly clear as the century wore on that modernization would be an important byproduct of *ressourcement*. The earlier recovery of medieval and scholastic sources had been so successful as to have restored and reinforced a fundamentally post-Tridentine theological edifice, with at least deference to—if not actual adoption and promotion of—the positions of Aquinas as its

3. Lindbeck, "Ecumenical Theology," in *The Modern Theologians*, ed. David F. Ford, Vol. II (Oxford: Basil Blackwell, 1989), 255–73.

cornerstone. This neoscholastic and neo-Thomistic revival supplied the means to refute the errors of modernity if not always to engage its challenge. But study of the biblical, liturgical, and patristic sources afforded theologians access to the immeasurably more pluralistic pre-scholastic period. In a strategic deployment of *ressourcement*, its practitioners sought to recover the greater tradition at the expense of what they considered the narrower post-Tridentine tradition enshrined by neoscholastic and neo-Thomistic theology. For neoscholastic theologians, *ressourcement* had provided access to an arsenal; for biblically and patristically oriented theologians, it seemed to unlock a treasure.

Thus it transpired that the later phase of the 20th century *ressourcement* had a powerfully modernizing edge. It cut into the neoscholastic hegemony through the radically pluralizing introduction of biblically and patristically based theological positions in dialogue with modern culture and philosophy. The passion at the core of the *ressourcement* program stemmed, nonetheless, from a tradition-minded reaffirmation of Catholic Christian identity. *Ressourcement* theologians shared the confidence that the richness of the Christian tradition, once displayed in all its wonderful diversity and breadth, could not fail to win a favorable hearing in the modern world.

While this conception of the balance of *ressourcement* and *aggiornamento* remained in place throughout the Council, it did not fare well in the postconciliar period. In the popular American reception of the results of the Council, it never even had a chance. Almost from the start, the program of *aggiornamento* was seen by the public and the media as providing the key to the conciliar deliberations and actions. Vatican II came rather quickly to be viewed as representing a sharp break with the previous centuries and as charting a new course for the Church as it entered the twenty-first century. In part, this reception was fostered by the early implementation of the Constitution on the Sacred Liturgy. This document, in addition to recommending the reform of the liturgy, was also understood to signal a vast overhaul of Catholic life. Reform and renewal were widely viewed as equivalent with modernization rather than with the reaffirmation of Christian identity implicit in the *ressourcement*. Modernization came to entail in practice a vigorous engagement in dialogue and in socially transformative action.

With massive consequences for the future of Catholic theology in the U. S., the program of *aggiornamento* prevailed in American Catholic reception of the Council from the outset. In theology, the priority of *aggiornamento* over *ressourcement* entailed more than simply the updating of forms of life and expression. It often meant a readiness to appropriate the agenda of modernity, especially in correlationist and revisionist modes of theological reflection. In correlationist conceptions of the relation of faith and modern culture, culture asks the questions to which faith provides the responses. In revisionist conceptions, faith tailors its claims with an eye to prevailing canons of reasonability and applicability. Both theological styles in varying degrees embodied an accommodationist appropriation of the modern agenda that was not favorable to the affirmation of traditional Christian claims about revelation, the status of Scripture, the person of Jesus Christ, and meaning of human life.[4] But, even where correlationism and revisionism were not operative as explicit methodological commitments, the priority of *aggiornamento* fostered a climate in which modern criteria of rationality were perceived to be in competition with fidelity to the Christian doctrinal tradition.

American Catholic theology increasingly came to display a typically modern profile. The characteristic concerns of modern theology, singly or in combination, gained prominence in theology over the final decades of the twentieth century: the primacy of the category of experience—whether religious or common human experience; the subjective turn, with its emphasis on the structures of human existence as affording the chief context for theological affirmation; the centrality of theological anthropology; universalism

4. Peter Berger, "A Sociological View of the Secularization of Christianity," *Journal for the Scientific Study of Religion* 6 (1967): 3–16.

in the doctrine of revelation; pluralism in the attitude to other religions; insistence on the historically conditioned nature of formulations of the faith; the ascendancy of historical-critical approaches to the study of Scripture; antipathy to doctrinal norms; the centrality of critique and dissent with reference to the tradition and magisterium; a preference for procedural over thematic ecumenism; in ethics, the centrality of obligation and the autonomous agent. In addition to these familiar characteristics of modern theology, some current American Catholic theology drew from liberation theology an emphasis on political activism and the notion that certain experiences, especially those of the oppressed, afford a privileged access to the meaning of revelation.

PROTESTANT LIBERALISM AND CATHOLIC *AGGIORNAMENTO*

While George Lindbeck helped me to understand mid-twentieth-century Catholic theology in the light of postconciliar trends, it was especially in listening to Hans Frei's lectures on nineteenth-century Protestant thought that I began to see the parallels between Protestant liberalism and Catholic *aggiornamento*.

Frei's *The Eclipse of Biblical Narrative* was published during my first year in New Haven. This enormously important book eventually led biblical scholars and theologians to question the hegemony of historical-critical methodologies for mediating the meaning of the Scriptures for theological, doctrinal, and other churchly uses. Frei was critical of the modern theory and practice of biblical hermeneutics and persuasively underscored the validity of pre-critical narrational and typological hermeneutics, which had read the Scriptures as a unified account of revelation and salvation with Jesus Christ at the center.

Later it would be clear that Frei's book had opened the way for the recovery of a doctrinally and liturgically structured reading of the Scriptures that is central to postliberal theology. But much more influential for me at the time were his lectures on nineteenth-century philosophy and theology, and his seminars on Karl Barth. Though I had studied them in history of philosophy courses in Dover, I had never read Kant's *Critique of Pure Reason* and *Religion Within the Limits of Reason Alone*, or Hegel's *Phenomenology of Spirit* and *Lectures on the Philosophy of Religion*, or Schleiermacher's *On Religion: Speeches to Cultured Despisers* and *The Christian Faith*. Barth had not figured significantly in my theological studies. But now I read his *Church Dogmatics* and *Protestant Theology in the 19th Century*. Frei's lectures and his brilliant essay on "Niebuhr's Theological Background"[5] were my guides. When I chose the somewhat playful title for this lecture—"Taking the Cure at Yale"—what I had in mind chiefly was the intellectual epiphany I experienced when reading nineteenth-century philosophy and theology.

Like so many young theologians of my generation, I had become a fledgling Rahnerian after braving the daunting obscurities of transcendental philosophy to write my STL thesis on Rahner's theology of grace and the Trinity. For many of them and certainly for me, transcendental Thomism had swept into the vacuum created by the postconciliar eclipse of classical Thomism.

But, I now saw, as I wrote later in an essay on philosophical theology, that "the 20th century transcendental turn in Catholic theology, associated especially with the work of Karl Rahner, roughly parallels the 19th-century turn to the subject in Protestant theology. The prevailing Rahnerian (if not Rahner's) theology in the Catholic community exhibits remarkable formal and material similarities to modern Protestant theological positions."[6] What I now saw, to put it briefly, was that there was another way and that there were very good reasons not to think of Kant's critique of metaphysics as a definitive block to robust Christian affirmation. But more on this later.

---

5. Hans W. Frei, "Niebuhr's Theological Background," in *Faith and Ethics: The Theology of H. Richard Niebuhr*, ed. Paul Ramsey (New York: Harper and Row, 1957), 9–64.

6. J. A. Di Noia, "Philosophical Theology in the Perspective of Religious Diversity," *Theological Studies* 49 (1988): 411.

More broadly, Frei and Lindbeck helped me to see that the postconciliar Catholic experience in effect seemed to represent a compressed and accelerated recapitulation of the nineteenth- and twentieth-century Protestant experience. I found that study of the range of Protestant responses to modernity would prove to be instructive for understanding developments in Catholic theology and in Catholic life generally in the aftermath of the Council.

The kind of polarization that divided the Protestant churches into conservative and liberal branches at the turn of the nineteenth century emerged in the postconciliar Catholic Church. In both the Protestant and Catholic situations, issues turned on how to understand and deal with the challenge of modernity. In both Catholic and Protestant circles in the U. S., the conservative/liberal split became more significant than denominational differences. Progressive Catholics and liberal Protestants found themselves allied against tradition-minded Catholics and evangelical Protestants. Evangelical Protestantism continued its rapid growth, in comparison with a long-range decline in liberal Protestantism. This trend confirmed the prediction that Christian communities with a clear sense of their distinctive identity vis-à-vis the wider culture possessed a competitive advantage over those whose accommodationist strategies had blurred their distinctively Christian profile.

But the modernizing accommodationist strategies typical of modern Protestant theology (and with them, the forms of institutional adjustment they inspired) were already showing signs of exhaustion. One could predict that, over the long haul, *aggiornamento* would not sustain a fully Catholic Christian theology and a vital Church life. The agenda of modernization by itself turned out to be an inadequate program for the practice of Christian theology. Prevailing trends within the history of Christian thought suggested that *ressourcement* supplied a more lastingly potent principle of theological energy. In fact, within American Catholic theology, there was a growing movement that sought to reassert the priority of *ressourcement* over *aggiornamento* in the appropriation of Vatican II and in the theological enterprise generally. There was no question of reversing the tremendous gains in flexibility, in collegiality, in religious freedom, in social and political awareness, in commitments to dialogue with other Christians, other religious people, and nonbelievers, in respect for diversity within the world Church, and so on—all achieved in the name of *aggiornamento*. Rather, there was a recovery of the astute insight that fueled the work of the original *ressourcement* theologians: an uncompromising, unapologetic but open reaffirmation of the fullness and richness of the Christian tradition is in itself a powerful form of engagement with modernity.

In combination with wider cultural and intellectual trends, these developments produced a favorable environment within Protestant and Catholic theology in the U. S. for the emergence of a complex set of approaches that would eventually come to known as postliberal theology. I was hooked.

POST-LIBERAL THEOLOGY

Naturally, when I arrived in New Haven in 1974, I had never heard of postliberal theology, and neither had anyone else. It was only ten years later in 1984, after the publication of Lindbeck's *The Nature of Doctrine*, that it entered common discourse. The group of graduate students whom I found at Yale in 1974 and those who later joined us there formed deep bonds of intellectual and spiritual friendship that have endured to this day. Some of them are sitting in this room today. We didn't have a name for it then, but we knew that something quite remarkable was taking shape there and that we were very fortunate to be among its early beneficiaries.

Forty years ago we probably would have called it the "Yale School"—comprising not only theologians like Lindbeck, Frei, and David Kelsey, but also the philosopher of religion William Christian, the historian of doctrine Jaroslav Pelikan, and the scripture scholars Brevard Childs and Wayne Meeks, just to mention the most prominent. Despite considerable differences among them, these

Yale professors—and others elsewhere who shared their convictions—believed that new opportunities for Christian affirmation were emerging as theology freed itself from the strictures imposed by characteristically modern presuppositions. Not unlike the *ressourcement* theologians in Catholic circles, the postliberal theologians among these thinkers in varying degrees turned to premodern and classical sources of philosophy and theology—not in order to repristinate the past as if the modern era had never occurred, but in order to make these sources speak anew in the irreversibly pluralized postmodern era.

Among several that could be cited, three elements imparted a distinctively postliberal flavor to the new theological initiatives. In the first place, in the service of a broader conception of rationality, postliberal theologians rejected the modern (Cartesian) quest for a foundation for all knowledge, modeled on mathematical or scientific paradigms of rationality. As a Thomist might say, reasonability and certainty are analogous concepts, applicable to diverse domains of knowledge in ways that are dependent on the principles operative from one context to another. Scientific claims are truth-bearing in ways that are distinctive from claims in other fields like philosophy, ethics, religion, history, literary criticism, and so on. In assessing claims to rationality and truth, it was axiomatic for postliberal theologians to attend to the context in which these claims are embedded. Truth and rationality are far broader notions than modern thinkers were generally prepared to acknowledge. In this connection and in sharp contrast to modernity, postliberal theologians insisted on the centrality of tradition and authority in legitimating and supporting truth and rationality (not only in the religious but in the scientific and philosophical fields as well).

Two other characteristic elements in postliberal theology were the insistence on the role of texts and narratives in shaping thought and culture, and its stress on the importance of relationships and community in fostering intellectual and personal identity. These emphases challenged rationalism and positivism in modern philosophy of language and epistemology, and individualism in modern moral and political philosophy. In part, the postliberal insistence on the culture- and identity-shaping roles of language was the outcome of the so-called "linguistic turn"—a series of developments in continental and Anglo-American philosophy stemming from the thought of Heidegger and Wittgenstein respectively. Postliberal theologians sought to secure the objectivity and realism of knowledge with reference, not to the inner workings of consciousness (as in rationalism) or to their correspondence to objective facts (as in positivism), but to a shared world of meaning and truth embodied in the linguistic practices of a community. In addition, postliberal theology saw personal identity, not as an individualistically cultivated sense and performance of moral duty, but in a communally and relationally shaped life of virtue.

AQUINAS AND POSTLIBERAL
THEOLOGICAL APPROACHES

Traditionally, the Yale divinity faculty was known to welcome confessional commitments among its graduate students. Whether Anglican, Catholic, Lutheran, Reformed, or otherwise, these confessional backgrounds were regarded as the natural seedbed of theology. In seminars, Lindbeck would routinely invite students to speak to the issues under discussion out of their distinctive doctrinal or theological traditions. You can imagine my alarm when Lindbeck turned to me in a seminar to inquire about what Aquinas had to say about the matter under discussion. Thus, it happened that another important aspect of the "cure" I took in those six years in New Haven was to return to the study of St. Thomas so that I would be able reply to Lindbeck intelligently.

But once I began teaching, my recovery of Aquinas began in earnest. My teaching responsibilities included the first forty-three questions of the Prima Pars of the *Summa Theologiae*—that is, the courses on the nature of theology, and on the doctrine of God One and

Three. Later they would extend to the doctrine of creation and theological anthropology, and even, occasionally, sacramental theology.

As my rediscovery of Aquinas reshaped my thought, I found that my developing Thomism and newly formed postliberal sympathies made for quite congenial partners. The characteristic postliberal determination to overcome the legacy of modernity's turn to the subject in epistemology and ethics resonated with Thomistic metaphysics and the modest place within it occupied by epistemology. Like postliberal theology, Thomists reject the modern equivalence of consciousness with the true self, insisting instead on the fundamental importance of bodiliness—and hence on the immersion of human beings in a natural cosmic order and on patterns of activity in a community of social and personal relations—as a constitutive element of personal identity. In postliberal theology, thought, bodiliness, agency, and community replace subjectivity, consciousness, and the autonomous self as fundamental anthropological categories. Read straightforwardly—rather than in the modernizing construal given him by transcendental Thomism—Aquinas supports precisely this displacement of the Cartesian separations of mind and matter, of spirit and body, of subject and object, and of moral self and moral agent. As the years of teaching unfolded, I found that my reading of Aquinas and my reading of postliberal theologians were mutually enriching in ways that I could not always specify. Looking back on those twenty years of teaching here at DHS, I can identify four areas in which characteristic elements of postliberal theology coalesced with my understanding of Aquinas to produce a distinctive—and one hopes not incoherent—style of theological affirmation.

Biblical hermeneutics was one of the first areas in which the impact of postliberal thought, was felt, particularly its insistence on the interplay between the communal reading of texts and their community-shaping power. Although it was generally admitted that historical-critical approaches have much to contribute to Christian understanding of the Bible, in the practice of theology these approaches are logically subordinate to the doctrinally and liturgically shaped reading of the Bible precisely as Scripture.[7] I saw that Aquinas's understanding of the appropriation of the results of other disciplines by *sacra doctrina* in terms of the subalternation of sciences can be helpful in sorting out the complex logic of the relation of historical and literary exegesis to theology. Directly relevant to a reading of Aquinas on these issues was the fact that the movement from *lectio* to *quaestio* in his own theological work represented the cresting of one of the most potent movements of *ressourcement* in the history of Christian thought.

Another area in which postliberal theology bore fruit in my teaching was in my whole approach to systematic theology. If in modern theology the basic question was, how can a modern person believe this doctrine? then in postliberal theology the basic question became, how can the deep intelligibility of this doctrine be exhibited? From the outset, postliberal theology avoided posing skeptical questions about the Christian scheme of doctrine. There was a deep suspicion of the Cartesian methodological starting point of doubt. The assumption was not that religious claims inevitably challenge and bend accepted canons of rationality. Rather, canons of rationality in the religious realm have their own integrity and scope, and, although they do not isolate the religious domain from other domains, they nonetheless involve a distinctive logical structure. Systematic theology in the postliberal vein begins by trying to discern and exhibit this structure. The initial assumption is that a doctrinal scheme and the religious pattern of life it commends make good sense in theory and in practice. The task of Christian theology is to explicate the inherent intelligibility of a particular doctrine in connection with the whole body of Christian doctrines. Again, Aquinas's vision of the fundamental and integral intelligibility of the mysteries of the Christian faith is very attractive to postliberal theology. In his employment of metaphysical and other conceptions in the service of

---

7. See David H. Kelsey, *The Uses of Scripture in Recent Theology* (Philadelphia: Fortress Press, 1975).

this explication, he was careful to avoid forcing the Christian scheme onto a philosophical grid.

What is more, in postliberal theological approaches and in marked contrast to those of modernity, Christianity's particularistic claim to universality constitutes not an embarrassment but a necessary feature of its commitment to and proclamation of the truth about God's dealings with us in Christ. The postliberal emphasis on the narrational and communal sources and embodiment of a community's claim to truth renders the Christian insistence on the uniqueness of Christ intelligible and, incidentally, comparable to the particularistic claims of other religious communities. Universal meaning is embedded in the particularistically depicted and narrated story of the passion, death, resurrection, and glory of Jesus of Nazareth, delivered to us as Christ and Lord. The motto of von Balthasar's theology is pertinent here: "the greatest possible radiance in the world in virtue of the closest possible following of Christ." The replication of the pattern of Christ, in the *imitatio Christi*, is not only the vehicle through which Christian personal and communal identity is shaped. It is also the particularistic medium in which the universally applicable, though not universally accessible apart from revelation and evangelization, truth of Christ is made known to the whole world beyond the visible ambit of the Christian community. The scandal of particularity is no scandal for postliberal theology. Despite much well-intentioned defense of the interplay of history and metaphysics in Aquinas, particularity is no scandal for his theology either. At the center of his theology is a doctrine of salvation, embedded in a Christologically shaped narrative. The objective of theological explication is to provide as complete as possible an account of the principal characters upon whose agency the movement and action depicted in the narrative depends: God, angels, humans, and Christ. The narrative is not universalized by the introduction of metaphysical concepts. Rather, its particularistic claim to universal relevance is secured by a web of exegetical, theological, philosophical, and other patterns of argumentation.

Finally, postliberal theology helped me to understand that the interweaving of philosophical analysis and construction in the web of theological argument in the *Summa* is in the service of properly theological affirmation. The outcome is not a theological/philosophical system, but a highly ramified complex of interrelated dialectical arguments, always open to embracing or engaging alternative positions that can be rationally justified. The *principle* of unity and coherence is supplied by the mysteries of the faith in their own interconnection and intelligibility, itself rooted in the *scientia divina*. The exigencies of doctrinal and theological affirmation are seen to demand a robust theological realism, and it is for this reason that wide-ranging appeals are made to philosophy and other non-theological disciplines. At each turn in the larger argument, such appeals function as needed to secure the intelligibility of the doctrine under consideration, whether it be the concept of relation in the Trinity, or the concept of making in creation, or the concept of end in moral life, or the concept of disposition (*habitus*) in grace and the virtues, and so on.

The *Summa's* sparing methodological passages support this reading of the role of philosophy in the explication of the Christian faith. Though transposed to a new—a "supernatural"—level of activity, ordinary patterns of human perception, thought, and language are internal to knowledge and talk about God in faith and, ultimately, in vision. According to Aquinas, the life of grace involves not the infusion of a set of capacities geared exclusively to engagement with God, but the transformation and empowerment of natural capacities for exercise at a new level. Hence, wherever relevant and appropriate, the results of nontheological inquiries as well as the logic of assertion and argument can be brought to bear on the theological explication of the contents of Christian faith. With respect to its overarching formal interest, theology is thus a field-encompassing field (Stephen Toulmin), and nontheological disciplines contribute to its pursuit of understanding and explication of divine revelation. Because of the prominence of the role of philosophy here, these issues are usually considered under the rubric "theology and philosophy." But other nontheological disciplines contribute to theological understanding and explication, notably literary criticism, history, sociology, psychology, and the natural sciences.

The role of the philosophical component in Aquinas's theological arguments can be seen in Aquinas's discussion of the triune God in *Summa Theologiae* I, q. 2–43. That the discussion of the existence and nature of God in I, q. 2–26 has a properly theological role to play is clear from Aquinas's prior description of the nature of theological inquiry (I, q. 1). To assert that theology gets its subject matter from revelation entails that faith in God constitutes one of the principles of the inquiry now getting underway. The triune God is already "in place," so to speak, in his full Christian characterization. The burden of the argument in I, q. 2 on the existence of God is to assert that the one confessed as Father, Son, and Holy Spirit is the cause of the world. Through an interweaving of philosophical and scriptural premises, the subsequent argument in I, q. 3–26 exhibits something of the kind of life the triune God enjoys as cause of the world. The force of these arguments is to secure the particularistic claim to universality which the Christian community makes for its doctrines.

Philosophically-shaped arguments concerning God's existence function to secure this universal claim. Starting with observable features of the world, such arguments affirm the divine agency as the source of these features and of the world order as a whole. Whatever their logical merits or probative force, their position at the beginning of the theological inquiry signals the logical space that Christians' claims are understood to occupy. This discussion functions to locate Christian worship, nurture, practice, and belief with respect to the widest possible conceptual map. The triune God who is adored, confessed, and proclaimed in the Christian community has not only a local, narrative, or contextual reference within the usage of a particular cultural and linguistic community. He is none other than the cause of the world.

While developed in connection with scientific and metaphysical claims, such arguments are subsumed in a properly theological and scripturally-based inquiry. They do not displace, but rather presuppose the reading of Scripture as a "canonically and narrationally unified and internally glossed ... whole centered on Jesus Christ, and telling the story of the dealings of the Triune God with his people and his world in ways that are typologically ... applicable to the present."[8] In effect, philosophical analysis and construction enable Aquinas to address the question (here and in subsequent discussions of the divine nature and agency, of angelic and human natures, and, finally and decisively, of Jesus Christ as divine-human agent): what must be true of the main characters of the Christian narrative for it to have the features Christians claim for it, truth and "followability"? Philosophy and other nontheological disciplines contribute as needed to filling out these complex characterizations. A literary analogy may help at this juncture. In a critical study of Melville's *Moby Dick*, for example, the complex narrative need not be continually retold in the course of literary analysis of the motivations and structure of the main characters. In somewhat the same way in the *Summa Theologiae*, Aquinas presumes his readership's detailed familiarity with the Christian narrative in order to show—or, more accurately, to remove obstacles to seeing—that its central claims are true and its chief injunctions followable.

Aquinas thus provides a powerful model of theological affirmation and realism over against alternatives that locate the reference for Christian talk about God either in human experience of God or in the linguistic practices of the community. The philosophical component in his discussion of the existence and nature of the triune God serves purposes internal to this properly theological project. In this discussion, the triune God is not left behind but presupposed. The central affirmation of I qq. 2–26 is that the Father, Son, and Holy Spirit are together one God, sharing the single divine life of sheer existence (*ipsum esse per se subsistens*).

8. George A. Lindbeck, *The Church in a Postliberal Age*, ed. James J. Buckley (Grand Rapids, MI: Eerdmans, 2002), 203.

CONFRONTING THE *QUAESTIONES*

My conversations with George Lindbeck continued after I moved on to the Dominican House of Studies—both in New Haven and here in Washington. *Especially* during the fall semesters when I was teaching the nature and method of theology, we often reprised the theme of *ressourcement* and *aggiornamento*. We talked about the affinities between postliberal theology and the *ressourcement* agenda in Catholic theology. Like *ressourcement,* postliberal theology favors tradition-mindedness over traditionalism, on the one hand, and revisionism and correlation, on the other. In contrast to the program of *aggiornamento,* postliberal theology sees systematic importance in the reaffirmation of Christian identity as a means of promoting Christian fidelity and Christian proclamation. When accorded primacy over *ressourcement, aggiornamento* looks to postliberal eyes as if always on the verge of running out of breath as the culture rushes several steps ahead. Conceived simply as the updating of theology, *aggiornamento* is never finished catching up; conceived more grandly as modernization, it is already far behind.

On the other hand, *ressourcement* theology has sometimes shown itself unable or unwilling to confront and resolve the conceptual problems—the *quaestiones,* as Aquinas might say—that the sources themselves serve up. *Lectio* is not always enough. Lindbeck and I talked about this often. We agreed that Aquinas provides a set of strategies for the disciplined appropriation of the results of nontheological intellectual inquiries—like philosophy, philosophical ethics, history, and psychology—in order to advance the analysis and resolution of such problems. The vastly pluralized postmodern contexts in which theology is undertaken today accentuate the challenge. Though sympathetic to the *ressourcement* agenda, postliberal theology has never shared its unfortunate antipathy for Thomism. The rigorous philosophical analysis and sound patterns of argumentation fostered in the Thomistic tradition are skills and habits of mind that are also much valued in postliberal theology.

Lindbeck appreciated and imitated what he called the "question approach" of Aquinas. In a 2007 interview, speaking about the ecumenical purpose of *The Nature of Doctrine*, he said:

[Like Aquinas] you raise a question, and then there is an objection to the position that you're going to take, and they you try to answer the objection. I would say that what I'm trying to do in *The Nature of Doctrine*—to develop a so-called rule theory of doctrine, a grammatical rule theory of doctrine—is an attempt then to provide a supporting conceptuality for seeing how this 'question method' proceeds and how apparently contradictory views can be shown not to contradict each other [if one introduces] the appropriate distinction.[9]

One can see how appropriate it has been for the Thomistic Institute to organize this gathering on postliberal theology and Thomism. I am grateful to have had the opportunity to think more systematically and self-consciously about the influence of postliberal theology on my own thinking and that of my close friends and colleagues. I have tried to convey something of the gradual way I came in varying degrees to absorb it the over years of studying and teaching. You will have grasped from the other presentations and the discussion that postliberal theology is more than anything else the name of a particular family of approaches to theological construction that, as John Webster put it, "has sought to revisit Christian doctrine, asking not so much what might be wrong with it but what resources it may contain to redefine or illuminate current perplexities."[10]

We owe a considerable debt of gratitude to our teachers, especially to Frei and Lindbeck. Frei we lost early and very suddenly in 1988. Lindbeck is still with us, now well over ninety years old and living in a Lutheran retirement home in Boca Raton.

When he visited DHS, Lindbeck loved to participate in the Liturgy of the Hours in the chapel. He especially loved chanting the Psalms. I remember once, after Midday Prayer, he turned to me

---

9. John Wright, *Postliberal Theology and the Catholic Church* (Grand Rapids, MI: Baker Academic, 2012), 72.

10. John Webster and George Schner, SJ, eds., *Theology After Liberalism* (Oxford: Blackwell, 2000), 55.

and said, "You know, Joe, I think I could have been a Dominican." That was over thirty years ago. In the 2007 interview I quoted above, when asked if his work was a preparation for the future, Lindbeck replied: "The one advantage of living a long time is that one mistrusts entirely predictions of what the future will bring.... At any rate, given the revolutions that are likely to be taken and the way we find ourselves reacting to reality, I can't help but think that there is at least a good chance that the sorts of things that drove the church to what we call neo-orthodoxy that required a sizable interest in the visible unity of the churches, is something we won't escape in this century either. That's the way I look at the future. Therefore, I think of what I have been doing all my life in working for the visible unity of the church ... might very well be very valuable in the things that will be happening in the not very distant future. So, I am quite willing to leave this life, and quite optimistic about my life's work."[11]

11. Wright, *Postliberal Theology and the Catholic Church*, 73–75.

CHAPTER 9

Knowing and Naming the Triune God
The Grammar of Trinitarian Confession

"O Abyss! O eternal Godhead! O deep sea!" exclaims St. Catherine of Siena in the prayer to the Trinity that concludes *The Dialogue*: "What more could you have given me than the gift of your very self?"[1] In St. Catherine's eloquent prayer, the awestruck Christian heart cries out in praise of the great mystery of the gift of the triune God's very self through the grace of Christ. The mystery defies expression but invites wonder, worship, and love. Although no words can exhaust it, the final test for the adequacy of any words that dare to name this mystery is that they be true to its reality.

This essay considers some recent suggestions for revisions in the Christian community's manner of speaking of the triune God who abides with that community in grace. One measure for assessing the Christian aptness of these proposals is furnished by the reality of the gift itself. Do the proposed ways of speaking permit the full reality of this gift to come to expression?

Originally published in *Speaking the Christian God: The Triune God and the Challenge of Feminism*, ed. Alvin F. Kimel, Jr. (Grand Rapids, MI: Eerdmans, 1992), 162–87.
1. Catherine of Siena, *The Dialogue*, trans. Suzanne Noffke, OP, *The Classics of Western Spirituality* (New York: Paulist Press, 1980), 365.

THE GIFT OF GOD'S VERY SELF

As Christians have understood it, to affirm the presence of God's "very self" in grace is to affirm the personal presence of the Blessed Trinity. Christ himself promised this: "Anyone who loves me will be true to my word, and my Father will love him; we will come to him and make our dwelling with him" (Jn 14:23). In the central action of the great narrative that recounts God's divine engagement with humankind, the presence promised by Christ is enacted and achieved. For in the person of the Word, God is united with human nature, and through his suffering, death, and glory, human beings are reconciled with the triune God, "for through him we both have access in one Spirit to the Father" (Eph 2:18). Indeed, it could be said that the whole economy of salvation is directed by God to nothing less than the incorporation of created persons into personal communion with the uncreated Trinity.[2]

How such a communion can come about St. Catherine intimates elsewhere in her prayer. "O eternal Trinity, fire and abyss of charity ... by the light of understanding within your light I have tasted and seen your depth ... and the beauty of your creation. Then, when I considered myself in you, I saw that I am your image. You have gifted me with power from yourself, eternal Father, and my understanding with your wisdom—such wisdom as is proper to your only-begotten Son; and the Holy Spirit, who proceeds from you and your Son, has given me a will, and so I am able to love."[3] The triune God so transforms and empowers human capacities as to become

2. See recent discussions of the doctrine of the Trinity: Karl Rahner, *The Trinity*, trans. Joseph Donceel (New York: Herder & Herder, 1970); William J. Hill, *The Three-Personed God* (Washington, DC: The Catholic University of America Press, 1982); Robert W. Jenson, *The Triune Identity* (Philadelphia: Fortress Press, 1982); Walter Kasper, *The God of Jesus Christ*, trans. Matthew J. O'Connell (New York: Crossroad, 1984); and Eberhard Jüngel, *God as the Mystery of the World*, trans. Darrell L. Guder (Grand Rapids, MI: Eerdmans, 1983). For the history of the doctrine, see Bertrand de Margerie, *The Christian Trinity in History*, trans. Edmund J. Fortman (Still River, MA: St. Bede's Publications, 1981).

3. Catherine of Siena, *The Dialogue*, 365.

known and loved in his inner being as Father, Son, and Holy Spirit. The gift of the triune God's "very self" entails not an intensification of the divine presence but a transformation of human personal and social existence. For how could it be possible for the God who actively sustains all things in existence to become "more" present to his creatures? Divine indwelling supersedes divine omnipresence, so to speak, because in grace the triune God occasions and enables human engagement with the personal Father, Son, and Holy Spirit.

Indeed, as St. Catherine's prayer suggests, this engagement itself possesses a trinitarian structure. Aquinas makes a similar point. The knowledge of the triune God given in grace partakes of the Son's knowledge, and hence, through the Spirit, it is the sort of knowledge that breaks forth into love.[4] The gift of God's very self thus entails the incorporation of human persons into the inner life of the Father, Son, and Holy Spirit. In an important way, the structure of this incorporation replicates the mutual relations of the persons of the Trinity. Christ's sonship is the principle of our coming to life in grace—our adoption—as sons and daughters who can with Christ speak the name of the Father in the power of the Spirit: "God sent forth his Son ... so that we might receive adoption as sons. And because you are sons, God has sent the Spirit of his Son into our hearts, crying, 'Abba! Father!'" (Gal 4:4–6). Moreover, Christ's sonship is also the principle of a reconciled and restored human community, as his own prayer makes clear: "Holy Father, keep them in your name, which you have given me, that they may be one, even as we Are one" (Jn 17:11).

"What more could you have given me than the gift of your very self?" Scripture, creeds, liturgy, sacramental rites, catechesis, preaching, theological tradition—all, like St. Catherine's prayer, are suffused with faith in the reality of the gift of God's very self in grace. As embodied in Christian utterance and practice, this faith defines the context for any consideration of the knowability and speakability of the trinitarian mystery.

---

4. Aquinas, *Summa theologiae* I, q. 43, a. 5, ad 2um.

The triune identity of the God who gives us his very self is knowable, strictly speaking, only through revelation. But even though the mystery is known, it permanently eludes human comprehension. Thus St. Catherine sounds another traditional theme when she prays, "You, eternal Trinity, are a deep sea: The more I enter you, the more I discover, and the more I discover, the more I seek you."[5] The mystery of the presence of the three-personed God to human knowledge and love in grace is inexhaustible and, in that sense, never fully comprehensible or expressible. To be sure, faith is the source of our knowledge of this mystery. But since its object is the transcendent God, this knowledge can never be complete or comprehensive.

It follows that, along with understanding, language itself falters before this mystery. The challenge to speak appropriately of this mystery has confronted the Christian community and its theologians in every generation. For the unknowable and unspeakable mystery at the heart of the Christian narrative and the life it fosters are found to be renderable in human utterance if for no other reason than to give voice to the truth of God's nearness. Just as God is the first teacher of trinitarian truth, so also is it God who provides the first lesson in trinitarian grammar: "When we cry, 'Abba! Father!' it is the Spirit himself bearing witness with our spirit that we are children of God" (Rom 8:15–16). Or as Christ's promise in a different context has it, "When they deliver you up, do not be anxious how you are to speak or what you are to say; for what you are to say will be given to you in that hour; for it is not you who speak, but the Spirit of your Father speaking through you" (Mt 10:19–20). The speakability of the otherwise unspeakable mystery of the triune God presupposes the gift of God's very self and depends on resources that come with that gift. It is a possibility rooted in the very presence whose reality faith affirms, a presence that supersedes the limitations of human understanding and utterance in the face of the radically transcendent creator. The Christian aptness of proposed forms of speech about the triune God must be measured at least by this criterion: Can these

5. Catherine of Siena, *The Dialogue*, 364.

proposed forms of speech do justice to the reality of the gift of God's very self?

PROPOSALS FOR THE REFORMULATION
OF CHRISTIAN LANGUAGE

Over the past two decades, a number of theologians have argued that standard forms of Christian speech about the triune God enshrine masculinist conceptions of God.[6] These conceptions are said to affect women adversely in at least two ways. First, they legitimate patterns of male domination and patriarchy in the church and in society at large. Second, they make it difficult if not impossible for women to relate to the divine in a way that is religiously meaningful.

Would it not be desirable to reformulate language about the triune God so that it would better reflect our diverse experiences of God? Some have argued not only that it would be advantageous to do so but also that it is necessary to do so in order to redress actual harms done to women which came to be legitimated and reinforced by androcentric language about God. Furthermore, it is hoped that such reformulation would foster the equality and liberation of women. To be sure, since the offending linguistic practices are embedded in the scriptural, liturgical, doctrinal, and theological traditions of all

---

6. For readers unfamiliar with this literature, a good start can be made with Ann Loades, "Feminist Theology," in *The Modern Theologians*, vol. 2, ed. David F. Ford (Oxford: Basil Blackwell, 1989), 233–52. Indispensable for understanding the case for the proposed reformulations of traditional trinitarian language are the following works: Mary Daly, *The Church and the Second Sex* (San Francisco: Harper & Row, 1975); Rosemary Radford Ruether, *Sexism and God-Talk* (Boston: Beacon Press, 1982); Elisabeth Schüssler Fiorenza, *In Memory of Her* (New York: Crossroad, 1985); Sallie McFague, *Models of God* (Philadelphia: Fortress Press, 1987); and Anne E. Carr, *Transforming Grace* (San Francisco: Harper & Row, 1987). The Viennese feminist theologian Susanne Heine has mounted a vigorous critique of standard feminist theology in two works: *Women and Early Christianity*, trans. John Bowden (Minneapolis: Augsburg, 1987), and *Matriarchs, Goddesses, and Images of God*, trans. John Bowden (Minneapolis: Augsburg, 1989). A helpful analysis of general feminist theory is found in Jean Bethke Elshtain, *Public Man, Private Woman* (Princeton, NJ: Princeton University Press, 1981).

Christian communities, the proposed reformulation would affect all aspects of Christian public discourse. In fact, proposals in this vein have already given rise to provisional biblical and liturgical texts, primarily for use in public worship.[7]

Among the proposed reformulations, the following are prominent. With respect to customary trinitarian language, the names of the first and second persons of the Trinity—"Father" and "Son"—and the manner of conceiving their relationship are singled out as instances of androcentrism. It is proposed that names like "Creator," "Redeemer," and "Sanctifier" (and variants) be adopted to replace "Father," "Son," and "Holy Spirit." Some suggest that "Father/Mother" or "Mother" replace "Father" in references both to God and to the first person, and that the traditional "Word" or newly proposed "Child" replace "Son" in references to the second person. Others propose that the Holy Spirit be considered feminine and be referred to by feminine personal pronouns (*she* and *her*). Others eschew all gendered pronouns when referring to God and suggest the repetition of the word *God* in place of *he, him,* and *his,* and the substitution of *Godself* for *himself.*

Some have further argued that classical Christian theism enshrines androcentric conceptions in the divine attributes (in particular: simplicity, immutability, eternity, omniscience, and omnipotence) in that they project the ideal of a distant, detached, and omnicompetent male. This conception is seen to be in need of amplification or replacement by one in which female attributes of relationality and engagement figure.[8] This proposal ventures beyond

7. See, for example, *The New Companion to the Breviary* (Indianapolis: Carmelite Monastery, 1988).

8. This issue will not be considered in this paper. See discussions of the matter in, for example, Carr, *Transforming Grace,* 145, and notably in an influential essay by Elizabeth A. Johnson, "The Incomprehensibility of God and the Image of God Male and Female," *Theological Studies* 45 (1984): 441–65. Two recent philosophical discussions of the divine nature, while critical of classical theism at various points, do not take up the feminist critique: Edward R. Wierenga, *The Nature of God* (Ithaca, NY: Cornell University Press, 1989), and Christopher Hughes, *On a Complex Theory of a Simple God* (Ithaca, NY: Cornell University Press, 1989). A passage from a work by Anglican Carter Heyward entitled *The Redemption of God* (Lanham, MD: University Press of America, 1982), will perhaps convey some idea

the field of linguistic practice and advances a more nearly theological agenda.

Some authors, while agreeing that Christian talk about God is androcentric, nonetheless judge the proposed reformulations to be implausible and unenforceable. The view that Christian talk and conceptions of God are incorrigibly masculinist furnishes for some the grounds for departing from the Christian community to newly formed post-Christian feminist communities or simply to a personally shaped post-Christian religiosity.[9] Some of these propose some form of goddess religion.[10]

Still, reformist as distinguished from post-Christian feminists continue to press for the desired reformulation of Christian linguistic practices, often arguing that such reformulation serves not only the cause of women's equality but also that of negative theology. Some reformists contend that exclusively androcentric conceptions of and language for God can become idolatrous.[11] In order to safeguard the incomprehensibility and ineffability of the transcendent, such language must be complemented by categories and terms derived from women's experience.

---

of the feminist critique of traditional conceptions of God: "It is in the nature of our idol to be intolerant of ambiguity. His first and only love is Himself. He is an impassible unflappable character who represents the headship of a universal family in which men are best and women least. He is the keeper of an ethical scorecard on which 'reason' gets good marks and 'relation' fails. He is a master plan-maker who maps out and, by remote control, directs our journeys before we have learned to walk. His narcissism is unquenchable. He demands that he be loved. The cold deity is the legitimating construct of the patriarchal desire to dominate and control the world. He is the eternal King, the Chairman of the board, the President of the institution, the Guru of the youth, the Husband of the wife, the General of the army, the judge of the court, the Master of the universe, the Father of the church. He is our superior, never our friend. He is a rapist, never a lover, of women and of anyone else beneath Him. He is the first and final *icon of evil* in history" (156).

9. A powerfully argued case for post-Christian feminism is Daphne Hampson, *Theology and Feminism* (Oxford: Basil Blackwell, 1990). This book is indispensable reading.

10. See Ruether, *Sexism and God-Talk*.

11. For the frequently reiterated charge that the traditional conception of God is idolatrous, see the influential article by Gail Ramshaw Schmidt, "*De Divinis Nominibus:* The Gender of God," *Worship* 56 (1982): 117–21. See also Sallie McFague, *Metaphorical Theology* (Philadelphia: Fortress Press, 1982), 147–48; and Carr, *Transforming Grace*, 138, 140–41. See the illuminating discussion of this issue in Garrett Green, *Imagining God* (San Francisco: Harper & Row, 1989), 91–97.

Is the customary trinitarian language of the Christian community revisable in the ways proposed by reformist feminist theologians? Some critics say no.[12] But on the assumption that the cause is a good one—that is to say, promotes the equality and dignity of women—let us entertain the reformist (as distinct from post-Christian) proposals as potentially appropriate revisions of Christian linguistic practices.[13] In order to assess these proposals, let us consider them in the light of the grammar of Christian patterns of discourse about the triune God, particularly as these patterns are meant to secure the reality of the faith in the presence of God in grace and the incorporation of human persons into the life of the Trinity. Although some critics argue that these revisions compromise central Christian beliefs about the triune God, let us assume here that the reformist case presses not for a radical revision of Christian doctrine but simply for the reformulation of Christian language.[14] Some of the proposed reformulations have a basis in tradition, while others are more clearly innovative. In defense of the innovations, reformists argue that the Christian tradition has shown itself to be remarkably pliable and flexible in its appropriation of new ways of speaking and thinking when these seem suited to new circumstances. Why not adopt some of the revisions suggested? Don't the experiences reported by some women (and men) imply the advent of a new opportunity for creative evolution in the linguistic practices of the community? If the commonly proposed reformulations can do justice to the central convictions of the Christian faith about the triune God's gift of his very self, then at least on this score they would appear to be Christianly apt.

12. Important nonfeminist critiques of feminist theology are Donald G. Bloesch, *The Battle for the Trinity* (Ann Arbor, MI: Servant Publications, 1985), and William Oddie, *What Will Happen to God?* (San Francisco: Ignatius Press, 1988).

13. Typical descriptions of the goal of feminist theology are, for example, "promoting the human dignity of women" (Johnson, "The Incomprehensibility of God," 442) and "the equality of women and men" (Hampson, *Theology and Feminism*, 87).

14. Since feminist theology presents a variety of positions, this generous presumption will not be verified in all cases. Thus, for example, the post-Christian feminist Daphne Hampson doubts whether the Christian feminist Sallie McFague is a theist (see *Theology and Feminism*, 158–60). And throughout *What Will Happen to God?* William Oddie contends that the feminist agenda is universally a radical one.

ESSENTIAL VS. PERSONAL TERMS

Consider first the suggestion that the names "Creator," "Redeemer,"
and "Sanctifier" (or "Sustainer") be substituted for "Father," "Son,"
and "Holy Spirit." A variant of this proposal is the triad "God, Christ,
and Spirit."

In favor of such a substitution are two main considerations. First,
it eliminates in one stroke the masculinist associations of the terms
father and *son*, along with the male conception of the processions
and relations between the first and second persons of the Trinity.
Second, the substitution employs terms that are unimpeachably traditional. "Creator," "Redeemer," and "Sanctifier" occur widely in the
characteristic discourse of the Christian community as equivalents
for "Father," "Son," and "Holy Spirit," both individually and triadi-
cally.[15] These factors explain the increasing appeal of this proposal.
Some worshiping communities, persuaded of the legitimacy of the
reformist case, have adopted the proposed triad as an apt substitution for the classical doxology and occasionally also as a substitute
for the classical baptismal formula.

Critics of this reformulation can appeal to several considerations.
For some, the substitution of "Creator," "Redeemer," and "Sanctifier" (and its variants) for "Father," "Son," and "Holy Spirit" in classical liturgical settings is precluded on the grounds that such revision
of traditional forms of worship is simply inappropriate. Traditional forms should not be tampered with.[16] At this point, reformists
can respond that previous generations of Christians neither recognized nor acknowledged that women were oppressed. Awareness of
this situation today makes it difficult for women and many men to
participate in worship whose language canonizes and protects the
androcentrism now in retreat in most sectors of society. Reformists
contend that the understandable reluctance to alter hallowed texts

15. See Bloesch, *The Battle for the Trinity*, 50–55.
16. See Roland M. Frye, "Language for God and Feminist Language: Problems and
Principles," *Scottish Journal of Theology* 41 (1988): 446.

and formulas must yield to the just demand for inclusive forms of language for God.

Opponents of the proposed substitution appeal not only to the non-optional status of the traditional language but also to doctrinal and theological considerations. There are two important objections of this kind.

According to the first objection, the terms "Creator," "Redeemer," and "Sanctifier" are not in fact, as alleged by reformists, equivalent to "Father," "Son," and "Holy Spirit." For one thing, "Father," "Son," and "Holy Spirit" are personal names, while "Creator," "Redeemer," and "Sanctifier" are functional terms.[17] What is more, the names "Father," "Son," and "Holy Spirit" are unsubstitutable self-descriptions of the persons of the Trinity.[18] These are the names by which God has chosen to be known. In intimate relationships with other persons, we usually refer to them by their names, not by the functions they perform, and we respect their preferences in matters of nicknames, and so on. Since the only knowledge we possess of the triune God comes from Scripture, it follows that the names of the Father, Son, and Holy Spirit are non-optional in a strong sense. This defense of traditional trinitarian language appeals not simply to the authority of Scripture but also to the scripturally and narrationally warranted self-description of the triune God.

A second important objection suggests that the proposed substitution is crypto-modalist in its implication that the triadic structure of the economy of salvation—represented by the threefold actions of creation, redemption, and sanctification—exhibits nothing of the internal life of the triune God. Characteristic of modalism in its historic and implicit forms is the conception of an internally undifferentiated deity who appears in the forms of Father, Son, and Spirit respectively in order to create, redeem, and sanctify humankind. Thus, precisely as replacements for "Father," "Son," and "Spirit," the terms

17. For a careful and thoroughly informed theological critique of reformist proposals, see Jenson, *The Triune Identity*, chap. 1.
18. See Bloesch, *The Battle for the Trinity*, 50.

"Creator," "Redeemer," and "Sanctifier" possess unexpungeably modalist implications.[19] Advocates of the substitution insist that a revision of Christian public utterance that does not exclude women is compatible with the profession of orthodox trinitarian belief and indeed necessary for it in present circumstances. It is at this point that such variants as "God, Christ, and Spirit" or "Source, Word, and Spirit" are advanced to correct the modalist implications of "Creator, Redeemer, and Sanctifier."

Beyond simply reiterating the case in favor of some version of the proposed substitution, reformists can pursue two lines of counterargument at this juncture. One reformist response might be that, as products of a patriarchal and male-dominated culture, the Scriptures themselves are susceptible of critique and revision. But this line of counterargument ventures perilously close to a post-Christian rather than a strictly reformist position and poses issues that lie beyond the scope of the present essay.[20] A second line of counterargument appeals to the incomprehensibility of God and the inadequacy of all human talk about him. This reformist response will be considered in the next section of this essay.

But the arguments so far considered both for and against the substitution of "Creator," "Redeemer," and "Sanctifier" for "Father," "Son," and "Holy Spirit" do not directly address the issue of the adequacy of the proposed formulation when measured against the reality of the triune God's self-gift.

In order to apply this measure, let's consider a useful distinction between essential and personal terms in the grammar of trinitarian confession.[21] Essential terms are those that identify all that is common to the three persons of the Trinity, while personal terms are

19. Bloesch, *The Battle for the Trinity*, 50.
20. The issue of the authority of Scripture in feminist theology is a complex one. See the essays in *Interpretation* 42 (1988): 3–57.
21. This discussion is dependent on a reading of the grammar of trinitarian confession provided by Aquinas in *Summa theologiae* I, qq. 32–42. My reading of these questions is informed throughout by T. C. O'Brien's remarkable commentary as presented in his notes and appendices in the Blackfriars edition of St. Thomas Aquinas, *Summa Theologiae*, Vol. 7 (New York: McGraw-Hill, 1976).

those that identify what is proper to each of the persons. Thus, to move directly to the matter at hand, terms that identify relations of the created order to the Trinity function as essential names for God, while terms that identify the relations of the trinitarian persons to each other serve as personal names for them. "Creator," "Redeemer," and "Sanctifier" are each instances of essential names because they identify the agential interaction of the triune God with the creaturely order. On the other hand, "Father," "Son," and "Holy Spirit" are personal names that refer precisely to the relations of the persons with each other.

What is at stake doctrinally in this distinction? Since the three persons are equally God, eternally subsisting within the divine being, no causal or agential interaction is possible between them. By definition, the causal activity of the triune God has the creaturely as its object. In creation, redemption, and sanctification, the triune God functions as the agent of created outcomes in the created order. The persons of the Trinity exercise agency not with respect to each other but only with respect to the creaturely realm. The suggestion that terms denoting agential interactions—for example, "Creator," "Redeemer," and "Sanctifier"—could appropriately name the persons in relation to each other would be inescapably subordinationist because it would introduce a hierarchy of causality into the Trinity. An agential understanding of the processions of generation and spiration entails a subordinationist account of the being of the Son and the Spirit. To avoid this pitfall, a sophisticated grammar of trinitarian confession evolved in the historic Christian mainstream that safeguarded the truth of the eternity of the processions and the complete absence of differentiation in being in the Father, Son, and Holy Spirit. Even the personal names "Father" and "Son" have to be understood analogously (as we shall see subsequently), to correct for the connotations of superiority and subordination in creaturely fatherhood and sonship.

It follows that essential names are not equivalent to personal names and are applied to the persons only according to the linguistic rule of "appropriation." This rule—implicit in Christian linguistic practice—allows that terms denoting the common being and agency of the triune God with respect to the created order are ascribed to one or another of the three persons according to their affinity with the personal properties or the missions of the persons. Thus, Father, Son, and Holy Spirit can be named, respectively, "Creator," "Redeemer," and "Sanctifier" by appropriation of the common activities of creation to the Father (unbegotten), of redemption to the Son (because of the visible mission of the incarnation), and of sanctification to the Holy Spirit (by virtue of the invisible mission of the indwelling). In the characteristic discourse of the Christian community, there are other examples of such appropriations of essential names to the three persons.

It is clear, then, that the terms of the triad "Creator, Redeemer, and Sanctifier" cannot serve as personal names for the Trinity. Similar considerations apply to such variants as "God, Christ, and Spirit" and "Source [or Ground], Word, and Spirit." The terms "Spirit" and "Word" are proper names and hence unobjectionable. But since each of the three persons can be called "God," the name specifies nothing proper to the first person. In this combination, however, its application in the post-Nicene church to the first person entails a subordinationist conception of the second and third persons. "Christ" names the incarnate divine hypostasis of the second person in human nature but fails to name the Son in relation to the Father and the Spirit. The difficulty with the use of terms like "Source" or "Ground" for the first person is that such terms have agential connotations. The use of an essential name for any one of the three persons in combination with personal names for the other two entails subordinationism in suggesting either inequality in divinity or a causal interaction between them.

These considerations supply an important test for the suitability of "Creator," "Redeemer," and "Sanctifier" (and variants) as substitutes for "Father," "Son," and "Holy Spirit." The preceding analysis demonstrates that the proposed substitutes fail to be equivalent for or interchangeable with "Father," "Son," and "Holy Spirit." Moreover, the grammar of trinitarian confession implies something profound about the Christian life in God's conception of it. Names that apply specifically only to the inner life of God—names, in other words, that belong properly only on the lips of the Father, Son, and Holy Spirit speaking to each other—are given to be spoken by creatures. That human beings are invited to adopt God's own names and to share God's own life is the goal of the trinitarian action of creation, redemption, and sanctification. Our employment of the triad "Creator, Redeemer, and Sanctifier" identifies our reception of the benefits of this action; our employment of the names "Father," "Son," and "Holy Spirit" signifies our recognition and enjoyment of these benefits. Surely, no considerations—no matter how compelling—can justify a preference for terms that identify the effects of divine agency over names that identify the divine relations themselves. Accordingly, it is clear that, as substitutes for "Father, Son, and Holy Spirit," the triads like "Creator, Redeemer, and Sanctifier" fail to do justice to the full reality of the presence of the triune God and of our incorporation in grace into the inner-trinitarian life.

RESPECTING THE INCOMPREHENSIBILITY AND INEFFABILITY OF GOD

At this juncture, proponents of the reformulation of customary trinitarian language could mount a potentially strong counterargument. Granted—reformists might argue—that the triad "Creator, Redeemer, and Sanctifier" is vulnerable in that it replaces personal names with essential terms. In this way, the triad fails to identify relations internal to the Trinity and names external relations instead. Perhaps other alternatives to the androcentric "Father, Son, and Holy Spirit" could be found that avoid the confusion entailed by the employment of triads like the preceding one. "Father/Mother, Child, and Spirit" is one candidate that comes to mind.

But, more seriously, the defense of traditional trinitarian language advanced in the preceding section seems to have fallen under the spell of literalism. Is it an implication of this defense that the first person is literally Father and the second person literally Son? If so, then haven't the rules of negative theology been violated? Divine reality cannot be captured by human concepts or identified with human expressions. If God is incomprehensible, then there can be no literal description of the inner life of the Trinity nor a set of non-optional proper names for the trinitarian relations.[22]

Reformists appeal to the incomprehensibility and ineffability of God in order to relativize the prevailing androcentric conventions in language about the triune God. If God is incomprehensible and all claims to knowledge and forms of utterance about him radically inadequate, then the masculinist set of conventions is in no way privileged. Furthermore, reformists argue, a plurality of divine names will be more successful than a narrowly defined set at referring to the God who is beyond human comprehension and expression. Divine attributes and names that draw upon women's experience can correct deficiencies in conceptions of God that draw exclusively upon men's experience. Since reformists can lay claim to the tradition of negative theology, their program of reformulating customary trinitarian language has relevance for the entire community, not just for its women members.[23] The literalism of the defense of traditional trinitarian language in the preceding section of this essay effectively blocks the path to needed revision of trinitarian language, a path that advocates of such revision feel justified in identifying with the objectives of the classical *via negativa*.

The reformist case against literalism also draws strength from a variety of theories of the semantic force of Christian language. Prominent among these is the view that this language is to be understood as metaphorical and expressive of experiences of the transcendent. This combination of experiential with metaphorical theology

22. "The Incomprehensibility of God and the Image of God Male and Female" by Elizabeth Johnson is fundamental for most feminist discussions of this issue.
23. Elizabeth Johnson, "The Incomprehensibility of God and the Image of God Male and Female."

provides the prevailing theoretical justification for the negative theology fundamental to the reformist case in most of its current versions.[24]

The metaphorical/experiential argument for revision of traditional trinitarian language runs roughly as follows. Religious language refers primarily to our experience of the divine being. In itself, the divine being is utterly transcendent and unknowable. It is knowable only on the basis of the impact it makes on human religious consciousness. The adequacy of religious language must be assessed at least in part by its capacity to express the experience of the divine. Since no literal forms of speech can capture its meaning and truth, only nonliteral (chiefly metaphorical) language is suited to the symbolization of this range of experience.

Feminist theory supplies the additional premise that women's experience is distinctive in ways that can be specified (despite disagreements among feminists about the content of this specification). In order to be meaningful and true, Christian speech about God must express women's experience as well as men's. But traditional trinitarian language is thoroughly biased in favor of men's experience. Such language must therefore be corrected for its androcentric bias if it is to continue to refer successfully to God in present circumstances. Since God is in any case incomprehensible and ineffable, it follows that such language will adequately express our experience of him only insofar as it is morally inclusive—insofar, that is, as it redresses the harms done to women by the hegemony of androcentric language and thinking, and encourages the reform of social structures massively legitimated by this language in the past. Apparently literal forms of speech embedded in the tradition can be reconstrued to possess a metaphorical force. In addition, if this goal is to be achieved, new metaphors must be developed and fielded for Christian use. This broad theological project must be preceded by revisions of the public discourse of the Christian community so that

24. The representative and influential sources for this argument are the already cited works of Sallie McFague.

it reflects the appropriateness of language that ascribes to the triune God feminine as well as masculine names and traits.

We can make headway in grasping the force of this argument if we consider two examples of assertions about God that occur in the customary discourse of the Christian community: "God is the rock who saves us" and "God is faithful." Compare these assertions about God with the following statements: "Kristen is a rock" and "Kristen is faithful." These utterances pick out a trait of Kristen's character. One employs the term *rock* to suggest Kristen's solidity and constancy; the other uses the term *faithful* its primary meaning to ascribe to Kristen the quality in question. It is not controversial to distinguish the two remarks about Kristen by noting that the first is an instance of metaphorical utterance and the second an instance of literal utterance. The reformist argument sketched in the preceding paragraphs implies that the distinction between metaphorical and literal utterances, while applicable to ordinary speech, is inapplicable to Christian speech.

But if this is the outcome of the claim that all religious speech is metaphorical in character, then the reformist case—at least insofar as it depends on this claim—seems implausible as an account of Christian discourse about God. Users of Christian discourse have at their disposal and in fact employ speech that has the form both of literal utterance and of nonliteral utterance.[25] The reformist case just outlined is implausible in requiring that all apparently literal speech about God be reconstrued as nonliteral and, in particular, metaphorical speech.

In noting the at least prima facie distinction between literal and metaphorical speech in Christian discourse about God, there is no

25. In *Metaphor and Religious Language* (Oxford: Clarendon Press, 1985), Janet Martin Soskice defines metaphor as "that figure of speech whereby we speak about one thing in terms which are seen to be suggestive of another" (15). At the level of complete utterances, metaphor is a form of nonliteral speech (along with allegory, parable, and so on) and is contrasted with literal or "accustomed" speech, in which terms are used according to their primary meanings (69). Soskice's important work is crucial to sorting out the issues discussed in this section.

question here of preferring literal speech to metaphorical speech. It is inconceivable to imagine that Christians could dispense with the one or the other. Rather, the point is to try to account for the one without reducing it to an instance of the other. There is reason to think that one test of the adequacy of theories about Christian discourse (as well as of the discourse of other religious communities) would lie in their capacity to field nonreductionist accounts of this discourse in all its variety and peculiarity.

It would be a mistake to draw the distinction between literal speech and metaphorical speech as if the former were "reality-depicting" or referential while the latter were not. Substantial affirmative predications about God can have either metaphorical or literal form. In common versions of the reformist case (such as that outlined here), metaphorical utterances are contrasted with literal utterances in a way that conflates "literalism" with "realism." This conflation results in part from premises drawn from experiential theology about the force of religious utterances. As noted previously, experiential theology holds that religious discourse refers to human experience of the transcendent (partially knowable and expressible) but fails to refer to the transcendent in itself (unknowable and inexpressible). A thorough examination of these premises would take us far afield of the chief burden of the reformist case.[26] The possibility that metaphorical speech about God can be no less "reality-depicting" than literal speech about him is not directly at issue here.[27] Because of the reformist deployment of the claim that all religious language is metaphorical, what is needed here is a defense of the possibility of literal speech about God.

Granted the difficulty of speaking about the transcendent realm and the healthy determination to avoid bald rationalism in this area,

26. For a discussion of these issues, see my essay entitled "Philosophical Theology in the Perspective of Religious Diversity," *Theological Studies* 49 (1988): 408–16.

27. For the term "reality-depicting" and for a realistic account of metaphor, see Janet Martin Soskice, "Theological Realism," in *The Rationality of Religious Belief*, ed. William J. Abraham and Steven Holtzer (Oxford: Clarendon Press, 1987), 105–19; see also her *Metaphor and Religious Language*, passim.

Christian traditions of theological inquiry have sought to account for the force of utterances about God that have the form of literal speech. There are good reasons for trying to make sense of these utterances. Even traditions with a strong preference for negative theology have wanted to avert sheer agnosticism in their accounts of discourse about God.[28] As posed for us by the reformist case, the issue is this: Can a nonreductionist account of literal utterances like "God is faithful" be consistent with an affirmation of the radical incomprehensibility and ineffability of God? The answer to this question will have important consequences for the shape of trinitarian language and its expression of God's self-gift.

But a defense of the possibility of literal speech about God seems to commit us to the implausible claim that some kinship obtains between the statements "Kristen is faithful" and "God is faithful." We think we know what it means to ascribe faithfulness to Kristen: we know what faithfulness means, and we know what it means for persons to possess or lack this trait. But we have no way of knowing what being faithful is for God. It may turn out that the kinship between the two statements is no more than grammatical. In their endeavor to avoid a rationalistic account of Christian talk about God, some have arrived at precisely this conclusion. They have argued that the term *faithful* possesses no more the same meaning when applied to God and Kristen than does a homonym like *bark* when applied to the covering of a tree and the sound a dog makes. In each case the terms are identical, but the things to which they refer are utterly disparate. Christian talk about God employs terms like *faithful* and *good* but with unknown meanings. Other thinkers have understandably

---

28. I have gained much in my understanding of the issue of the divine incomprehensibility and other issues considered in this essay from the monumental two-volume dissertation of Gregory P. Rocca, *Analogy as Judgment and Faith in God's Incomprehensibility: A Study in the Theological Epistemology of Thomas Aquinas* (Ann Arbor: University Microfilms, 1989). See his article entitled "The Distinction between *Res Significata* and *Modus Significandi* in Aquinas's Theological Epistemology," *The Thomist* 55 (1991): 173–97. [Editor's note: See his book, *Speaking the Incomprehensible God: Thomas Aquinas on the Interplay of Positive and Negative Theology* (Washington, DC: The Catholic University of America Press, 2004).]

judged this account of Christian discourse as leaning too far in the direction of agnosticism. They have suggested that the meaning of the term *faithful* is identical whether it is applied to Kristen or to God. But when applied to God such terms single out perfections that exist in God to a supereminent degree.

A shorthand characterization for these alternative accounts of the kinship between literal utterances about God and those about Kristen goes like this: rationalist views take *faithful* to apply univocally to God and Kristen, while agnostic views take it to apply equivocally. But can the literal force of statements like "God is faithful" be understood in a way that avoids agnosticism on the one hand and rationalism on the other?

It may be helpful at this point to call upon a distinction that Aquinas found useful in sorting out these issues and advancing his own proposal for construing such statements in Christian discourse.[29] Drawing on the earlier work of grammarians, he distinguished three elements in utterances: the *res significata* (that to which reference is being made—e.g., a quality in Kristen), the *ratio nominis* (the concept by which this quality is specified—e.g., faithfulness), and the *modus significandi* (the grammatical form of the utterance, in this case a predication). According to this account, what makes a predication equivocal is that the *ratio nominis* of, for example, the homonym *bark* is different when it is applied to dogs than when it is applied to trees. What makes a predication univocal is that the *ratio nominis* of, say, the term *faithful* is the same whether it is applied to Kristen or to Jack. Sometimes, however, the terms we use cannot be classified in either of these ways. For instance, in the statements "Chocolate is good" and "Kristen is good," the *ratio nominis* of *good* applies to both subjects in some sense. Goodness in human beings is different from goodness in sweets, but it is perfectly appropriate to use *good* to cover both instances. This example helps us to see that univocal and equivocal predications do not exhaust the

29. Aquinas, *Summa theologiae* I, q. 13. See also Rocca, *Analogy as Judgment and Faith in God's Incomprehensibility*, 616–41.

range of literal utterances. Terms like *good* resist classification within these alternatives. Such terms support analogous predications because in their various legitimate uses the *ratio nominis* is both the same and different with respect to the various *res significata* to which such predications apply.

Aquinas thought that this point was an important one for understanding a certain class of statements about God that have the form of literal utterances and ascribe some positive attribute to him, like "God is faithful" and "God is good." He thought that theories which explained these statements by reconstruing them as negative statements that deny limitations in God (like "God is unchangeable") or relative statements that affirm the outcome of his agency (like "God is the cause of goodness") were implausible in a way similar to theories which reconstrue them as nonliteral or metaphorical. Suppose that, like the term *good* when it is used to describe people and chocolate (and many other things as well), certain terms of perfection are predicated of God in an analogous way. In this case, one could say, to return to the example of goodness, that when we assert that "God is good," the *res significata* is the supreme reality of goodness as it exists in God identical with his very being, even though the *ratio nominis* is based on our ordinary uses of the term for the things familiar to us through our experience. On this account the crucial insight of negative theology is preserved at two points. First, the *ratio nominis* derives from the created order and in no way functions as a conceptualization of God's being. For this reason, such predicates are employed analogously rather than univocally or equivocally in assertions about divine being and activity. Second, the *modus significandi* of Christian talk about God—although taking the grammatical form of predications of attributes in the created order—could never capture the way in which such attributes exist in God. We have no way of specifying linguistically (indeed, we have no way of knowing) how God, who is sheer existence, can be said truly to be good, faithful, and so on without seeming to ascribe qualities to him in a way that implies potentiality and composition. To insist that the *modus significandi* of such predications of God differs from predications of created beings is to provide a linguistic rule that continually corrects for implications of our way of speaking that can never be true of God.

These remarks open the way to distinguishing literal from metaphorical predications in Christian discourse about God.[30] Terms of perfection have a literal but analogous sense in predications about God in that the perfections they ascribe are found supereminently in God, who is their cause in creatures. Such terms have a nonunivocal sense in that their *ratio nominis* derives from creaturely concepts and in that their *modus significandi* is more appropriate to creatures than to God. Some terms of perfection can function in literal predications about God because their meaning is separable from their creaturely embodiments. Nothing prevents the literal ascription of such attributes as goodness, faithfulness, wisdom, and mercy to God because the meaning of these attributes does not entail the limitations characteristic of such perfections when they exist in the created order. Hence it can be said that predications of such attributes are more true of God than of creatures, even though we have neither a concept of divine goodness nor a way of signifying the goodness of God. Terms used literally of God apply primarily to him and secondarily to creatures. Recognition that the *modus significandi* differs with respect to predications about God corrects for any creaturely limitations associated with such terms. Thus, for example, in the assertion "God is the Creator, Redeemer, and Sanctifier," the fact that the divine agency produced temporal effects does not entail change or temporality in God. We correct for such limitations by noting that, while this assertion is literally true of God, we cannot specify this truth without using temporal categories.

Other terms (some of which are terms of perfection) function in metaphorical predications because the meaning of these terms

---

30. As Soskice states clearly in *Metaphor and Religious Language*, analogy is a type of literal speech: "The categories of univocal, equivocal, and analogical are different in kind from that of metaphor. Thus, when we speak of God as infinite, perfect, or transcendent, we speak analogically of God ... but not, as some have suggested, in a flagrantly pictorial or metaphorical way" (66).

is logically inseparable from their creaturely embodiments. The following assertions are examples of metaphorical predications (though nonetheless clearly reality-depicting): "God is angry," "God stretched out his mighty arm to save us," "God is a rock." Having an arm or being a rock are things attributed to God metaphorically because they entail the possession of bodily being, while anger entails bodiliness and emotions. Terms used metaphorically of God apply primarily to creatures and secondarily to God. The classification of such predications as metaphorical is a logical remark. There is no suggestion that such expressions are "merely" metaphorical or that they should always be "translated" into literal speech (although there might be occasions when this would be appropriate).

This nonreductionist account can specify the logical force of some of the different forms of utterance available to users of Christian discourse. To distinguish metaphorical from literal forms of predication and to defend the possibility that customary trinitarian language contains literal forms of speech is not to fall under the spell of an unwarranted literalism, as prominent versions of the reformist case imply. Rather, this account shows that a vigorous realism about the trinitarian presence in grace does not contravene the tradition's equally vigorous insistence on the incomprehensibility and ineffability of God.

THE NAME "FATHER"

We are now in a position to consider a second widely advocated revision of language about the triune God: the substitution of "Father/Mother" or "Mother" for the name "Father." There are two main arguments for this revision. The first is that here is the crucial instance where patriarchy is canonized and where it must be eradicated. The exaltation of fatherhood in God constitutes the chief legitimation of patriarchal patterns that have been oppressive of women and supportive of their exclusion from equal participation in the church and in society at large. This nearly metaphysical foundation for conceptions of female inferiority must at all costs be shaken and toppled. Christian women who feel the urgency of this objective have come to be persuaded that unless God can be called "Mother" it will be impossible for them to continue to participate in good conscience in the life of the Christian community.[31]

The second set of considerations favoring the use of "Mother" has a basis in the tradition itself. On this view of the matter, to call God "Mother" exploits resources furnished by strands in the tradition in which feminine traits are attributed to God. While it is admitted that the Bible never calls God "Mother," it describes him in terms of feminine and maternal characteristics. In addition, mystical literature is replete with feminine characterizations of the deity.[32]

This widely debated proposal has provoked objections from feminists and their critics as well. Some feminist authors argue that the attribution of feminine characteristics to God simply confirms the androcentric conceit of a superior male divinity who can with ease encompass feminine as well as masculine traits.[33] Others have argued that calling God "Mother" and attributing feminine traits to him reinforces the very stereotyping of women that feminists deplore.[34] Some feminists share with their critics doubts about a fundamental premise in the reformist case for calling God "Mother." There is no evidence that societies in whose religions goddesses were prominent had a social structure any less patriarchal than those with male deities.[35] Still, while some feminists advocate a goddess religion either on the periphery of Christianity or in self-consciously post-Christian communities, others regard this suggestion as uninviting and alien, particularly if it involves the selective and artificial reconstruction of extinct polytheistic religions (whether ancient

31. See Carr, *Transforming Grace*, 141.

32. See the discussion in Hampson, *Theology and Feminism*, 92–96; see also Johnson, "The Incomprehensibility of God," 462.

33. See Hampson, *Theology and Feminism*, 94.

34. See Heine, *Matriarchs*, 28.

35. See Heine, *Matriarchs*, especially Chap. 3, and Elshtain, *Public Man, Private Woman*, 212–15.

Egyptian, Mesopotamian, or Hellenistic, or combinations of these).[36] Some feminists argue that, while it might be desirable for God
to be reconceived in feminine terms, such a reconceptualization
would involve so profound a transformation of traditional Christianity as to be unworkable. It may well be thought that the incidence
in the Bible of feminine imagery for God hardly supplies the basis
for the conception of a feminine God in Christianity.[37] This admis-
sion might be a reason to develop another religion—not necessarily
a goddess religion, but rather one in which the deity is not conceived
in personal terms at all.[38]

In this connection, it is recognized that if the deity is thought to
be personal, then talk about it cannot be gender-neutral or, for that
matter, double-gendered. Some feminists view as muddled the suggestion that God be called "Father/Mother" in that it is impossible
to visualize anything being both in any meaningful way, short of an
unacceptable introduction of androgyny into the divine being. It is
hard to see how any human could identify or pick out so utterly alien
a being.[39] Some nonfeminist critics of the proposal under consideration voice the same objection and argue further that the language
"Father/Mother" introduces a range of sexual images into the Christian conception of the deity that the Bible and the tradition scrupulously resisted.[40] There is plenty of evidence of a deliberate avoid-
ance of such conceptions in the formative periods of Israel's faith
when the community sought to distinguish itself from surrounding
religious conceptions. The language "Father/Mother" seems to rein-
troduce conceptions decisively rejected a long time ago. This consideration also bears on the proposal to refer to the Holy Spirit as "She."
Whatever advantages such usage may seem to have from the feminist

36. See Heine, *Matriarchs*, 44–48, and Hampson, *Theology and Feminism*, 157–58.
37. See Hampson, *Theology and Feminism*, especially Chaps. 3 and 5.
38. Hampson adopts this position in *Theology and Feminism*; see especially Chap. 5.
39. See Heine, *Matriarchs*, Chap. 1.
40. See Elizabeth Achtemeier, "Female Language for God: Should the Church
Adopt It?" in *The Hermeneutical Quest*, ed. Donald G. Miller (Allison Park, PA: Pickwick
Publications, 1986), 97–114.

perspective, it introduces gender differentiation into speech about God and, in effect, sexual differentiation into the divine being. In addition, it is argued that "Father/Mother" and similar locutions in effect replace a trinitarian with a quaternitarian conception of God.[41]

The case against the substitution of "Mother" or "Father/ Mother" for "Father" in talking about God and about the first person of the Trinity seems a strong one. But considerations suggested by the grammar of trinitarian confession can render this case decisive—particularly when viewed in the perspective of the divine invitation to created persons to enjoy the inner life of the Trinity.

It is possible to distinguish three senses in which the term *father* can be applied to God: metaphorically to the triune God, by appropriation to the first person, and literally and properly to the first person.[42] The third sense is absolutely crucial to Christian forms of speech that do justice to the reality of our incorporation in grace into the inner-trinitarian life.

In the first place, the term *father* can be used to refer to the triune God. In this way of speaking, the attribution of fatherhood to God is metaphorical. First, the term *Father* is meant to suggest the creator or personal principle of all that exists. Since fathers play an important role in the generation of their children, we use the term *father* as a metaphor for productions of various sorts, as when we say that someone has fathered an idea or an institution. On this basis, we can say that the triune God is the Father of the created order. While this is not a uniquely Christian way of speaking about God, there is plenty of biblical warrant for it. The suggestion is that God's creative agency in regard to the human race is describable in terms that evoke the intimacy, concern, attention, and engagement of a good father. Second, the term *Father* is metaphorical in reference to God in that

41. See Frye, "Language for God and Feminist Language," 449.

42. See O'Brien's commentary in the Blackfriars edition of *Summa Theologiae*, 239–51. See also Alvin F. Kimel, Jr., "The Holy Trinity Meets Ashtoreth: A Critique of the Episcopal 'Inclusive' Liturgies," *Anglican Theological Review* 21 (1989): 26. John W. Miller offers a defense of the name "Father" from the perspective of developmental psychology in *Biblical Faith and Fathering* (New York: Paulist Press, 1989).

its meaning entails the limitations of human fatherhood. Generation of progeny requires both a father and a mother and suggests sexual differentiation and engagement. For this reason, the metaphorical naming of the triune God as "father" does not absolutely exclude the metaphorical naming of God as "mother." As we noted previously, the difficulties posed by such usage and the lack of unqualified biblical support for it rule the simple substitution of the name "Mother" for "Father" in the public discourse of the community when the triune God is mentioned. But there seems to be no reason why private devotion and prayer might not afford scope for such usage—though not, as I shall argue subsequently, as a substitute name for the first person of the Trinity.

In addition to the metaphorical predications of the triune God as Father, the rule of appropriation permits the first person of the Trinity to be named "Father" just as he can be named "Creator." The personal property of unbegottenness provides the basis for such appropriation. As we saw earlier, an activity common to the three persons can be attributed by appropriation to the first person without implying that he acts independently of the other two when acting externally. Viewed as an essential term denoting the agential interaction of the triune God with creaturely reality, the name "Father" can be appropriated to the first person.

In its third use, the term *Father* serves as the preferred personal name of the first person of the Trinity. As we saw earlier, personal names of God are those that refer not to the agential interaction of the triune God with creatures but to the internal relations of the persons. They refer to what is true in God independent of the existence of creaturely reality and describe the intimate, eternal reality of the three persons. These personal names are inaccessible to creatures except by virtue of the divine revelation and the invitation to communion that this revelation entails.

The personal names "Father" and "Son" describe a familial intimacy of a particularly intense form. According to the Scriptures as they are read in the church, the "comings forth" *in* God are distinct from the coming forth of things *from* God. The trinitarian processions do not involve creation or causation of any kind, but they give rise to real relative opposition in God. The theological tradition has been challenged to the utmost of human reflective powers to show how this mystery can be understood, but there can be no way of gaining access to it except as invited and occasioned by the triune God. Thus we know that the first person is the Father because the Son calls him by that name; it is the Son's personal way of speaking of the Father. The same is true of the name of the Spirit. These names do not originate in our experience of God and his agency in the world, as do many of the essential names we use to speak of God. We have no basis for naming the persons of the Trinity by their proper names except their own "usage." Insofar as we become intimates of the Trinity be grace, we can learn to use these names as well. Since we have no uninvited basis for naming the persons, we have no grounds to prefer other terms to these personal names for the Trinity. These names are proper because they identify nonagential relations internal to the Trinity itself. The exclusive warrant for their aptness lies in Christ's revelation of the inner-trinitarian life. This consideration supports a decisive case against the substitution of the name "Mother" for "Father" when speaking of the first person of the Trinity.

This consideration is connected with the very structure of the revelation of the nearness and presence of God and what it promises for us. Christ is the son by "nature," and we are sons and daughters by adoption. What this means is that we are invited by the triune God to enter into the most intimate possible relation with the three persons, in that we are entitled to call the first person by the same name by which the Son calls him, by that proper, private, family name that is the Son's divine prerogative. In a treatise on the Lord's Prayer, St. Cyprian wrote, "Let us pray as God our master has taught us. To ask the Father in words his Son has given us, to let him hear the prayer of Christ ringing in his ears, is to make our prayer one of friendship, a family prayer. Let the Father recognize the words of his

Son. Let the Son who lives in our hearts be also on our lips."[43] God's entire salvific initiative is seen to be the full and perfect incorporation of human beings into the life of the triune God. The adoptive filiation of human beings—their participation in the life of the Trinity in grace—is grounded in the natural filiation of the Son.

A final comment is in order concerning two further proposed revisions of traditional trinitarian language. Although the substitution of "Child" for "Son" cannot be positively excluded, it should be noted that it blurs rather than enhances the personal reality suggested by the relationship of son to father. At the same time, it carries a connotation of immaturity that the name "Son" does not.[44] Similarly, a string of impersonal or suprapersonal terms for God—"Heavenly Parent, Source, Eternal Spirit, Ground of Being"—while not thoroughly objectionable, strike one as inadequate. In terms of the analysis offered earlier, as substitutes for the metaphorical name "Father" as applied to the triune God, these expressions miss the very point of using "father" in this sense. They replace the connotations of the personal engagement of God with an impersonal, more nearly deistic conception of the Supreme Being. To be sure, as has been noted, some feminists admit that an impersonal conception of the deity is preferable to a masculine one and more plausible than a feminine one—an idea that seems to point the way toward post-Christian forms of feminist religiosity. It is hard to see how it is possible to remain true to the Christian conviction about God's nearness and presence to us if personal categories for speaking about this mystery are abandoned. To speak of God in impersonal or suprapersonal terms constitutes not a revision of Christianity but an alternative to it. In this connection one is reminded of St. Paul's rebuke to the Galatians: "Formerly, when you did not know God, you were in bondage to beings that by nature are no gods; but now that you have come to know God, or rather to be known by God, how can you

---

43. A passage assigned for the Readings on Tuesday during the first week of Lent in *The Liturgy of the Hours*, Vol. 2 (New York: Catholic Book Publishing Co., 1976), 105.

44. See Bloesch, *The Battle for the Trinity*, 46.

turn back again to the weak and beggarly elemental spirits, whose slaves you want to be once more?" (Gal 4:8–9).

ANDROCENTRISM AND THE DISTINCTION BETWEEN METAPHORICAL AND LITERAL PREDICATION

The concern to avoid androcentrism in our talk about God is an urgent one. In fact, of course, the tradition is unanimous in rejecting the sexual or androcentric connotations of the personal names "Father" and "Son." This is precisely the point of affirming that these names apply literally to the first and second persons of the Trinity. As we reviewed them earlier, the rules for construing literal predications about God require the exclusion of any limitations associated with the meaning of the predicates "father" and "son" when used to refer to creatures. Chief among these are connotations of superiority and subordination in generation, and the male characteristics of bodily beings who are men. In addition, the sexual differentiation presupposed to human generation is excluded, since there is no active/passive partnership in the generation of the Son.[45] When "Father" and "Son" are predicated of God, the *modus significandi* of these predications corrects for all creaturely limitations, including androcentrism. Male characteristics can be attributed to God only

45. In the *Summa Contra Gentiles* IV, Ch. 11, n.19, Aquinas states, "One should note carefully that the fleshly generation of animals is perfected by an active power and by a passive power; and it is from the active power that one is named 'father,' and from the passive power that one is named 'mother.' Hence, in what is required for the generation of offspring, some things belong to the father, some things belong to the mother: to give the nature and the species to the offspring belongs to the father, and to conceive and bring forth belong to the mother as patient and recipient. Since, however, the procession of the Word has been said to be in this: that God understands Himself; and the divine act of understanding is not through a passive power, but, so to say, an active one; because the divine intellect is not in potency but is only actual; in the generations of the Word of God the notion of mother does not enter, but only that of father. Hence, the things which belong distinctly to the father or to the mother in fleshly generation, in the generation of the Word are all attributed to the Father by sacred Scripture; for the Father is said not only 'to give life to the Son' (cf. John 5:26), but also 'to conceive' and 'to bring forth'" (Vol. 4, trans. and with an introduction by Charles J. O'Neil [Notre Dame, IN: University of Notre Dame Press, 1975], 90).

by way of metaphor, since such characteristics suppose bodiliness in their very meaning. It is crucial to the reformist feminist cause that the distinction between metaphorical and literal predications about God be recognized and maintained. This distinction provides the principal basis upon which to exclude androcentrism from conceptions of God.

In the absence of such a distinction, revision of traditional trinitarian language will appear to be the only means available by which to achieve this important objective. But in that case and in the name of negative theology, we would run the risk of subverting or obstructing the loving initiative of God the Father, Son, and Holy Spirit through our anxiety to find adequate words in which to address them—rather like a lover whose anxiety to find the right words to speak to her beloved leads her to postpone and delay indefinitely the intimacy beyond words for which her beloved longs. The speakability of the otherwise unspeakable mystery of the triune God is rooted in the gift of God's very self to us in grace.

Customary trinitarian language expresses the reality of the mystery of the triune God and our participation in the communion of life of the three persons. The triune God "who stands in need of no one gave communion with himself to those who need him," wrote St. Irenaeus.[46] Feminist objectives can be served neither by altering the language that names this mystery nor by preferring language that fails to do justice to its reality. No considerations of any kind can be advanced that would warrant the revision of the language in which the Father, Son, and Holy Spirit invite us to speak with them. "O abyss! O eternal Godhead! O deep sea! What more could you have given me than the gift of your very self?"

---

46. From the treatise *Against Heresies* (4.14.2–3) assigned for Readings on Wednesday during the second week of Lent in *Liturgy of the Hours*, 2:177.

CHAPTER 10

---:---

Imago Dei—Imago Christi
The Theological Foundations of
Christian Humanism

It has been widely recognized that the documents of the Second Vatican Council represent a notable reaffirmation of the theology of the *imago Dei*.[1] For a variety of reasons, in some traditions of Catholic theology after the Reformation and Enlightenment periods, this element of classical theological anthropology had not received the attention it properly deserved. But in the first half of the twentieth century, both in neo-Thomistic and *ressourcement* circles, the theology of the *imago Dei* enjoyed a significant revival. Inspired in part by this retrieval of classical theological anthropology, the council Fathers sought to recover the Christological and eschatological contexts which had been essential in the theology of the *imago Dei* of the best patristic and scholastic authors. Among the conciliar documents, none was more complete in its articulation of the theology of the *imago Dei* than *Gaudium et Spes*.[2]

Presented to the International Congress of the Pontifical Academy of St. Thomas Aquinas, Rome, September 21–25, 2003. [Subsequently published in *Nova et Vetera* 2 (2004): 267–77—Editor's note.]

1. See Luis Ladaria, SJ, "Humanity in the Light of Christ in the Second Vatican Council," in *Vatican II: Assessment and Perspectives*, ed. René Latourelle, Vol. II (New York: Paulist Press, 1989), 386–401.

2. See the comprehensive treatment in George Karakunnel, *The Christian Vision of*

The importance of the connection between anthropology and Christology both for a correct interpretation of *Gaudium et Spes* and for an authentic Christian humanism was noted early on. Over thirty years ago, in one of the first theological commentaries on *Gaudium et Spes*, the now Cardinal Joseph Ratzinger argued that it is essential to take into account the intrinsic linking of anthropology with Christology (and thus with eschatology) which unfolds across the entire text and which in his view constitutes its crucial insight. Any properly comprehensive interpretation of the theology of the *imago Dei* in *Gaudium et Spes* would need to balance passages which speak of man as created in the image of God (such as article 12) with those which speak of Christ as key to the mystery of man (such as the crucial article 22). The perfect image of God is the Incarnate Word who is both the exemplar of the created of God in man and the pattern for its graced transformation.[3] The concrete human person who is created in the image of God is always *in via*, always being drawn to the Father, but partly impeded by sin; he is redeemed by Christ, yet still undergoing a lifelong transformation in the power of the Holy Spirit, with a view to the final consummation of a life of communion with the Blessed Trinity and the saints. The image of God is always, as it were, a work in progress. From the moment of creation, the perfection of the image of God—more simply, holiness—is already intimated as the end of human life. A Christian theology of creation "is only intelligible in eschatology; the Alpha is only truly to be understood in the Omega."[4] Thus, according to Cardinal Ratzinger's early essay, *Gaudium et Spes* presents "Christ as the eschatological Adam to whom the first Adam already pointed; as the true image of God which transforms man once more into likeness to God."[5]

Man: A Study of the Theological Anthropology in "Gaudium et Spes" of Vatican II (Bangalore: Asian Trading Association, 1984).

3. Joseph Ratzinger, "The Dignity of the Human Person," in *Commentary on the Documents of Vatican II*, ed. Herbert Vorgrimler et al, Vol. V (New York: Herder and Herder, 1969), 115–63.

4. Ratzinger, "The Dignity of the Human Person," 121.

5. Ratzinger, "The Dignity of the Human Person," 159. See the discussion of these issues in Walter Kasper, "The Theological Anthropology of *Gaudium et Spes*," and David

Subsequently, as is well known, Pope John Paul II made this cluster of themes the hallmark of his pontificate. The dominant interest
in anthropology, which had characterized his entire career as a philosopher and theologian, now in his papal magisterium blossomed
prodigiously into the fullblown reaffirmation of an authentic Christian humanism.[6] A distinctive element in Pope John Paul's teaching about the *imago Dei* has been his stress on the relational character of the image: creation in the image of God is the basis for and
is realized precisely in the communion of persons. In addition, the
Holy Father has made his own the distinctive blend of anthropology
and Christology which is the mark of conciliar teaching. Pope John
Paul II frequently invokes the words of *Gaudium et Spes*, §22 which
state that "it is only in the mystery of the Word made flesh that the
mystery of man truly becomes clear." Beginning with his programmatic first encyclical, anthropology and Christology are always to
be found interwoven in the relational theology of the *imago Dei* expounded by the Holy Father.

The juxtaposition of *imago Dei* and *imago Christi* in the title of
my paper is meant to capsulize the Christocentric anthropology that
is characteristic of patristic and scholastic theology of the image of
God and that has been expressed anew by the Second Vatican Council, by Pope John Paul II, and by Cardinal Ratzinger and other theologians. It can truly be said that, according to this vision, the human person is created in the image of God (*imago Dei*) in order to
grow into the image of Christ (*imago Christi*). This Christocentric
vision of the human person is the foundation of authentic Christian
humanism. What is more, *Gaudium et Spes* and the magisterium of
Pope John Paul II testify to the immense relevance of this vision for

---

L. Schindler, "Christology and the *Imago Dei*: Interpreting *Gaudium et Spes*," *Communio:
International Catholic Review* 23 (1996): 129–41 and 156–84.
    6. See Kenneth Schmitz, *At the Center of the Human Drama: The Philosophical An-
thropology of Karol Wojtyla/Pope John Paul II* (Washington, DC: The Catholic Universi-
ty of America Press, 1993), and Jarosław Kupczak, OP, *Destined for Liberty: The Human
Person in the Philosophy of Karol Wojtyla/John Paul II* (Washington, DC: The Catholic
University of America Press, 2000).

the new evangelization and for theology today as the Church confronts a wide range of challenges in her proclamation of the truth about man.

The challenges to authentic Christian humanism today are of at least two kinds, though the first arises from within the Christian theological tradition itself and is represented by the lingering influence of nominalist patterns of thought in moral theology and in the anthropology that it implies. A second kind of challenge has sources largely external to the Christian tradition, and is represented by the variety of secular humanisms and anti-humanisms which advance alternative accounts of the meaning (or lack of it) in human existence. Another important kind of challenge arises from the distinctive religious visions of the human espoused by Buddhism, Hinduism and Islam, but I shall not be considering it here. The two kinds of challenge I do want to consider can be seen to be convergent in their final outcomes, and I want to suggest that the theology of the *imago Dei* of St. Thomas Aquinas can be of particular assistance in facing them.

We have seen that the Christocentric anthropology of Pope John II and the Second Vatican Council highlights the intrinsic link between what human beings are as such and what they can hope to become. Implicit in this anthropology is the conviction that human fulfillment and religious consummation are themselves intimately connected. The holiness (or religious consummation) that is Christ's gift in the Holy Spirit constitutes the perfection of the image of God (integral human fulfillment). Created in the image of God, human persons are meant to grow into the image of Christ. As they become increasingly conformed to the perfect man, Jesus Christ, the fullness of their humanity is realized. There is thus a finality built into human nature as such and, although its realization is possible only with the assistance of divine grace, this realization is in a real sense continuous with the tendencies and even aspirations essential to human nature as such. The cultivation and fulfillment of the human person through seeking the good in a graced moral life enables one to enjoy the Good that is beyond life.

It is precisely this identification of human fulfillment with religious perfection that is, in different ways, severed or negated by the lingering nominalism of some Catholic moral theology and by the competing secular humanisms and anti-humanisms of Western modernity. The result in both cases is a spiritual crisis in which the goods of human life are disengaged from the desire for transcendence. Nominalism divorces human moral fulfillment from the possibility of the enjoyment of a transcendent good, while secular humanisms and anti-humanisms declare the desire for this transcendence to be itself irrelevant and even injurious to integral human fulfillment. Let us consider these challenges in turn.

The features of nominalist thought that are crucial to my argument here will be familiar to students of the history of late medieval philosophy and theology.[7] Nominalist thinkers famously sought to preserve the divine freedom by stressing the unlimited possibilities available to the absolute power of God (the *potentia absoluta*) which cannot be regarded as in any way constrained by the existing order of things in creation and redemption established by the divine *potentia ordinata*. To a certain extent under the influence of Scotus, who had already made Aquinas the target of his criticism,[8] nominalists explicitly denied that which Aquinas had affirmed, namely, the existence of a rationally ordered universe reflecting the divine wisdom and accessible to human experience and knowledge. Whereas for Aquinas there is a congruence between the knowable divine law inscribed in human nature (natural law) and human aspirations

7. For details, see Frederick Copleston, *A History of Philosophy*, Vol. 3 (New York: Doubleday, 1963), 43–122, and *The Cambridge Companion to Ockham*, ed. Paul Vincent Spade (Cambridge: Cambridge University Press, 1999), especially the essays by Peter King, Marilyn McCord Adams, A. S. McGrade, and Alfred J. Freddoso.

8. See Thomas Williams, "How Scotus Separates Morality from Happiness," *American Philosophical Quarterly* 69 (1995): 425–45. See also Copleston, *A History of Philosophy*, Vol. 2, 476–551, and *The Cambridge Companion to Scotus*, ed. Thomas Williams (Cambridge: Cambridge University Press, 2003), especially the essays by James Ross and Todd Bates, William E. Mann, Hans Möhle, Thomas Miller and Bonnie Kent. For the contrast between Scotus and Aquinas, and the links between nominalism and Scotus on these issues, see especially Anthony Levi, *Renaissance and Reformation: The Intellectual Genesis* (New Haven, CT: Yale University Press, 2002), 30–67.

for fulfillment, on the one hand, and the enjoyment of supernatural beatitude, on the other, for nominalism God is completely unconstrained in enjoining moral laws. The moral law imposes obligations which reflect neither the rational character of God's activity nor the inbuilt finalities of human nature. Moreover, since absolutely free, God's decision to save or damn particular individuals could not be in any way dependent on their fulfillment, or lack of it, of these obligations. Rather than being the intrinsic principle of the moral life, as in Aquinas, beatitude becomes an external reward whose enjoyment may or may not reflect the moral character of a particular human life. Since moral law is the expression of the divine will and thus ceases to depend upon the ontological constitution of human nature, moral theology is detached from theological anthropology and from any exemplary Christology. Yielding its place in theological anthropology and moral theology, Christocentrism in the form of intense devotion to Christ became a persistent feature of the spirituality of the *devotio moderna*, which was itself a religious strategy designed to bypass the troublesome philosophical and theological perplexities of nominalist *via moderna*. In an important recent book, Anthony Levi has argued that nominalist theology gave rise to an "intolerable spiritual tension, deriving from the separation of moral achievement from religious fulfillment," principally because individuals "could not know what unalterable fate God had decreed for them without reference to the exercise of autonomously self-determining powers during life."[9] With the divorce of moral achievement from religious perfection, religious practices and observances served to allay this tension independently of the moral state of the individual.

Father Servais Pinckaers has convincingly demonstrated that certain fundamental presuppositions of nominalist theology are embedded in the casuistic moral theology of the manuals in use from the seventeenth century to the eve of the Second Vatican Council.[10]

9. Levi, *Renaissance and Reformation: The Intellectual Genesis*, 64.

10. Servais Pinckaers, OP, "La nature de la moralité: morale casuistique at morale thomiste," in *Somme théologique: Les actes humains*, Vol. 2, trans. S. Pinckaers (Paris: Desclée & Cie, 1966), 215–76. See also his *The Sources of Christian Ethics* (Washington, DC:

Among these, perhaps the most important for our theme are the centrality accorded to obligation in the moral life and the eclipse of beatitude as an intrinsic principle of moral action. In this tradition of moral theology, the categories of the obliged and the forbidden are prior to the categories of good and evil in actions. Actions are bad or wrong because they are forbidden, rather than vice versa. Actions that are bad or wrong merit punishment, while those that are good or right merit reward. But there is no intrinsic connection between these actions as such and the punishment or reward they merit. Since nominalist philosophical theology does not survive in the casuist worldview, the predestinating deity has vanished. God is now understood to confer reward or punishment in view of an individual's success or failure in meeting moral obligations. Under the influence of nominalism, casuist moral theology has no need for an account of how moral agents become good by seeking the good. It is significant, as Father Pinckaers has pointed out, that the treatise on beatitude disappeared from manualist moral theology while the treatise on the virtues was consigned to the realm of spiritual theology.

Although I cannot pursue the point here, the prevalence of this kind of moral theology gave rise to the intolerable tensions experienced by many Catholics in the face of the moral teaching of *Humanae Vitae*—and eventually the entirety of Christian teaching about human sexuality—which seemed to impose an outdated moral obligation whose connection with the human good was either denied or dismissed or, more commonly, simply not apparent. The proportionalist and consequentialist moral theories devised with a view to allaying these tensions failed to question, and indeed often presupposed, the very edifice of casuistic moral theology that had made these tensions almost inevitable.

The fundamental difficulty here—echoing Levi, one might speak

---

The Catholic University of America Press, 1995), 327–53. For a helpful summary of Pinckaers's argument, see Romanus Cessario, OP, *Introduction to Moral Theology* (Washington, DC: The Catholic University of America Press, 2001), 229–42.

of an "intolerable spiritual tension"—is that many people can no longer discern an intrinsic link between the moral law and their good,
and, furthermore, no longer view religious achievement (the reward
of happiness) as intrinsically connected with moral or human fulfillment. Religious practices—often in the form of eclectic spiritu-
alities—are now often seen as unconnected from moral obligations,
whose specific content is in any case exiguous. Morality, even when
faithfully observed, is viewed as disengaged from, and indeed is often regarded as in conflict with, basic human aspirations for a good
and happy life. In addition, a good and happy life here is not seen as
continuous with the life of beatitude as such. Heaven is inevitable
in any case, while hell is unthinkable and purgatory unintelligible.

In accounting for the revolution that came with modernity and
saw the emergence of secular humanism and, more recently, of
neo-Nietzschean anti-humanisms, one can certainly point to the
spiritual mentality fostered by casuist moral theology as among the
likely contributing factors. Certainly, Charles Taylor is right in seeing
affective and spiritual factors as crucial in fostering this revolution
and maintaining the West in what he terms a "post-revolutionary"
climate.[11] It is not simply the loss of belief in God and in other central Christian dogmas that contributed to this revolution, but possibly, in the terms of the argument of this paper, the long-term insup-
portability of the edifice of casuist moral theology with its divorce
of human and moral fulfillment from religious perfection. Be that
as it may, according to Taylor, secular humanisms and postmodern
anti-humanisms agree in affirming a good to human life without the
need to invoke any good beyond life. What distinguishes them is the
anti-humanist insistence that a comprehensive affirmation of human
life must embrace (and even celebrate) suffering and death. But both
secular humanism and post-modern anti-humanism simply deny
that religious aspirations have any relevance for human and moral fulfillment. The desire for transcendence is a kind of human and

11. Charles Taylor, "Iris Murdoch and Moral Philosophy," in *Iris Murdoch and the
Search for Human Goodness*, ed. Maria Antonaccio and Michael Schweiker (Chicago:
University of Chicago Press, 1996), 3–28.

moral dead end. "Immortal longings," to use Fergus Kerr's felicitous phrase, may not be good for one's moral health or, indeed, for one's humanity.[12] For Taylor, the "horizon of assumptions" that "shapes the pervasive outlook toward religion in our culture" includes the view that for us "life, flourishing, driving back the frontiers of death and suffering, are of supreme value" and that what prevented people from seeing this sooner and more widely was "precisely a sense, inculcated by religion, that there were higher goals," a good beyond life. In the postrevolutionary climate, "to speak of aiming beyond life is to appear to undermine the supreme concern with life in our humanitarian, 'civilized,' world."[13]

One can readily see, in the terms of Taylor's persuasive analysis of the rejection or marginalization of religion in Western modernity, that in order to seek the good of human life, one must give up pursuing a good beyond life or, at least, one must define the good beyond life in nonreligious terms. Religious perfection is seen not only as irrelevant to human fulfillment but as an actual obstacle to it. We can also readily see, if we recall the fundamental features of the Christocentric anthropology of Pope John Paul II and the Second Vatican Council, how radical a challenge is posed both by moral theology in the nominalist-casuist vein and in its current variants, and by the secular humanisms and anti-humanisms of Western modernity.

According to the Christocentric anthropology sketched earlier, there is an intrinsic link between what human beings are as such and what they can hope to become. There is a link, not a contradiction, between human fulfillment and religious consummation. Holiness (religious consummation) is the perfection of the created image of God (human fulfillment). The legacy of nominalism in casuistry and in the moral theories that sought to correct it is such as to make it very difficult to grasp the terms of an authentic Christian humanism even when they are forcefully presented. (Consider, in this connection, the cool reception still accorded to *Veritatis Splendor* in some

12. Fergus Kerr, OP, *Immortal Longings* (Notre Dame, IN: University of Notre Dame Press, 1997).

13. Taylor, "Iris Murdoch and Moral Philosophy," 23.

quarters). Without a moral theology that is thoroughly integrated with anthropology and Christology, it will be difficult to withstand the variety of secular humanisms and anti-humanisms of Western modernity. Indeed, in the climate of contemporary culture, there is a powerful temptation for some religious people, including Catholics, tacitly to accept the "horizon of assumptions" of Western modernity and to promote precisely (and sometimes chiefly) those aspects of their faith that can be seen as contributing to the good of human life. The documents of the Second Vatican Council have themselves sometimes been subjected to readings employing this strategy with an eye to well-meaning programs of renewal that, without denying the good beyond life, do not always leave much room for it in practice. It may well be that the divorce between human/moral fulfillment and religious perfection, embedded in prevailing forms of Catholic moral reflection, makes it difficult for Catholics influenced by them to respond to the challenges posed by non-religious or anti-religious humanisms for which the presumption of this divorce is axiomatic.

I am convinced that a recovery of Aquinas's theology of the *imago Dei* can and has already begun to make a significant contribution to the Catholic response to these challenges. Here I can only sketch briefly the possibilities as I see them in the time left to me. That Aquinas's theology affords such resources may not be obvious to everyone. Certainly, many will readily admit that, in linking anthropology, Christology and eschatology in its theology of the *imago Dei, Gaudium et Spes* had recovered important strands in the patristic doctrine of the *imago Dei*. Perhaps less widely known is how thoroughly Christological and eschatological is the theology of the *imago Dei* advanced in the writings of St. Thomas Aquinas. One of the more refreshing aspects of recent scholarship on Aquinas is the emergence of a broad appreciation of this central element of his theology.[14]

14. For an orientation to the literature on this topic, see Jean-Pierre Torrell, OP, *St. Thomas Aquinas: Vol. II: Spiritual Master*, translated by Robert Royal (Washington, DC: The Catholic University of America Press, 2003). See also: Emile Bailleux, "A l'image du Fils premier-né," *Revue Thomiste* 76 (1976): 181–207; Romanus Cessario, OP, *Christian Faith and the Theological Life* (Washington, DC: The Catholic University of

A crucial feature of this more comprehensive appraisal of Aquinas's theology of the *imago Dei* has involved the recognition that his explicit consideration of the matter as part of the theology of creation in question 93 of the *prima pars* cannot be treated in isolation but must be located within the broader context of the overall argument of the *Summa theologiae*.[15] It is well known that the structure of this argument is framed in terms of Aquinas's distinctive appropriation of the *exitus-reditus* scheme. This structure has immense significance for his theology of the *imago Dei*: the human being created in the image of God is by the very fact of his human nature and from the very first moment of his existence directed toward God as his ultimate end.[16] Contrary to a widespread misrepresentation of his

America Press, 1996), 38–48; Michael A. Dauphinais, "Loving the Lord Your God: The *Imago Dei* in St. Thomas Aquinas," *The Thomist* 63 (1999): 241–67; Ignatius Eschmann, OP, "St. Thomas Aquinas, the Summary of Theology I-II: The Ethics of the Image of God," in *The Ethics of St. Thomas Aquinas: Two Courses*, ed. Edward A. Synan (Toronto: Pontifical Institute of Medieval Studies, 1997), 159–231; L.-B. Gillon, OP, *Cristo e la Teologia Morale* (Roma: Edizioni Romane Mame, 1961); Thomas Hibbs, "*Imitatio Christi* and the Foundation of Aquinas's Ethics," *Communio: International Review* 18 (1991): 556–73, and *Virtue's Splendor: Wisdom, Prudence and the Human Good* (New York: Fordham University Press, 2001); Fergus Kerr, OP, *After Aquinas: Versions of Thomism* (Oxford: Blackwell, 2002); Matthew Levering, *Christ's Fulfillment of Torah and Temple* (Notre Dame, IN: University of Notre Dame Press, 2002), 83–107; D. Juvenal Merriell, *To the Image of the Trinity: A Study in the Development of Aquinas's Teaching* (Toronto: Pontifical Institute of Medieval Studies, 1990); Luc-Thomas Somme, *Fils adoptifs de Dieu par Jésus Christ* (Paris: Vrins, 1997); Batista Mondin, "Il bene morale come perfezione della persona," in *Pontifical Academy of St. Thomas*, *Atti della III Plenaria 2002*, 127–37.

15. See Ghislain Lafont, *Structures et méthode dans le Somme théologique de saint Thomas d'Aquin* (Paris: Cerf, 1961), and, more recently, Servais Pinckaers, "Le thème de l'image de Dieu en l'homme et l'anthropologie," in *Humain à l'image de Dieu*, ed. P. Bühler (Geneva: Ed. Labor et Fides, 1989), 147–63 (English translation: "Ethics and the Image of God" in *The Pinckaers Reader*, ed. John Berkman and Craig Steven Titus [Washington, DC: The Catholic University of America Press, 2005], 130–43). See also Thomas S. Hibbs, "The Hierarchy of Moral Discourses in Aquinas," *American Catholic Philosophical Quarterly* 64 (1990): 199–214; and A. N. Williams, "Mystical Theology Redux: The Pattern of Aquinas' *Summa Theologiae*," *Modern Theology* 13 (1997): 53–74, and "Deification in the *Summa Theologiae*: A Structural Interpretation of the Prima Pars," *The Thomist* 61 (1997): 219–55.

16. In this paper, I have not dealt with the controversy that has surrounded the "nature and grace" of theological anthropology which originated in the work of Henri de Lubac and has been sharpened lately in the writings of David Schindler and others in the "communio" school. It will be evident to the careful reader that, with Aquinas and

thought (which while losing much its currency remains entrenched in certain quarters), for Aquinas the theology of the *imago Dei* constitutes not a static and thus ahistorical conception of human nature, but rather a fundamentally dynamic and active one.[17]

This is already explicit in question 93. The dynamism is that of the *exitus-reditus*, a movement rooted in the divine purposes in creation and redemption and inscribed in the created order by the very finalities of human nature. In addition, Aquinas's account of the *imago Dei* explicitly asserts that it is primarily in acts of knowing and loving God through faith, hope and charity that the imaging of God is realized.[18] According to Father Romanus Cessario, "Aquinas contends that we should look for the image of God, not primarily in the intellectual capacities of the soul, but in the very acts of those operative capacities or habits." [19]

Looking beyond question 93, to the *secunda* and *tertia pars*, we can see that the theology of the *imago Dei* within the overall argument of the *Summa theologiae* secures the intrinsic link between moral theology, anthropology and christology, and thus the

---

many other Thomists, I both hold for the description of a natural end for human nature *and* deny a double order of nature and grace extrinsically related to one another. A teleological understanding of human nature is crucial to maintaining the link between religious perfection and integral human fulfillment. For a perspective on this controversy touching on the issues raised in this paper, see Romanus Cessario, OP, "On Bad Actions, Good Intentions and Loving God: Three Much Misunderstood Issues about the Happy Life that St. Thomas Aquinas Clarifies for Us," *Logos* 1 (1997): 100–122. On the broader issues, see the comprehensive treatment of Schindler's position in Tracey Rowland, *Culture and the Thomist Tradition* (London: Routledge, 2003). For a splendid survey of the twentieth-century controversy, see Lawrence Feingold, *The Natural Desire to See God* (Rome: Appolinare Studi, 2000). See also: Benedict Ashley, OP, "What is the End of the Human Person? The Vision of God and Integral Human Fulfillment," in *Moral Truth and Moral Tradition*, ed. Luke Gormally (Dublin: Four Courts Press, 1994), 68–96; Steven A. Long, "On the Possibility of a Purely Natural End for Man," *The Thomist* 64 (2000): 211–37; Peter A. Pagan-Aguiar, "St. Thomas Aquinas and Human Finality: Paradox or *Mysterium Fidei*?" *The Thomist* 64 (2000): 374–99; and Jacob Wood, *To Stir a Restless Heart: Thomas Aquinas and Henri de Lubac on Nature, Grace, and the Desire for God* (Washington, DC: The Catholic University of America Press, 2019).

17. See Ian A. McFarland, "When Time Is of the Essence: Aquinas and the *Imago Dei*," *New Blackfriars* 82 (2001): 208–23.

18. *Summa theologiae* I, q. 93, a. 4.

19. Cessario, *Christian Faith and the Theological Life*, 43.

connection between human/moral fulfillment and religious perfection, or beatitude. For one thing, we find that the entirety of the *secunda pars*—Aquinas's expansive treatise on the moral life—unfolds as an explication of what it means for man to made in the image of God. Here the dynamic character of the *imago Dei* is clear: human beings must be active in the grace-enabled actualization of the image of God within them. Coming from God, they are active participants in the movement of their return to him. What draws them is their pursuit of the good of human life which is continually revealed as the Good beyond life. No one demonstrates better than Aquinas the continuity between the inbuilt desire for the good and the enjoyment of the Good beyond all limited goods which is beatitude. Hence the capital importance of the meditation on the nature of beatitude which begins Aquinas's treatise on moral theology: only the supernatural beatitude of communion actualizes the movement of the human person towards his or her fulfillment.

In the *tertia pars*, Aquinas arrives at the culmination of the theology of the *imago Dei* when he shows how Christ, the perfect image of the Father, is the principle and pattern of the restoration and the perfection of the image of God in us.[20] All the mysteries of Christ's life, but especially his passion, death and resurrection, bring about the work of transformation in us by which the image of God, damaged by original sin and by our own personal sins, can be restored and perfected. Configured and transfigured in the *imago Christi* by the power of the Holy Spirit, we return to the Father, and come to enjoy to the communion of trinitarian life which is the essence of beatitude.

In the terms of the argument of this paper, and contrary to

20. In addition to the works by Torrell, Gillon, Hibbs, Levering, Somme, and Williams cited in footnote 14 above, see also Jean-Pierre Torrell, OP, "Le Christ dans la 'spiritualité' de saint Thomas," in *Christ among the Medieval Dominicans*, ed. Kent Emery and Joseph P. Wawrykow (Notre Dame, IN: Notre Dame University Press, 1998), 197–219, and J. A. Di Noia, OP, "*Veritatis Splendor*: Moral Life as Transfigured Life," in *Veritatis Splendor and the Renewal of Moral Theology*, ed. J. A. Di Noia, OP, and Romanus Cessario, OP (Princeton: Scepter, 1999), 1–10.

both nominalist moral theology and to the secular humanisms and anti-humanisms of Western modernity, Aquinas can be construed as advancing a theology of the *imago Dei* that shows how in the gracious plan of divine providence religious perfection is central to human and moral fulfillment. The human person is created in the image of God in order to grow into the image of Christ. This truth about man is the foundation of the authentic Christian humanism central to the teaching of Vatican Council II and John Paul II. A critical task of Christian anthropology in every age is precisely to supply an adequate basis for moral theology. Among the most significant of Pope John Paul's encyclicals, *Veritatis Splendor* corrects the unfortunate legacy of casuist moral theology and its contemporary progeny and, more importantly, presses upon us the profound links between anthropology and Christology that establish the basis of an authentic Christian humanism.

CHAPTER 11

The New Christian Humanism

The Legacy of Pope Saint John Paul II

INTRODUCTION: HUMANISM, SECULAR AND CHRISTIAN

Christian humanism? Although lately we have become accustomed to this expression, it must be acknowledged that the juxtaposition of the terms Christian and humanism is not an uncontroversial one. For a long time—and still in the minds of some people— humanism signifies an alternative to rather than an instance of the Christian vision of human life. In fact, in the form of a rich theology of the *imago Dei*, Christian humanism is as old as Christianity itself.[1] Secular humanism, on the other hand, is a relatively recent phenomenon. There is a long and complex history here that would make for a whole lecture of its own.[2]

This evening we have something else in our sights: the recovery and reaffirmation of an authentic Christian humanism by Pope Saint

---

Paper presented at the Dominican House of Studies (Washington, DC) on April 22, 2015.

1. See J. Augustine Di Noia, "Imago Dei-Imago Christi: The Theological Foundations of Christian Humanism," *Nova et Vetera* 2 (2004): 267–78. [Reprinted in this volume as Chapter Ten—editor's note.]

2. See Benedict Ashley, OP, *Theologies of the Body: Humanist and Christian* (Braintree, MA: The Pope John XXIII Center, 1985).

John Paul II. "As the rescue of the Western humanistic tradition from its decay into skepticism and nihilism had seemed to [Pope John Paul II] a fitting task for Vatican II, so the re-presentation of Christian doctrine through the prism of a thoroughly humanistic Christian analysis of the human person seemed to him a useful, and perhaps imperative, papal contribution to the Church and the world on the threshold of the third millennium—and at the end of a century in which false ideas of who and what human beings are had made an abattoir of history."[3]

Pope Saint John Paul II schooled us to engage in this endeavor. If Christ is the measure of man, then only in Christ can we grasp what it means to be human. No force on earth—neither the Nazis nor the Communists, neither the secular general public nor the lukewarm Catholics, not even the criticism of dissident theologians—could deflect him from the endeavor to rescue and express humanism in its properly Christian form.

In pursuing this project, Pope John Paul can be seen to have created the conditions for a new level of engagement with the wider culture on the part of the Church. With the benefit of hindsight, we can see that the inspiration of his teaching and example permanently altered the agenda for the dialogue of Catholic faith and modern culture.

We can say with confidence that, among all the major teaching pontificates, Pope John Paul's will undoubtedly come to be regarded as one of the most important in the history of Christendom. His rich and profound magisterium touched on nearly every aspect of Catholic faith and life and has profoundly influenced the pontificates of Pope Benedict XVI and Pope Francis. He affirmed the power of the Gospel of Christ to transform culture, society, and individual human persons to their very depths, and thus relaunched the worldwide movement of Catholic renewal envisaged by Vatican Council II.

At the core of Pope John Paul's message was a vision of a new,

3. George Weigel, *The End and the Beginning: Pope John Paul II—The Victory of Freedom, the Last Years, the Legacy* (New York: Doubleday, 2010), 472.

or at least a newly formulated, Christian humanism. Already in his homily at the Mass for the inauguration of his pontificate on 22 October 1978, he sounded the theme in what would become one of the most famous utterances of his twenty-seven-year-long pontificate:

Brothers and sisters, do not be afraid to welcome Christ and accept his power. Help the Pope and all those who wish to serve Christ and with Christ's power to serve the human person and the whole of mankind. Do not be afraid. Open wide the doors for Christ. To his saving power open the boundaries of States, economic and political systems, the vast fields of culture, civilization and development. Do not be afraid. Christ knows "what is in man." He alone knows it. So often today man does not know what is within him, in the depths of his mind and heart. So often he is uncertain about the meaning of his life on this earth. He is assailed by doubt, a doubt which turns into despair. We ask you therefore, we beg you with humility and trust, let Christ speak to man. He alone has words of life, yes, of eternal life. (§5)

This evening I shall present a synthesis of Pope John Paul's Christian humanism as he expressed it in the programmatic first encyclical of his pontificate, *Redemptor Hominis*, and then briefly explore essential elements of this vision as they were expounded in three of his most important encyclicals: *Evangelium Vitae, Veritatis Splendor,* and *Fides et Ratio.*

REDEMPTOR HOMINIS: A NEW CHRISTIAN HUMANISM

While waiting for a Washington Metro train recently, I watched a group of children comparing their heights. "Who's the tallest? Let's see who's the tallest?" one of them was shouting. To a neutral observer like myself, it was obvious which one of them was the tallest. But they went through with the ritual of standing against one of the concrete pillars in the Brookland-CUA station, stretching perfectly straight, trying to inch toward the highest marking. To be as tall as the tallest—I suppose you might say that's what each of those children wanted. To know their own heights, to stretch even beyond

them, they had to be able to measure themselves against the tallest
of them. A relatively insignificant personal attribute, physical height.
Suppose that in a matter incomparably more significant, in the matter of knowing the reality and possibilities of our nature as human
beings, in the matter of knowing not just our present heights, but
of stretching beyond them—suppose that in this matter there were
someone to measure ourselves by, some "tallest" so to speak.

If you can suppose this, and indeed if you can affirm your conviction that there is someone by whom to measure the full stature and
unimaginably exalted destiny of our nature as human beings, you
can grasp the heart of Pope John Paul's encyclical, *Redemptor Hominis*. In this first encyclical of his pontificate, published in March 1979
after less than a year in the See of Peter, Pope John Paul presented
a traditional, yet distinctive spiritual doctrine in which Christ the
Redeemer is depicted not only as revealing and achieving the full
measure of human dignity in himself, but also as enabling all other
human beings with whom he is united in grace to realize and attain
their value and greatness.

In *Redemptor Hominis* Christ is the measure of what human beings are and can become. The encyclical presented a context in which
the starting points and possibilities of human progress and development—personal and social—can only be discovered by turning our
minds and hearts to the "Redeemer of Man, Jesus Christ, who is the
center of the universe and of history" (§1). Thus, *Redemptor Hominis*
provided a theological basis for a spirituality of human personal and
social progress that is comprehensive enough to include every significant area where that progress is desired and pursued. Considering the encyclical almost forty years later, it is clear that it contained
in germ almost all the themes of this great teaching pontificate.[4]

As was noted at the time of its publication, the encyclical reflected Pope John Paul's considerable philosophical and theological

4. See George Weigel, *Witness to Hope: The Biography of John Paul II* (New York:
Harper Collins, 1999) and *The End and the Beginning: Pope John Paul II—The Victory of
Freedom, the Last Years, the Legacy.*

learning (comprising among other things a thorough knowledge of the Thomistic tradition and of contemporary phenomenology) in presenting a profoundly personalist and unitive spiritual doctrine.[5] But it should be noted that no technical philosophical or theological background is required to grasp its meaning: its style is luminously clear and its message directly accessible.

"While the ways on which the Council of this century has set the Church going … will continue for a long time to be the ways that all must follow, we can at the same time ask: How, in what manner should we continue? What should we do in order that this new advent of the Church connected with the approaching end of the second millennium may bring us closer to him whom the Scripture calls 'Everlasting Father?'" To his own question, Pope John Paul answered: "A fundamental and essential response must be given: our spirit is set in one direction, the only direction of our intellect, will, and hearts is towards Christ our Redeemer, towards Christ the Redeemer of Man" (§7). As this passage suggests, the doctrine of *Redemptor Hominis*—the mystery of our redemption in Christ—supplied the framework within which Pope John Paul II would come to articulate the main lines of the program of his pontificate.

Signaling the enormous significance that he attached to the teaching of Vatican Council II, this first encyclical constituted an extended commentary on the famous paragraph 22 of the Pastoral Constitution on the Church in the Modern World (*Gaudium et Spes*): "The truth is that only in the mystery of the Incarnate Word does the mystery of man take on light … Christ the new Adam in the very revelation of the mystery of the Father and his love, fully reveals to himself and brings to light his most high calling … He who is the image of the invisible God is himself the perfect man who has restored in the children of Adam that likeness to God which had been disfigured ever since the first sin. Human nature, by the very

5. See Jaroslaw Kupczak *Destined for Liberty: The Human Person in the Philosophy of Karol Wotyła/John Paul II* (Washington, DC: The Catholic University of America Press, 2000).

fact that it was assumed, not absorbed in him, has been raised in us also to a dignity beyond compare. For by his Incarnation, the Son of God, in a certain way united himself with each man"— "He," Pope John Paul added after quoting this passage in full, "he, the Redeemer of Man" (§8).

Perhaps only in retrospect have we been able to grasp the range and profundity with which Pope St. John Paul mined this passage of *Gaudium et Spes* to develop what I have been calling a new Christian humanism that was in fact a highly original recovery of traditional Christian anthropology.[6]

His frequent references to this passage of *Gaudium et Spes* and to others from the documents of Vatican Council II exhibited Pope John Paul's determination to frame the program of his own pontificate in terms of continuing and advancing the program of renewal initiated by this council. Significantly, he sounded the dominant theme of his own message here by quoting Vatican Council II. In addition, in the first chapter of *Redemptor Hominis*, Pope John Paul enthusiastically embraced the legacy of his immediate predecessors in the See of Peter—John XXIII and Paul VI—whose initiatives in fostering collegiality and the ecumenical movement he warmly applauded and commended. Pope John Paul offered an analysis of the situation of modern man in order to depict concretely the condition of the human partner in the redemptive union.

Following the lead of Vatican Council II, but deepening its analysis of the human condition in ways that we would come to recognize as characteristic of his thinking, Pope John Paul argued that, since by redemption Christ is united in a certain way with each man and since the Church must pursue Christ's way, the Church needs to be sensitive to whatever serves man's true welfare and alert to whatever obstructs it. Human beings are in fact threatened by their own achievements whenever material progress is not matched by a corresponding progress in ethical and spiritual awareness. A "menace

6. See Romanus Cessario, "The Light of Tabor: Christian Personalism and Adoptive Sonship," *Nova et Vetera* 2 (2004): 237–48.

to man" arises today from a variety of sources, the encyclical argued, notably from arsenals of self-destructive weaponry and the growing disparity between rich and poor. True conversion will be needed if there is to be real progress in overcoming this menace and in ensuring the future of human society about which *Gaudium et Spes* had spoken with such eloquent optimism.

At the core of *Redemptor Hominis* is a spiritual doctrine of union with Christ the Redeemer. As a new creation, the redemption by Christ overcomes the effects of sin and reveals man to himself. And this is achieved precisely through union—through Christ's union with us. "Christ, the Redeemer of the world, is the one who penetrated in a unique unrepeatable way into the mystery of man and entered his heart" (§8).

Christ reveals the love of God, the Creator who in redeeming shows himself to be faithful to his promises and to his love for humankind. "The redemption of the world"—to quote one of the encyclical's most striking phrases—" is, at its deepest root, the fullness of justice in a human heart, the heart of the first-born Son, in order that it may become justice in the hearts of many human beings" (§9). This constitutes what the encyclical calls the "divine dimension of the Mystery of Redemption." Christ reveals man to himself—the "human dimension" of the mystery. Christ reveals the greatness, dignity, and value that belong to human nature.

Pope John Paul wrote: "The man who wishes to understand himself thoroughly—and not just in accordance with immediate, partial, and often superficial and even illusory standards and measures of his being—he must ... draw near to Christ. He must enter into him with all his own self, he must appropriate and assimilate the whole reality of the Incarnation and Redemption in order to find himself. If this profound process takes place, he then bears fruit not only of adoration of God but also of deep wonder at himself. In reality, the name for that deep amazement at man's worth and dignity is the gospel, the Good News" (§10).

Therefore, redemption is accomplished through Christ's entering

into union with all human beings, revealing God fully and fully realizing human dignity and worth. The Mystery of Redemption calls
every human being to a lifelong endeavor through which this union
with Christ is strengthened and deepened, extended and shared.
"Christ's union with man is power," transforming man inwardly "as
the source of a new life that does not disappear ... but lasts to eternal life. This life ... is the final fulfillment of man's vocation ... this
truth about man enables him to go beyond the bounds of temporariness at the same time to think with particular love and solicitude of
everything within the dimensions of temporariness that affect man's
life and the life of the human spirit" (§18). Thus, Christ's union with
each human being is sustained by grace, constitutes a participation
in the divine life itself, and culminates in that complete union with
God which is the destiny of every person.[7]

The transformative aspects of the experience of union with Christ
are framed by the encyclical in terms of the Christian vocation to
kingly service. If in the light of Christ's attitude, "'being a king' is truly possible by 'being a servant' then 'being a servant' also demands
so much spiritual maturity that it must really be described as 'being a
king.' In order to be able to serve others effectively we must be able to
master ourselves, possess the virtues that make this mastery possible.
Our sharing in Christ's kingly mission ... is closely linked with every
sphere of both Christian and human morality" (§21).

Servanthood is not just a functional designation entailing a generous readiness to be at the service of others, but, to be faithful to
the "kingly" quality of Christ's service, entails the grace-sustained
struggle for self-mastery through growth in the life of virtue. For the
Christian, therefore, pursuit of the life of virtue does not represent a
self-centered preoccupation with one's own perfection, but a transformation patterned on Christ's kingly service.[8]

7. See Avery Dulles, "John Paul II and the Mystery of the Human Person," in *Church
and Society: The Laurence J. McGinley Lectures 1988–2007* (New York: Fordham University
Press, 2008), 414–29.

8. See Chapter 10 of this collection, "*Imago Dei—Imago Christi*: The Theological
Foundations of Christian Humanism."

Membership in the Christian community cannot be viewed simply as a sociological allegiance: it represents for each person a response, in grace, to a particular vocation to membership in Christ's body. For each person and class of persons in the Church, this vocation takes individual forms. Each Christian is called by a "singular, unique and unrepeatable grace" to union with Christ in the community of his faithful disciples. Hence, "it is precisely the principle of 'kingly service' that imposes on each of us, in imitation of Christ's example, the duty to demand of himself exactly what we have been called to, what we have personally obliged ourselves to by God's grace, in order to respond to our vocation" (§21).

Christian life involves union with Christ, initiated, achieved, and sustained by him, revelatory and redemptive for us, still partial but pledging consummation in eternity, and requiring persevering struggle on our part to be transformed according to the full stature of Christ.

In the Christian humanism advanced by *Redemptor Hominis*, Christ is the true measure of man. The encyclical's robust personalism—emphasizing the precisely personal nature of the individual's union with Christ—is balanced by a strong ecclesiology. Each person who is united with Christ, who is addressed by his intimate invitation "Follow me," is thereby united in community with Christ's other disciples. Despite all the deficiencies that beset communities as human institutions, the Church is one because Christ forms it together with his disciples. It is within the Church that the Mystery of Redemption in Christ is faithfully proclaimed and made present in teaching and sacrament.

For Pope John Paul, any account of the nature and possibilities of human development must start with the mystery of Christ the Redeemer. Any account that omits reference to him at every point will be partial and illusory at best, and possibly harmful as well. This deep conviction provides the context for Pope John Paul's whole magisterium, for his subsequent encyclicals concerning family, peace, labor, economy, and, as we shall see briefly now, human life, freedom, and rationality. Such matters can receive adequate consideration only when set within a comprehensive doctrine of human life centered in the Mystery of Christ the Redeemer. Any humanism that leaves Christ out of the picture will fall short of the full truth about what it means to be human. This conviction is at the heart of the legacy of Pope St. John Paul II.

EVANGELIUM VITAE: THE GIFT OF LIFE

God loves the life and the goodness he creates. God calls out of nothingness those to whom he then calls out in love. This is the pattern of God's activity in creation and redemption: he creates the conditions that enable creaturely persons to love him.

Some modern thinkers have concluded that, if one accepts the Christian faith on this matter, then there is no space for human beings to be themselves; they are smothered, as it were, by God. Some modern thinkers have regarded this faith as antihuman and have concluded that human freedom and autonomy demand that God be erased. The eclipse of God, they argue, is the guarantee of human autonomy.

The deep flaw in this way of thinking, as Pope John Paul demonstrated in his encyclical *Evangelium Vitae,* "The Gospel of Life," is that it conceives the human condition as if it were a competition in which we can secure our place only if God recedes into oblivion. But Pope John Paul insisted that just the opposite is the case: God creates the very conditions for our existence and action. Human fulfillment lies not in autonomy but in theonomy. We embrace it in an ordered existence where life is God's gift and our happiness lies in our participation in the divine life, in our friendship with God.

The year 2015 marks the twentieth anniversary of the publication of *Evangelium Vitae* which appeared on the feast of the Annunciation in 1995. The words in its subtitle—*On the Value and Inviolability of Human Life*—signal the encyclical's key themes: the moral evil of taking innocent human life, of abortion, and of euthanasia.

But did the pope need almost two hundred pages of text to repeat the contents of the Fifth Commandment? I don't think so. The substance of this defense of life could be summarized in a few pages. In addition, however, Pope John Paul offered a penetrating analysis of what he famously termed the culture of death and its modern philosophical premises. He argued forcefully that, contrary to what some philosophers have thought, the experience of the twentieth century demonstrated that the eclipse of God conceals a terrible threat to human existence. When human beings stop seeing life as a gift from God, they see it as something over which they have authority and control. And then, my friends, as history shows, they are in the gravest danger.

With his sights set firmly on the monopoly that *secular* humanism holds in Western popular culture, Pope John Paul articulated a fundamental element in the new *Christian* humanism he sought to advance. To accept life as a gift and to be subject to God is not to obliterate the human, but to realize that which is most fully human.

Recall St. Thomas Aquinas's discussion of the sin of the angels. He pondered the nature of their sin. What sort of sin could it have been? After eliminating some of the obvious possibilities (e.g., if you don't have a body you can't sin by lust or gluttony!), Aquinas explained that, according to the tradition, their sin was a spiritual one: the fallen angels, it is said, wanted to be like God. But what is wrong with that, Aquinas asked, what's wrong with wanting to be like God? Nothing as such, said Aquinas, but the sin was that they wanted to be like God *as if it were their due*. They wanted to take from God something that could only be theirs as a gift, indeed something that God wanted to share with them in love.

In *Evangelium Vitae,* Pope John Paul did not want simply to demonstrate the moral evil of abortion and euthanasia. He wanted to expose the deep errors that feed the culture of death and in this way to show us that life is a gift that is not at our disposal. God gives it to us as a gift, and we must receive it as a gift. This recognition is at the core of the new Christian humanism. It is only in and through our faith in God, as revealed to us in Christ, that we can understand what it means to be human. If we do not understand that life itself, the life of grace, and, in the end, the life of glory are each and all a gift, we will be seduced by the culture of death or, worse, conspire with it. *Evangelium Vitae* presents a teaching about God's love for human life and thus about the necessity of proclaiming the *Gospel of Life*. This is the theological root for participation in the pro-life movement. It touches on the deepest truth about God and human beings: without God we are nothing, but with God we have everything. This is why the battle is worth fighting and, contrary to what some critics say, why it must be fought not only in the churches but also in the public domain. Fundamental elements of the new Christian humanism are at stake here.

VERITATIS SPLENDOR: THE NATURE OF FREEDOM

Published in 1993, the tenth year of Pope John Paul's pontificate, on the feast of the Transfiguration, the encyclical *Veritatis Splendor*—the "Splendor of Truth"—bears the subtitle *Regarding Certain Fundamental Questions of the Church's Moral Teachings*. Pope John Paul sought to correct some seriously erroneous moral theories (notably concerning the so-called fundamental option as well as proportionalism) and to lay out the authentic substance of Catholic moral teaching. Exploring the moral implications of a thoroughgoing Christian humanism, the encyclical argued that the divinely willed realization of human existence can be achieved only through our *free* embrace of the ultimate Good that Christ's grace makes for us.[9]

Remember our Lord's words to the disciples: "For whoever wishes to save his life will lose it, but whoever loses his life for my sake will find it" (Mt 16:24–26). What this means, in effect, is that,

9. See J. A. Di Noia and Romanus Cessario, eds. *Veritatis Splendor and the Renewal of Moral Theology* (Huntington, IN: Our Sunday Visitor Press, 1999).

unless we become like Christ, we will not find our true selves. Only the Son of God could say to the human race: you will only find your true self be becoming like me. In other words, to follow and imitate Christ is not to suppress our humanity and our freedom, and thus our human and personal identities. On the contrary. To become like Christ is not to become less of our true selves, but more uniquely and distinctively ourselves.

Christian moral life consists not in the observance of arbitrary commands but in the pursuit of the true good of human nature, a pursuit guided by the commandments, by divine grace, the infused moral virtues, by the sacramental life of the Church. In this way, we are continually being transformed in the image of Christ, becoming more and more like him through the course of our lives, and participating ever more deeply in the communion of the divine life which is our true end. It is only in this light that we can grasp the true meaning of human freedom. Real freedom is not simply the state of having an indefinite range of possible choices—including sin— but *the God-given capacity to embrace the kind of life that will make us truly happy.* Sin involves, not the exercise of freedom, but the failure of freedom. Our nature as personal beings, created in the image of God, with knowledge and free will, is such that we must willingly and freely embrace the ultimate Good that is nothing less than God himself. We cannot be compelled to do this—anymore than we can be compelled to love another human person. Love cannot be compelled; it must be free. God wants us to embrace him freely, and the freedom that is basic to human nature itself as well as the grace that sustains and directs it are God's gifts to us.

Tulips, and chipmunks, and cabbages flourish—or fail to—without making acts of the will. Some obstacles can short-circuit this flourishing, but it could not be that these creatures have failed to choose it. The drama—indeed the tragedy and sometimes the comedy—of human existence lies in this: unlike everything else in the universe, we are the only creatures who can fail to choose our true good.

As *Veritatis Splendor* affirmed, truth and freedom are entwined inextricably. An undifferentiated freedom, according to which one strives to define what the human is for himself or herself, can only lead to unhappiness because it fails to conform to the truth about human nature as God has created it. We can no more redefine our true nature than we can anything else in the created order. Our human nature is a divine gift. We must recognize the *truth* of what human beings are by nature in order to recognize that freedom lies in embracing that truth. In this way alone can we find happiness in communion with the triune God and with one another in him.

Free embrace of the ultimate good? To the postmodern mind, this complex teaching brims with incoherence. Once you accept the Gospel, according to some, your freedom to be yourself is constrained and your ability to explore the many possibilities that life offers is frustrated. The measure of what it means to be human—human nature—is not a socially constructed convention but a divinely created gift.

FIDES ET RATIO: HUMAN REASON ENLIGHTENED BY FAITH

Critical for the new Christian humanism was Pope John Paul's reaffirmation of the harmony of reason and faith and also, importantly, the capacity of reason to reach the truth. The circumstances were different from those of the middle decades of the nineteenth century when the pope had to defend faith against reason. Ironically, at the end of the twentieth century, he had to defend reason against unreason. While the situation at the end of the nineteenth century was one of reason triumphant, at the end of twentieth the situation was one of reason debased—a crisis of meaning brought on by the loss of confidence in the capacity of human reason to reach the truth.

More than a hundred years after the encyclical *Aeterni Patris* of Pope Leo XIII (1879), Pope John Paul turned again to the relationship between faith and reason. In the years since Leo XIII had raised the alarm against rationalism, Pope John Paul II saw the situation as having worsened. The exaggerated rationalism and humanism of the late nineteenth century led in the twentieth century to the antihuman totalitarian movements of communism and fascism. Published in 1998, Pope John Paul's encyclical *Fides et Ratio* marked the twentieth anniversary of his election as pope. With characteristic boldness, he challenged intellectuals to face a question fundamental to a truly humanistic vision of human beings: why is it that reason prefers to hold back from the truth when it is the very nature of reason to attain the truth? Reason is endowed with all that it needs to search for the truth. Yet various modes of philosophy today seek to glorify reason's weakness.

In his "*diakonia* for the truth," Pope John Paul II defended the greatness of reason. In a manner continuous with his earlier encyclicals *Evangelium Vitae* and *Veritatis Splendor*—where he pointed to moral truths that have been forgotten or misunderstood—*Fides et Ratio* was concerned with truth itself. This is not just an academic matter, to be discussed in the classroom or the scholarly monograph. For doubts about the possibility of reaching the truth touch the very depths of human existence. The answers to the questions of every human heart are at stake: Who am I? Where do I come from and where am I going? What will come after this life? The encyclical sought to defend the very possibility of finding reasonable answers to such questions.

In the first place, Pope John Paul wanted to address the erosion of the moral consensus that he saw as essential for the survival of free, democratic societies. This was a pope who had experienced the struggle to live internally free in societies where external freedom was impossible; a man who believed firmly in the possibilities and the potential of democratic society for preserving the dignity of the human person but was disturbed that at the end of the twentieth century the erosion of the moral consensus fundamental to a free society's survival threatened to undermine these societies.

In *Fides et Ratio* he wrote: "*There is growing support for a concept of democracy that is not grounded upon any reference to unchanging values*: Whether or not a line of action is admissible is decided by vote of a parliamentary majority. The *great moral decisions of humanity are subordinated to decisions* taken by institutional agencies" (§89).

The analysis of the problem provided by *Fides et Ratio* was that the gradual usurpation of philosophical inquiry by nihilistic, relativistic, and what Pope John Paul called undifferentiated and pluralistic systems of thought undermined people's confidence that they can achieve any kind of truth. The "possibility of discovering the real meaning of life is cast into doubt: *this is why many people stumble through life to the very edge of the abyss* without knowing where they are going" (§6). If meaning is socially constructed, then it is irreducibly diverse across cultures, and possibly also from one individual to the next. If the only meaning there is is the meaning we construct or confer upon reality, then whatever consensus is generated will essentially be one based not on universal values but on convention and possibly the sheer exercise of power. We will all agree, or be compelled to agree, to regard as true certain things just so that we can get on together.

According to the diagnosis advanced by *Fides et* Ratio, unless philosophers again reclaim the grandeur of their inquiry and its capacity to come to a knowledge of the truth, then nothing can ensure or ground the consensus upon which societies and polities depend. *Fides et Ratio* called upon philosophers to regain confidence in the possibility of inquiries that can arrive at the truth about what it means to be human. Here lay the most significant element of his message for the wider world. This encyclical was addressed to the bishops, primarily, but one can see it as addressed as well to an intellectually serious reading public in the Church and beyond it. Certainly, it was received as such.

From the erosion of a moral consensus based on the truth about man, *Fides et Ratio* turned to the emergence of a credulous piety in the realm of religion itself. History and experience show that not infrequently the greatest danger for religion is not skepticism but credulity. In the name of religion, people appear to be ready to believe almost anything. Without rigorous reflection and intellectual seriousness, without theology in its classical sense supporting the work of the proclamation of the Gospel, it is very easy for religion and spirituality to devolve into what the pope called superstition and mythology. "It is an illusion to think that faith, tied to weak reasoning, might be more penetrating; on the contrary, faith then runs the grave risk of withering into myth or superstition" (§48).

In the place of spirituality that is rooted in the mysteries of the faith—in the reality of God—piety turns in upon itself or merely to what might be called the epiphenomena of transcendence. "The Word of God refers constantly to things which transcend human experience and even human thought; but this 'mystery' could not be revealed, nor could theology render it in some way intelligible were human knowledge limited strictly to the world of sense experience.... A theology without a metaphysical horizon could not move beyond an analysis of religious experience" (§83).

Moreover, Pope John Paul insisted on the power of faith to illumine and enlarge rational inquiry. At the same time, "reason ... is not asked to pass judgment on the contents of faith, something of which it would be incapable.... Its function is rather to find the meaning, to discover explanations which might allow everyone to come to a certain understanding of the contents of faith" (§42). Pope John Paul posed again for theology the objective of seeking the intelligibility of revelation rather than what might be taken as its reasonability.

Classical theology accepted the entirety of revelation in faith and ascribed to it the presumption of truth and thus intelligibility—precisely as divinely revealed. It asked not, "Do the things we confess measure up to our standards of what is reasonable?" but "How do the things we believe come to be known ever more deeply *in their inner intelligibility*?"—God being infinitely intelligible and drawing the mind more and more to the Truth that he is. In the words of the encyclical: "Divine truth proposed to us in the Sacred Scripture and rightly interpreted by the Church's teaching enjoys innate intelligibility, so logically consistent that it stands as an authentic body of knowledge. The *intellectus fidei* expands this truth, not only in grasping the logical and conceptual structure of the propositions in which the Church's teaching is framed, but also, indeed primarily, in bringing to light the salvific meaning of these propositions" (§66).

In these ways, *Fides et Ratio*, among other things, reaffirmed crucial elements of an authentic Christian humanism: a robust confidence in the God-given capacity of reason to arrive at the truth along with an insistence on the fundamental harmony between faith and reason.

CHAPTER 12

---·---

Christ Brings Freedom
from Sin and Death

The Commentary of St. Thomas Aquinas
on Romans 5:12–21

INTRODUCTION: PAUL AND THOMAS

One night early in 1274, a Dominican friar in Naples had a dream about St. Thomas. In the friar's dream, Aquinas is lecturing on the letters of St. Paul when suddenly there enters into the hall none other than the Apostle himself. After acknowledging him with a slight bow, St. Thomas inquires whether his exposition of the text accords with the meaning that St. Paul intended. The Apostle Paul replies approvingly that Aquinas is indeed teaching "what could be understood from his epistles in this life," but that there would come a time "when he would understand them according to their whole truth."[1] And, with that, the Apostle takes hold of Aquinas's *cappa* and draws him from the lecture hall.

Torrell sees in this dream not just a touching premonition of the passing of Thomas Aquinas into eternal life—for, as it happens, the news of the death of Aquinas reached Naples three days later—but

Originally published in *The Thomist* 73 (2009), 281–98. Used with permission.

1. Jean-Pierre Torrell, *St. Thomas Aquinas: volume I, The Person and His Work*, 3rd ed. (Washington, DC: The Catholic University of America Press, 2023), 293–94.

also confirmation of his view that the final version of the commentary on Romans dates to a course of lectures given by Aquinas at Naples during the period 1272–73. We need not enter here into the controversy concerning the dating of the Aquinas's Pauline commentaries, except to note that, for the purposes of this paper, it is reasonable to assume that the section of the Romans commentary under consideration here represents the mature teaching of Aquinas.

What is more, we may take St. Paul's words of approval in this remarkable dream as an occasion to comment on the achievement of the Pauline commentaries of Aquinas, their scope, importance, and influence. Indeed, as other scholars will no doubt seek to show during this session of the academy, "the thinking of the Apostle is omnipresent" in the theology of Aquinas.[2] In a real sense, St. Thomas regarded the Apostle as a fellow master of theology, "the professor among the Apostles."[3] He saw in the letters of Paul a systematic vision of the faith and commented on them with meticulous attention and profound insight. St. Thomas considered the Pauline corpus to constitute a complete treatise, in three parts, on the grace of Christ: (1) nine of the letters concerning this grace as it exists in the *mystical body* (Romans, I and II Corinthians, Galatians, Ephesians, Philippians, Colossians, I and II Thessalonians); (2) four letters concerning the grace of Christ as it exists in the *chief members* of the Church, viz., the prelates (I and II Timothy, Titus, Philemon), and (3) one letter—Hebrews—concerning the grace of Christ as it exists in the *head* of the body, Christ himself.[4]

It is worthy of note that, in the friar's dream, the Apostle qualifies his approval of Aquinas's exposition of his letters by saying: what could be understood in this life is as yet partial in comparison to the fullness of truth that he would possess in the life to come. We should keep this cautionary note in mind as we take up the difficult topic of

2. Otto Hermann Pesch, "Paul as Professor of Theology: The Image of the Apostle in St. Thomas' Theology," *The Thomist* 38 (1974): 589.

3. Pesch, "Paul as Professor of Theology," 585.

4. *Lectura super S. Pauli Apostolam ad Hebraeos*, Prol., n. 11, in *Super Epistolas S. Pauli Lectura*, ed. Raphael Cai (Rome: Marietti, 1953).

original sin—a mystery of faith in the strictest sense—bedeviled in our time no less than Aquinas's by many errors, confusions, and misunderstandings.

SAINT THOMAS'S COMMENTARY
ON ROMANS 5:12–21

In his commentaries on the letters of St. Paul, as in his other exegetical and theological works, Aquinas used the edition of the Vulgate edited at the University of Paris at the beginning of the thirteenth century. In this so-called *Biblia Parisiensis* or "Bible of the University of Paris," the order of the sacred books and the chapter divisions (and, later, verses) within them correspond to those of our own modern editions.[5]

Thus Aquinas's outline of the structure of the section of the Letter to the Romans under consideration in this paper corresponds roughly to that recognized by most commentators, who see it as part of the long "doctrinal section" of the letter that stretches from Chapter 1, verse 16, through Chapter 11, verse 36.[6] According to this common view, the argument of this section moves through three stages, showing in turn: first, that through the Gospel the holiness of God is revealed as justifying the person of faith (1:16–4:25); next, that the love of God assures the salvation of those justified by faith (5:1–8:39); and, finally, that this plan of salvation does not contradict God's promises to Israel (9:1–11:36). Once St. Paul has announced the second stage of his overall argument at the beginning of Chapter 5, he moves on to discuss the threefold liberation which new life in Christ brings: freedom from sin and death (5:12–21), then freedom from self through union with Christ (Chapter 6), and freedom from the law (Chapter 7). The focus of our attention here is Aquinas's

---

5. Wiesław Dabrowski, "*La dottrina sul peccato originale nei commenti di san Tommaso d'Aquino allé lettere di san Paolo Apostolo,*" *Angelicum* 83 (2006): 560n.

6. See Joseph A. Fitzmyer, "The Letter to the Romans," in *The New Jerome Biblical Commentary*, ed. Raymond E. Brown, Joseph A. Fitzmyer, and Roland E. Murphy (Englewood Cliffs, NJ: Prentice Hall, 1990), 832.

commentary on Romans 5:12–21 which treats of the first element of the threefold liberation that Christ brings.

In accord with the common exegetical tradition, Aquinas states at the start of his commentary on this passage that St. Paul's theme in 5:12–21 is that through Christ's grace we are freed from the slavery of sin. Reflecting the logic of St. Paul's argument, Aquinas's exposition of these ten verses falls into two sections of two *lectiones* each: (1) *the history of sin* is taken up in two steps, first (in 5:12) the origin of sin and death and their entry into the world (*lectio* 3, nn. 406–20), and then (in 5:13–14) the existence of sin and death even under the law (*lectio* 4, nn. 421–29); (2) *the history of grace* concerns how Christ removed sin, first (in 5:15–19), insofar as it entered the world through one man (*lectio* 5, nn. 430–47), and then (in 5:20–21) insofar as it proliferated after the coming of the law (*lectio* 6, nn. 448–67).

Canon Dabrowski identifies the hermeneutical principle at work in the Pauline commentaries in two passages early in the Romans commentary where Aquinas calls Christ the "content of the Gospels" (*"materiam evangelii"*) and then where he states that "the Son of God is deservedly called the subject matter of the Holy Scriptures" (*"Convenienter autem Filius Dei materia Sanctarum Scripturarum esse dicitur"*).[7] This principle lends to the commentaries a Christological and Christocentric character, even as they present "a rich doctrine of original sin."[8] This point is of critical importance for a correct reading of Aquinas's exposition of chapter 5 of Romans. Not just the sin of Adam but the grace of Christ as well are at the center of our attention: not just the history of sin, but all the more so the history of grace. We need to know what sin and death are in order to grasp what Christ's grace has won for us.

The mature skills of a *magister sacrae paginae* are fully on display in Aquinas's commentary on Romans 5:12–21. A striking feature

---

7. *Expositio super S. Pauli Apostoli epistolam ad Romanos* (hereafter: *In Rom.*), c. 1, lect. 2, n. 28 and n. 29, in *Super Epistolas S. Pauli Lectura*; English translation, *Commentary on Romans*, by Fabian Larcher, OP (Steubenville, OH: Emmaus Academic, 2020).

8. Dabrowski, "La dottrina sul peccato originale nei commenti di san Tommaso d'Aquino," 561.

of the text of the commentary—something to which it will not be possible to do justice in this paper—is the constant and ample reference to texts from everywhere in the Bible. The classic Christian understanding of the Bible as one, internally cross-referenced book, centered on Christ and the economy of salvation, is at work here. A condition for such a comprehensive theological hermeneutics is, of course, a mastery of the content of the individual books of the Bible from Genesis to Revelation—precisely what was to be presupposed in a qualified "master of the sacred page." The unity and inner coherence of the Bible form the basis for the exegesis of each passage in what has lately come to be called a "canonical" interpretation.[9]

The theological hermeneutics at work in this commentary is not only comprehensive. It is also cumulative. Each passage and verse are to be read, not in an interpretive vacuum, but within the context of a tradition of reading, understanding, and teaching. A *magister sacrae paginae* like Aquinas is aware that he is not the first reader to have pondered the meaning of these verses. Thus, at crucial points in his commentary, one finds St. Thomas engaged with other key figures in the tradition of Pauline exegesis—principally, here, Ambrose and Augustine.[10] Especially where his interpretation seems to diverge from theirs, he is concerned to show the broad coherence they share with his reading—one which takes its place in a cumulative tradition of reading and interpretation which it both represents and then seeks to enlarge and deepen.

The hermeneutics of Aquinas is properly *theological*: here the doctrines of the Catholic faith function, we might say, rulishly. They guide the Catholic exegete, who reads these texts with the eyes of faith, to interpret the Sacred Scriptures in accord with the Revelation they contain. Although a reading that is consistent with

9. See Brevard S. Childs, *The Church's Guide for Reading Paul: The Canonical Shaping of the Pauline Corpus* (Grand Rapids, MI: Eerdmans, 2008), 1–27.

10. See Mark Johnson, "Augustine and Aquinas on Original Sin: Doctrine, Authority, and Pedagogy," in *Aquinas the Augustinian*, ed. Michael Dauphinais, Barry David, and Matthew Levering (Washington, DC: The Catholic University of America Press, 2007), 145–58.

Catholic doctrine is important for the entire Bible, it is particularly significant in the rare instances where the official Magisterium has construed a passage authoritatively, as is the case with Romans 5:12. Here the doctrine of the Church has been clear. "Revelation … enunciates one essential point about original sin: every man is heir to true sin just by being a member of the human race. This is the mystery."[11] The genre of the commentary entails verse-by-verse exegesis rather than a systematic presentation of the theology of original sin. For the complete teaching of Aquinas on these topics, one would have to consult the parallel discussions in his other works. Still, many of the key elements of the doctrine of original sin and our liberation from sin and death in Christ come up for discussion in the Aquinas's commentary on Romans 5:12–21.

THE HISTORY OF SIN: THE ORIGIN OF SIN AND DEATH (ROM 5:12)

The entirety of *lectio* 3 of Chapter 5 is devoted just to verse 12 in which St. Paul describes the entry of sin and death into the world: "*Propterea, sicut per unum hominem peccatum in hunc mundum intravit, et per peccatum mors: ita et in omnes homines mors pertransiit, in quo omnes peccaverunt*"; "Wherefore as by one man sin entered into this world and by sin death: and so death passed upon all men, in whom all have sinned."[12]

After noting that, against the Pelagians, St. Augustine construed this verse to mean that sin entered the world not only by imitation (of actual sins, that is, according to the Pelagians) but also by propagation, Aquinas plunges directly into the difficulties that this doctrine poses. The first difficulty he raises is perhaps the most acute. Aquinas says: "But it seems impossible that sin be passed from one person to another by carnal origin."[13] Sin is in the soul, and guilt

---

11. T. C. O'Brien, OP, "Introduction," *Summa Theologiae, volume 26 (1a2ae. 81–85): Original Sin* (New York and London: McGraw-Hill, and Eyre & Spottiswoode, 1965), xxii.

12. *In Rom.*, c. 5, lect. 3, *titolo*.

13. *In Rom.*, c. 5, lect. 3, n. 408.

must be voluntary: how can they be physically transmitted? As the exposition continues, more difficulties emerge. According to the Scriptures, Adam repented of his sin: if so, why didn't this repentance cancel out the inheritance of sin? Why have we not inherited the effects of the other sins of our first parents? What is more, according to Genesis, Eve sinned before Adam: should not Paul say that sin entered the world through a woman rather than through a man? Moreover, death is natural: how can Paul say that death is the consequence of sin when it is evident that all material things—anything that has a body—are perishable? If sin affects all the descendants of Adam, how come it doesn't affect Christ who is said to be sinless? And finally, does not St. Paul contradict our faith that Baptism removes sin?

Addressing these issues in turn, Aquinas begins with the seeming impossibility of the physical transmission of a spiritual property. Part of the answer lies in the receptivity of the body to the infusion of the soul which is adapted to the body according to the principle that whatever is received exists in the mode of the receiver.[14] But if a defect is transmitted by a source that is in some way defective, this does not involve guilt on the part of the one who inherits the defect. "Therefore, it must be admitted that as actual sin is a person's sin, because it is committed through the will of the person sinning, so original sin is the sin of the nature committed through the source of human nature."[15] To explain how this might be the case, Aquinas offers the analogy of the body and its various members. If the hand is involved in a sin, the source of the guilt for the action lies principally in the will of the person who uses his hand to commit the sin and only derivatively in the hand itself. In a similar way, the disorder of human nature derives from the will of Adam who is the source of human nature and this disorder carries with it "the notion of guilt in

14. *In Rom.*, c. 5, lect. 3, n. 408.

15. *In Rom.*, c. 5, lect. 3, n. 409: "*Et ideo dicendum est, quod sicut peccatum actuale est peccatum personae, quia per voluntatem personae peccantis committitur, ita peccatum originale est peccatum naturae, quod per voluntatem principii humanae naturae commissum est.*"

all who obtain that nature precisely as susceptible to guilt."[16] Just as an actual sin extends to the various members by reason of the personal act of the one who commits it, so original sin extends to each human being by the natural act of generation.

By generation, therefore, human nature is passed on along with the defect it acquired from the sin of the first parent. According to Aquinas, this defect is nothing other than the lack of original justice that was conferred by God upon the first parent not only as an individual person but also as the source of human nature. Original justice was to have been passed on to his progeny along with human nature. Instead, having lost it by his sin, the first parent could not pass on original justice. This defect has the aspect of guilt in his descendants in the way that the guilt of a person's members derives from the actual sin that he willfully commits.

Neither Adam's repentance for his first sin nor his subsequent actual sins—nor for that matter the sins of other men—can be passed on by generation because these are strictly personal acts. Only through the first sin could the good of nature, originally intended to be inheritable, be lost. What is more, Adam's repentance did not extend beyond him personally.[17] For this reason, St. Paul states that "sin" not "sins" entered the world through one man.[18] Even though Eve sinned before Adam, only through the sin of Adam—who was the source of human nature—could the resulting absence of original justice be transmitted to the human beings who followed.[19]

St. Paul's assertion that death entered the world through sin must be understood in the light of what has been said so far about the loss of original justice. Certainly, from the perspective of the structure of human nature as such, one could say that death is natural since, due to the presence of matter in its composition, the human body is perishable. But, in the state of original justice, the human mind was ordered to God, the lower powers of the soul to the human mind,

---

16. *In Rom.*, c. 5, lect. 3, n. 410.
17. *In Rom.*, c. 5, lect. 3, n. 411.
18. *In Rom.*, c. 5, lect. 3, n. 412.
19. *In Rom.*, c. 5, lect. 3, nn. 413–14.

the body to the soul, and all external things to man. Ordered to the soul, the human body would receive life from it uninterruptedly and would never be susceptible to harm on the part of any external agents. It was the plan of divine providence that "the rational soul, being incorruptible, deserved an incorruptible body."[20] Divine power thus provided to the soul whatever was lacking in human nature to maintain the body incorrupt. With the loss of original justice, "after man's mind was turned from God through sin," he lost the ability to control the lower powers and the body, as well as external things, and so became subject to death from within and to violence from without.[21]

Sin and death are indeed universal to human nature—lacking in original justice—as it has been passed on by Adam. But this is not true of Christ whose bodily substance derived from Adam through the Blessed Virgin but in whose generation the active principle was not Adam but the Holy Spirit. We derive human nature from Adam, both in bodily substance and in his role as active principle in our generation. For this reason, we inherit the lack of original justice which he passed on with human nature. But this is not true of Christ.[22]

Finally, to the question of the perdurance of the transmission of original sin after Baptism, Aquinas responds that through Baptism the mind is freed from sin, but not the flesh, and, since it is the flesh and not the mind that begets children, a man cannot transmit to his descendants the new life of Christ but only the old life of Adam.[23]

THE HISTORY OF SIN: THE EXISTENCE OF SIN AND DEATH UNDER THE LAW (ROM 5:13–14)

In *lectio* 4, Aquinas turns his attention to the relationship of sin and the law as St. Paul presents it in verses 13 and 14: "*Usque ad legem*

20. *In Rom.,* c. 5, lect. 3, n. 416.
21. *In Rom.,* c. 5, lect. 3, n. 416.
22. *In Rom.,* c. 5, lect. 3, n. 419.
23. *In Rom.,* c. 5, lect. 3, n. 420.

*enim peccatum erat in mundo. Peccatum autem non imputabatur cum
lex non esset. Sed regnavit mors ab Adam usque ad Moysen, etiam in eos
qui non peccaverunt in similitudinem praevaricationis Adae, qui est for-
ma futuri*"; "For until the law sin was in the world: but sin was not
imputed, when the law was not. But death reigned from Adam unto
Moses, even over those who did not sin after the likeness of the
transgression of Adam, who is a figure of him who was to come."[24]

The theme of these verses, as Aquinas reads them, is that, although neither the natural law nor the Mosaic Law could remove
sin or free us from death, they could nonetheless cause knowledge of
sins not previously recognized.[25] The original sin that is in the child
even before the use of reason (in this sense, *before* the natural law) is
reckoned by God even though it is not imputed by men. Before the
Law of Moses, actual sins not explicitly prohibited by the Law were
not imputed because they were not recognized as sinful, while sins
against the natural law were reckoned against those who violated the
precepts of the natural law. Although sins were not imputed before
the Law, death—both physical and spiritual (eternal damnation)—
reigned or exercised power over men. Aquinas suggests that St. Paul
is implying that we know that sin existed, though it was not imputed
before the Law, because death reigned even over children who committed no actual sins (i.e., those whose sins were not like the transgression of Adam).

Aquinas develops this point further in connection with an in-
triguing question to which St. Paul's language here and earlier gives
rise.[26] Having stated in the previous chapter that "where there is
no law, there is no transgression" (4:15) and in this chapter that
"through one man sin entered the world" (4:12), does not St. Paul
seem to imply that, as it is a transgression of the divine law, sin entered the world not through one man but through the Law? According to Aquinas, the words "until the law sin was in the world" are

24. *In Rom.*, c. 5, lect. 4, *titolo.*
25. *In Rom.*, c. 5, lect. 4, nn. 422–25.
26. *In Rom.*, c. 5, lect. 4, nn. 427–28.

introduced by St. Paul precisely to exclude this misreading. Both original and actual sin were in the world, but it was not "imputed"— it was not recognized as something to be punished by God since the law did not exist. But what St. Paul intends to convey is that original sin was in the world and that it entered through Adam. The fact that children and the just who did not sin mortally—who were, in other words, without personal sin—died nonetheless shows that Adam's sin had been spread to them by origin.

THE HISTORY OF GRACE: CHRIST REMOVES THE SIN OF ADAM (ROM 5:15–19)

Comparing the gift of Christ to the transgression of Adam, St. Paul turns from the history of sin to the history of grace when he states in verse 15: "*Sed non sicut delictum ita et donum. Si enim unius delicto multi mortui sunt, multo magis gratia Dei et donum in gratia unius hominis Iesu Christi in plures abundavit*"; "But the gift is not like the trespass. For if many died through one man's trespass, much more have the grace of God and the gift of grace of that one man Jesus Christ abounded for many."[27] The efficacy of Christ's grace far exceeds that of Adam's sin.[28] For sin is caused by the weakness of the human will, while grace flows from the immensity of the divine goodness. "The power of grace exceeds every sin."[29] Even though Adam's sin brought death to many, God's grace extends not only to the remission of Adam's sin but also to remove actual sins and to bestow abundant blessings.

In verse 16, according to Aquinas, St. Paul continues the comparison between the grace of Christ and the sin of Adam by considering their effects: "*Et non sicut per unum peccatum, ita et donum; nam iudicium quidem ex uno in condemnationem, gratia autem ex multis delictis in iustificationem*"; "And the gift is not like the effect of that one's

27. *In Rom.*, c. 5, lect. 5, *titolo*.
28. *In Rom.*, c. 5, lect. 5, nn. 431–34.
29. *In Rom.*, c. 5, lect. 5, n. 431.

man's sin. For the judgment following one trespass brought condemnation, but the free gift following many trespasses brings justification."[30] Christ's grace had a greater effect than Adam's sin.[31] Because the grace of Christ entails a more powerful agency than the sin of Adam, it produces a greater effect. Adam's sin brought condemnation on all men, while Christ's grace extends not only to original sin, but also to many actual sins and brings the complete cleansing of justification.

According to Aquinas's construal of this passage,[32] St. Paul in verse 17 offers the first part of a twofold proof for the affirmation contained in the preceding verse: "*In enim unius delicto mors regnavit per unum, multo magis abundantiam gratiae et donationis et iustitiae accipientes in vita regnabunt per unum Iesum Christum*"; "If, because of one man's trespass, death reigned through that one man, much more will those who receive the abundance of grace and the gift of justice reign in life through the one man Jesus Christ."[33] The first premise of the first proof, according to Aquinas, is contained in the words: "If, because of one man's trespass, death reigned through that one man," as St. Paul has argued up to this point. The words, "those who receive the abundance of grace and the gift of justice," express the minor premise. Explaining that the remission of sins cannot be won by any merits of ours but is due only to the grace of Christ, Aquinas refers to Romans 11:6: "If it is from works, it is no longer by grace." The conclusion of this first argument, fittingly introduced by the term "*igitur*," comes in verse 18: "*Igitur, sicut per unius delictum in omnes homines in condemnationem, sic et per unius iustitiam in omnes homines in iustificationem vitae*"; "Therefore as one man's trespass led to condemnation for all men, so one man's justice leads to acquittal and life for all men."[34]

But this conclusion seems to be false, according to Aquinas,

---

30. *In Rom.*, c. 5, lect. 5, *titolo*.
31. *In Rom.*, c. 5, lect. 5, nn. 435–37.
32. *In Rom.*, c. 5, lect. 5, nn. 438–40.
33. *In Rom.*, c. 5, lect. 6, *titolo*.
34. *In Rom.*, c. 5, lect. 5, *titolo*.

because, although all men do in fact die as a result of the sin of Adam, not all men are justified by Christ.[35] The point of the argument, however, is to affirm that all men *who are justified* receive justification through Christ. One could say that this justification is capable of justifying all men, but de facto it reaches only those who have faith in Christ. "As no one dies except through Adam's sin, so no one is justified except through Christ's righteousness, and this is brought about by faith in him"[36]—including those who lived before and after the resurrection.

According to Aquinas, St. Paul then states the second proof in verse 19: "*Sicut enim per inobedientiam unius hominis peccatores constituti sunt multi, ita et per unius obeditionem iusti constituentur multi*"; "For as by one man disobedience many were made sinners, so by one man's obedience many will be made just."[37] The argument appeals to the similarity between cause and effect: just as Adam's disobedience—*unrighteous* in character—made men unrighteous, so Christ's obedience—*righteous* in character—made them righteous.[38] While it is true that pride is the beginning of all sin (Sir 10:13), the first step of pride consists in an unwillingness to be subject to God's precepts, which pertains to disobedience. Thus, "man's first sin seems to have been disobedience, not as far as the outward action was concerned but in regard to the inner movement of pride, by which he wills to go against the divine command."[39] Christ's obedience, on the other hand, consisted in his acceptance of death for the sake of our salvation in accord with the Father's command.

---

35. *In Rom.*, c. 5, lect. 5, nn. 443–44.
36. *In Rom.*, c. 5, lect. 5, n. 444.
37. *In Rom.*, c. 5, lect. 5, *titolo*.
38. *In Rom.* c. 5, lect. 5, n. 445.
39. *In Rom.* c. 5, lect. 5, n. 446.

THE HISTORY OF GRACE: THE ABUNDANCE
OF THE GRACE OF CHRIST (ROM 5:20–21)

St. Thomas devotes *lectio* 6 to the final verses of chapter 5: "*Lex autem subintravit ut abundaret delictum. Ubi autem abundavit delictum, superabundavit gratia; ut sicut reganvit peccatum in mortem, ita et gratia regent per iustitiam in vitam aeternam per Iesum Christum Dominum nostrum*" ("Now the law entered in secretly that sin might abound. And where sin abounded, grace super-abounded, that as sin has reigned unto death, so grace might reign by justice unto life everlasting, through Jesus Christ our Lord").[40]

St. Paul's language in verse 20 creates a difficult problem, as Aquinas notes at the start. It seems to suggest that the purpose of the law was to make sin increase. Aquinas summarizes the solutions to this difficulty provided by a Gloss whose overall force is to suggest that the law was not the cause but more properly the occasion of the multiplication of sin.[41] Experience shows that what the law forbids is desired all the more. There are various psychological reasons for this. Things that are forbidden engage a greater level of energy than things that are easy to attain. Emotions and desires that are repressed for fear of punishment tend to build up when there is no outlet for them. We often do not bother about seeking things that we can have for the taking, but, when it comes our way, we jump at the opportunity to have what is forbidden. In the end, law seems more to exacerbate that to allay concupiscent desire. Contrary to the will of the legislator, human law—which cannot confer the grace of diminishing concupiscence—causes sin to multiply. It is true that the giving of the law caused sin to multiply in some people, but for those who love virtue, by the help of grace, the prohibitions of the law brought them to the perfection of virtue.

Aquinas adds his own explanation of the meaning of verse 20 by

---

40. *In Rom.*, c. 5, lect. 6, *titolo*.
41. *In Rom.*, c. 5, lect. 6, nn. 452–60.

distinguishing five senses of "law," each supported by a biblical citation. According to scriptural usage, the term can designate: (1) the entire Old Testament; (2) the five books of Moses; (3) the precepts of the Decalogue; (4) the entire content of the ceremonial precepts of the law; or lastly (5) a particular ceremonial precept. Aquinas suggests that, in this section of Romans, St. Paul uses the term "law" in a general way, referring to "the total doctrine of the Mosaic Law."[42] Given that the entire Mosaic Law includes the ceremonial precepts— which prescribe rites that did not give man the grace to fulfill the moral precepts or control concupiscence—it can be said that the law at least could not *reduce* sin and thus could be said to have increased it.[43] In this connection, the end of the law must be taken into account, as well as the different types of persons to whom it is directed: to the recalcitrant type of person, the moral precepts were enjoined by threats of punishment and the ceremonial precepts to prevent them from the worship of idols; to ordinary people, the law had a pedagogical function—the moral precepts advancing them toward justice and the ceremonial precepts restraining them in divine worship; for the perfect, the ceremonial precepts were given as a sign and the moral precepts as a consolation.[44]

That sin abounded under the law placed no obstacle in the way of God's plan for the salvation of the Jews and for the whole human race. St. Paul declares that where sin abounded, grace super-abounded. Aquinas gives two reasons for this. The first is that, just as a serious illness requires strong medicine, so an abundant grace is needed to heal an abundance of sin. The second reason is that, while some sinners despair at the enormity of their sins, others, with the help of grace, are humbled by them and thus obtain a more abundant grace.[45] So it is that, just as sin attained complete dominion over men and led them to physical and spiritual death, so the

42. *In Rom.*, c. 5, lect. 6, n. 461.
43. *In Rom.*, c. 5, lect. 6, n. 462.
44. *In Rom.*, c. 5, lect. 6, n. 463.
45. *In Rom.*, c. 5, lect. 6, nn. 465–66.

grace of God reigns in us through justice, and all this through the giver of grace, Jesus Christ our Lord.[46]

THE LASTING THEOLOGICAL SIGNIFICANCE OF THE COMMENTARY ON ROMANS 5:12–21

We may note some of the salient features of Aquinas's mature theology of original sin. We know from divine revelation *that*, but not *how*, sin passes to all of Adam's progeny. The doctrine itself neither proposes nor depends on a theory of transmission. The most fundamental elements of the Christian faith are in play here. God's intention in creating human persons was to make them participants in the divine life and to share the communion of trinitarian life with them. For this reason, according to Aquinas, the first human beings were created in grace. Only from divine revelation itself do we know that the first human beings momentously turned away from this invitation to share in divine life, and, further, that their doing so had inescapable consequences for the human race that could only be undone by Christ. According to Catholic doctrine, just by virtue of being part of the human race, all human beings are born in a state of sin—a state that is thus said to be acquired not by *imitation* but by *propagation*.[47]

We are all aware of the considerable intellectual difficulties that this doctrine poses. "[O]f all the religious teachings I know," writes the Evangelical author Alan Jacobs in a recent book on original sin, "none—not even the belief that some people are eternally damned—generates as much hostility as the Christian doctrine we call 'original sin.'"[48] As we have seen, Aquinas would concur with what Jacobs sees as the fundamental problem: even if one accepts

46. *In Rom.*, c. 5, lect. 6, n. 467.

47. See Rudi Te Velde, "Evil, Sin and Death: Thomas Aquinas on Original Sin," in *The Theology of Thomas Aquinas*, ed. R. Van Nieuwenhove and J. Wawrykow (Notre Dame, IN: University of Notre Dame Press, 2005), 143–66.

48. Alan Jacobs, *Original Sin: A Cultural History* (New York: HarperCollins, 2008), viii.

that there was such a thing as a "first sin," how could this act influence or cause subsequent sinful acts by human beings who come after the so-called "first parents"? Moreover, how could all their "progeny" be culpable or guilty of this first sin? How can someone be guilty prior to any personal choice or moral action?

It does not help to suggest, as G. K. Chesterton famously remarked, that, of all Christian doctrines, this the only one that can be demonstrated by empirical evidence.[49] For the doctrine of original sin is not the conclusion of observation and reflection on the presence of moral evil in the world. The most compelling *empirical* explanation for this undeniable feature of the human landscape is simply that people commit personal sins. There is no need to appeal to a theory of inherited sin. In fact, the doctrine of original sin is a *datum* of revelation. We learn about the peril of our state—the radical alienation from God which is the human condition—and our need for Christ the Savior only through the witness of the Sacred Scriptures and constant Tradition.[50]

These premises are fundamental to Aquinas's presentation. His method is to address the ways in which this doctrine can be made intelligible and can be shown to follow "the pattern of nature." As Aquinas says, "Where authority is wanting, we should shape our opinions to the pattern of nature."[51]

Aquinas's approach points the way to the resolution of the many of the difficulties the doctrine has posed over the centuries.[52] The history of theological reflection on this topic makes for fascinating reading. A series of articles helps us to track the twentieth century

---

49. Cited by Jacobs, *Original Sin*, x.

50. See André-Marie Dubarle, *Le Péché Originel: Ecriture et Tradition* (Paris: Les Editions du Cerf, 1999).

51. *Summa theologiae* I, q. 101, a. 1.

52. See Marie-Michel Labourdette, OP, *La Péché Originel et les Origines de l'Homme* (Paris: Alsatia, 1953); Marie-Michel Labourdette, OP, "*Anthropologie théologique et péché originel*," *Revue Thomiste* 73 (1973): 643–63; Marie-Michel Labourdette, OP, "*Aux origines du péché de l'homme d'après saint Thomas d'Aquin: Dans le courant de la tradition*," *Revue Thomiste* 85 (1985): 357–98; Jean-Hervé Nicolas, OP, "*L'Origine du Mal*," in *Synthése Dogmatique: Complément* (Fribourg: Éditions Universitaires Fribourg Suisse, 1993), 371–96.

developments[53] and thus supplement Henri Rondet's generally reliable account.[54]

Two critically significant elements in Aquinas's theology of original sin address some of the most vexing issues that have arisen in recent writing: (1) his insistence that the first personal sin of Adam was not merely the transgression of an arbitrary command, but an interior disobedience rooted in pride, that could be rectified only by the perfect obedience of the Son, and (2) his understanding of original sin in us as a lack of original justice—a lack of facility in choosing the good not a fatal inclination to evil. Thus, he locates the doctrine of original sin within the context of the factors that affect moral action.[55] These crucial elements, as we have seen, feature in his commentary on Romans 5:12–21 as well as in his other mature works.[56]

We have seen that he touches on many of the most neuralgic points in the doctrine of original sin, but some issues he did not consider explicitly. The most serious new objections come from modern biblical interpretation,[57] and evolutionary theory[58] and socio-

53. James L. Connor, "Original Sin: Contemporary Approaches," *Theological Studies* 29 (1968): 215–40; Stephen J. Duffy, "Our Hearts of Darkness: Original Sin Revisited," *Theological Studies* 49 (1988): 597–622; Brian McDermott, SJ, "The Theology of Original Sin: Recent Developments," *Theological Studies* 38 (1977): 478–512; Kevin A. McMahon, "The Christological Turn in Recent Literature on Original Sin," *The Thomist* 66 (2002): 201–29; Kevin A. McMahon, "Karl Rahner and the Theology of Human Origins," *The Thomist* 66 (2002): 499–517.

54. Henri Rondet, *Original Sin: The Patristic and Theological Background* (New York: Alba House, 1972).

55. See Terence W. Irwin, *The Development of Ethics: A Historical and Critical Study*, vol. 1. (New York: Oxford University Press, 2007), 635–38.

56. For a brief overview, see Joseph Wawrykow, "Original Sin," in *The Westminster Handbook to Thomas Aquinas* (Louisville, KY: Westminster John Knox, 2005), 103–4.

57. See Hans W. Frei, *The Eclipse of Biblical Narrative* (New Haven, CT: Yale University Press, 1974).

58. See Jerry D. Korsmeyer, *Evolution and Eden: Balancing Original Sin and Contemporary Science* (New York: Paulist Press, 1998); Jean-Michel Maldamé, "Que peut-on dire du péché originel à la lumière des connaissances actuelles sur l'origine de l'humanité: Péché originel, péché d'Adam et péché du monde," *Bulletin de littérature ecclésiastique* 97 (1996): 3–27; Daryl P. Domning and Monica K. Hellwig, *Original Selfishness: Original Sin and Evil in the Light of Evolution* (Aldershot: Ashgate, 2006).

biology.[59] Both sets of issues in a sense concern the historicity of the first parents and their first sin—something that Aquinas not only assumed but took to be fundamental to the Catholic doctrine of the economy of salvation. It has become commonplace to construe modern biblical criticism as entailing the view that the account of the first sin in Genesis as a myth that conveys a universal truth[60] rather than, with classical exegesis, as a historical narrative conveying factual truths. While it is clear that we cannot regard Genesis as strict history, we must nonetheless regard it—as did Aquinas and all traditional exegetes and theologians—as a symbolic rendering of what really happened, utilizing mythic elements in a kind of history-like or "realistic narrative,"[61] or "the history of the first human beings in the manner of traditional narratives."[62]

The approach of Aquinas in addressing difficulties of this kind, in stark contrast to much Enlightenment thinking, teaches us to take our methodological orientation from the criterion of intelligibility rather than the criterion of reasonableness. It is a theology that does not put God to the test, as it were calling him to the bar of human reason, but rather one that acknowledges the limits of human rationality and the unlimited character of the intelligibility of divine truth and the divine plan in which it is manifested. It is in this light that Aquinas offers his explanation of our membership in the human race as a way of understanding, in line with Catholic doctrine, how original sin could be said to have been transmitted—how sin and death entered the world through one man—and how, "as sin reigned unto death, so also grace might reign by justice unto life everlasting, through Jesus Christ our Lord." While the criterion of

59. See Patricia A. Williams, *Doing without Adam and Eve: Sociobiology and Original Sin* (Minneapolis: Fortress Press, 2001).

60. As, for example, Leon R. Kass, *The Beginning of Wisdom: Reading Genesis* (New York: Free Press, 2003) and, in a different way, Elaine Pagels, *Adam, Eve and the Serpent* (New York: Random House, 1988).

61. See Frei, *Theology and Narrative: Selected Essays*, ed. George Hunsinger and William C. Placher (New York: Oxford University Press, 1993), 142–43.

62. See Benedict Ashley, OP, *Theologies of the Body* (Braintree, MA: The Pope John XXIII Center, 1985), 373.

reasonableness allows only what makes sense to us, the criterion of intelligibility draws the human mind into the fullness of divine truth. No wonder, then, that in the friar's dream, after approving of Saint Thomas's teaching "what could be understood from his epistles in this life," Saint Paul should remind him that there would come a time "when he would understand them according to their whole truth."

CHAPTER 13

Not Born Bad
The Catholic Truth About Original Sin in a Thomistic Perspective

INTRODUCTION

According to James Boyce, Westerners have typically "believed that they were 'born bad' because they had inherited the sin of the first humans." In his recent book *Born Bad: Original Sin and the Making of the Western World,* Boyce argues that Christianity in the West "stood alone [among the religions] in seeing the eating of the forbidden fruit in the Garden of Eden as the original sin—not only the first sin in human history, but also one that subsequently became innate to the human condition."[1] Boyce is probably right that, whether or not they are Christians, many people do seem to believe that they were born bad. What lies behind this situation, however, is not an authentic Catholic doctrine of original sin, but a deeply flawed understanding of this doctrine—in some cases spawned within Christianity itself—according to which human beings are

This chapter began as the 2016 Edward Cardinal Egan Memorial Lecture, sponsored by the Magnificat Foundation, delivered at the New York University Catholic Center, 21 May 2016. This was subsequently published in *The Thomist* 81 (2017): 345–59. Used with permission.

1. James Boyce, *Born Bad: Original Sin and the Making of the Western World* (Berkeley, CA: Counterpoint, 2015), 3.

born with an essentially corrupted human nature along with an innate inclination to evil.

This misunderstanding is seriously in need of correction. "[O]f all the religious teachings I know," writes the Evangelical author Alan Jacobs in his book on the cultural impact of the doctrine, "none—not even the belief that some people are eternally damned—generates as much hostility as the Christian doctrine we call 'original sin.'"[2] Not only hostility but loss of faith and separation from the Church are among some other consequences of this misunderstanding. A straightforward presentation of the Catholic truth about original sin is the best antidote for this and other misunderstandings of the doctrine. Many have found the account presented by St. Thomas Aquinas in his *Summa Theologiae* to be the most balanced and intelligible account of this doctrine. This presentation will rely on him this evening.

THE NATURE OF THE FIRST SIN

Let's begin with what happened in the garden as recounted in the book of Genesis. What was the nature of the first sin? What fault was it, according to divine revelation, that Adam and Eve committed?

In his analysis of the nature of another fault—that of the fallen angels—St. Thomas Aquinas asks what sort of sin it could have been (*STh* I, q. 63, a. 1–3). Eliminating those capital sins which can be committed only by persons with bodies, he is left with the spiritual sin of pride: it is traditionally said that the sin of the fallen angels was that they wanted to be like God. But what is wrong with wanting to be like God, Aquinas asks; this seems to be an altogether admirable thing to desire. Their sin lay, he concludes, in their wanting to possess this likeness to God, not as his gift, *but as their due.*

The parable of the wicked husbandmen (Mt 21:33–44) dramatizes

2. Alan Jacobs, *Original Sin: A Cultural History* (New York: Harper Collins, 2008), viii.

just this sort of sin—by no means restricted to the angelic realm. The parable recounts the story of a landlord who sends servants to his vineyard to collect from the tenants his share of the harvest. The tenants treat the servants badly—beating, stoning and even killing them. In the end, the landlord sends his son, thinking that the tenants will respect him.

But when the tenants see the son, they say to themselves, "This is the heir; come let us kill him and get the inheritance." The situation here is one in which tenants could realistically expect to inherit the property of an absentee landlord upon the death of the last heir. Seeing the son, the tenants in this parable presume (wrongly) that the landowner is dead, and they kill the son and heir in order to get the vineyard for themselves—thus taking by violence what would eventually have been theirs as an inheritance or, more to the point, as a kind of gift.

Here we are close to the nature of sin—not only that of the fallen angels, but also that of Adam and Eve as it is recounted in the book of Genesis. Indeed, it is precisely the Devil, in the form of the serpent, who suggests to Adam and Eve the very sin that caused his own downfall. Encouraging them to eat from the only tree in the garden that God has forbidden to them, he concludes enticingly: "For God knows that when you eat of it your eyes will be opened and you will be like God, knowing good and evil" (Gn 3:5). This primordial sin of wanting to take from God what could only be given as a gift is tantamount to a rejection of the gift as such, the gift that would be nothing less than a share in His own divine life. Who can have the communion of life with God as his due? Only the Father, Son, and Holy Spirit. No creaturely person—angelic or human—clearly. To become "like" God in this sense can only come as a gift. The first sin was not simply the violation of a seemingly arbitrary command on the part of our first parents—to cite the frequent caricature—but a serious transgression affecting their relationship with God in a profound way.

To understand why this sin of our first parents had consequences for them and for us, and why God willed to take time to remedy these consequences through the Incarnation, Passion, Death, and Resurrection of his only-begotten Son, an analogy might help. Suppose that on a visit to your house, I deliberately break a precious Japanese vase in a fit of anger. Suppose that you forgive me for this action. Still, you cannot bring the vase back. Even if you have it repaired, it will always be that now-restored-broken vase. Consider a more serious example. Suppose I reveal to another something you tell me in confidence, indeed something that you above all want to conceal from that very person. Suppose that you forgive me. Still, what can undo the harm I have set in motion? Are you likely to confide in me again? I don't think so. These, and many other examples you could no doubt provide, may be taken to illustrate what might be called seemingly "irreparable" harms. Damage is done that cannot readily be undone. Words are spoken that cannot be withdrawn. Even where forgiveness is generous and ungrudging, the passage of time and appropriate measures are needed to repair the harm that lingers in the wake of certain words and deeds, both for the wrongdoer and for others affected by his actions. The sin of our first parents is like this.

Christian revelation teaches us that this actual sin on the part of our first parents had inescapable consequences for them and for their descendants, and that God—accommodating our salvation to the nature of the fault, and thus to our human nature—mercifully willed to take the time needed to prepare us for the coming of our "great Redeemer." By God's grace, the history of salvation coincides, we might say, with the history of the human race.

THE LOSS OF THE STATE OF ORIGINAL JUSTICE: CONSEQUENCES OF SIN FOR ADAM AND EVE

In order to understand the consequences of the sin of Adam and Eve for them, we need to understand something of the state of original justice in which they were created. Following St. Anselm,[3]

3. Jean Baptiste Kors, OP, *La justice primitive et le péché originel d'apres S. Thomas* (Le Saulchoir, Kain, Belgium: *Revue des sciences philosophiques et theologiques*, 1922), 23–24.

Aquinas maintained that original sin is the absence of original justice, "the disordered disposition rising from the dissolution of that harmony in which original justice consisted" (*STh* I-II, q. 82, a. 1–3). Aquinas insists that original justice entails that the first human beings be created in the state of grace—"concreated" to use the technical term. Given what we know from revelation about God's purpose in creating persons with whom to share his life, it would make no sense, Aquinas thinks, to create them from the start in a state where such participation would have been impossible. Thus, for Aquinas, original justice was a "concomitant of the nature of the species [*accidens naturae speciei*] not as being caused by the basic elements of the species, but as a gift given by God to human nature as a whole" (*STh* I, q. 100, a. 1). "Original justice was a particular gift of grace divinely bestowed upon all human nature in the first parent" (*STh* I-II, q. 81, a. 2).

This is a hugely important point. In God's plan for the human race, there is no room for an interval of time—however brief—in which creaturely persons would have existed outside the ambit of grace. To be sure, there had to be an opportunity for the free embrace of the grace of communion on their part, but such an embrace would only be possible for persons already in the state of grace. Thus, for Aquinas, both pure spirits—the angels—and embodied persons—human beings—were concreated in grace and thus free to embrace the communion on offer.

For the angels, with immediate intuitive knowledge, no interval of time was necessary to embrace, or fail to embrace, the divine offer of communion. Like the angels, human beings were concreated in grace; unlike them, some interval of time was needed for them freely to embrace divine communion and a share in divine life.

This gift of sanctifying grace is the essential element in the supernatural state of original justice—"supernatural" not only in being beyond human nature and entirely unmerited, but also and properly in entailing a share or participation in the divine life that transcends the possibilities of human nature on its own. The term "supernatural" in its proper theological sense signifies the transformed and elevated human nature of persons now enabled to live life at a new level of divine charity and communion. It is "natural" only to the three divine persons—each consubstantially sharing the one divine nature—to share simultaneously in this communion of trinitarian life. Only by grace can persons who are not God share in his life by adoptive participation in Christ and the Holy Spirit.

Within the state of original justice, sanctifying grace was the principle of the perfections of human nature as such. Not only was human nature drawn into a participation in the divine life, but it was also perfected in itself by other "preternatural" gifts. Freedom from bodily suffering and death was in keeping with the natural immortality of the soul. The gift of a harmony in human emotions was in accord with the control that right reason is meant to exercise. The ordering of the whole human person to the supreme love of God brought into harmony the whole ensemble.

PRIVATION OF ORIGINAL JUSTICE: CONSEQUENCES FOR US

St. Thomas's theology of original sin is located within the context of the human person's journey to God. His *Summa Theologiae* can be read as a commentary on a single verse of Scripture: "Beloved, we are God's children now; it does not yet appear what we shall be, but we know that when he appears we shall be like him, for we shall see him as he is" (1 Jn 3:2). The whole panorama of the economy of salvation is directed towards the accomplishment, the consummation, of our life in the communion of the Blessed Trinity through our adoptive participation in Christ—becoming like him through grace and the Holy Spirit. Only within this context can the doctrine of original sin be properly expounded and understood. Specifically, Aquinas locates the discussion of original sin within the treatment of the intrinsic and extrinsic principles of human action where it falls under the category of external causes of personal sin.

When Aquinas asks whether "sin caused by origin" is among the external causes of sin, what is the meaning of the affirmative answer that divine revelation requires of him? The question is framed in this way: "*Utrum primum peccatum hominis derivetur per originem in posteros*" (whether or not man's first sin passes by way of origin to posterity) (*STh* I-II, q. 81, a. 1). Since revelation tells us *that* sin is in every man born of Adam by propagation, and not merely by imitation, but does not tell us just *how* it is transmitted, Aquinas confines himself as strictly as possible to its natural origin and avoids speculation about the mode of transmission.

His restraint here is in marked contrast to positions advanced by theologians both before and after him. Especially among those following St. Augustine, transmission is associated with sexual intercourse itself—an act swept along by disordered libido. A kind of active concupiscence—a positive disorder or vice—comes to be identified as original sin transmitted in the act of generation.

Aquinas will have nothing to do with this line of explanation, in large part because he regards it as unnecessary. "Where authority is wanting," he famously wrote elsewhere, "we should shape our opinions according to the pattern of nature" (*STh* I, q. 101, a. 1). Human nature itself is the source of what is common to all human beings. Sin is derived through origin not because concupiscence in the act of generation infects the soul but because origin involves the human generation in which human nature is transmitted. Men receive their nature from Adam. Human nature is *this sort* of human nature, and not some other sort, because of its origins in the first parents. As an act of nature, generation itself is the sufficient explanation of the unity of the concrete human race with Adam. For Aquinas, the concupiscence that may be involved in the act of generation is not some sort of sinful lust but simply the *absence* in nature of an order that would have prevailed in the state of original justice.

Aquinas adheres strictly to this path in order to explain the voluntariness of original sin and thus its truly sinful nature. "So too the disorder which is in an individual man, a descendant of Adam, is not voluntary by reason of personal will, but by reason of the will of the first parent, who through a generative impulse [*motione generationis*] exerts influence upon all who descend from him by way of origin, even as the will of the soul moves bodily members to their various activities" (*STh* I-II, q. 81, a. 1). Aquinas rejects explanations that suggest that all men *ratify* Adam's personal sin, or that they *acted in* Adam, or were *represented by* Adam—theories without foundation in divine revelation. Original sin is voluntary, not by the will of the individual agent, but by the will of Adam. All men can be considered as one man because all are one in that the nature they share is derived from one source. Adam's causality is limited, just as the "sin" in original sin is analogous. "Adam's influence is verified only with the exercise of the active reproductive powers.... They alone contract original sin who descend from Adam through the exercise of these powers derived from him by way of origin" (*STh* I-II, q. 81, a. 4).

Because of his personal sin (*peccatum originale originans*), Adam lost the state of original justice that he would have been able to pass along with human nature to his posterity. The state of original sin in his posterity (*peccatum originale originatum*) is nothing other than the privation or absence of original justice and the resulting disorder in the powers that is called concupiscence.

Formally, then, original sin is the absence of sanctifying grace in the substance of the soul. It does not involve what is proper to actual sin: there is no conscious turning away from God and toward the creaturely instead of him. That positive orientation to God that is at the root of original justice is absent, and with it an effective moral direction is also lacking. "As a result [of the loss of original justice,] all the powers of the soul are in a sense lacking an order proper to them, their natural order to virtue" (*STh* I-II, q. 85, a. 3). Man's moral powers are thus in need of healing grace to overcome ignorance, malice, weakness, and concupiscence.

With the loss of original justice, sanctifying grace comes to us, not by way of the human nature inherited from Adam, but by redemption through the new Adam, Jesus Christ. Original sin is not an inclination to evil, but a lack of facility in choosing the good. Its character is essentially privative not positive. *We are not born bad.* Without the grace of original justice that once directed them, man's natural powers are no longer aimed at the ultimate Good. Their restoration now involves a struggle against sin and a formation in the moral life according to the pattern of Christ's cross and resurrection, death to sin and life on high in Christ Jesus.

ORIGINAL SIN IN CONTEMPORARY CONTEXT

The most fundamental elements of the Christian faith are in play in the doctrine of original sin. God's intention in creating human persons is to make them sharers in the divine life and thus in the communion of trinitarian life. For this reason, the first human beings were created in grace or at least immediately thereafter constituted in grace. Only from divine revelation itself do we know that the first human beings momentously turned away from this invitation to share in divine life and, further, that their doing so had inescapable consequences for the human race that could only be undone by Christ. According to Catholic doctrine, just by virtue of being part of the human race, all human beings are born in a state of sin—a state that is thus said to be acquired not by *imitation* but by *propagation*.

Two crucially significant elements of Aquinas's theology of original sin address some of the most vexing issues that have arisen in recent writing: (1) his insistence that the first personal sin of Adam was not merely the transgression of an arbitrary command, but an interior disobedience rooted in pride, which could be rectified in the divine economy of salvation only by the perfect obedience of the only-begotten Son, and (2) his understanding of original sin in us as a lack of original justice—a lack of facility in choosing the good, not a fatal inclination to evil. By considering original sin within the context of the factors that affect our capacity for moral action, Aquinas leaves us with a remarkably sober and relatively optimistic account of the consequences of Adam's sin. Clearly for him, we are not born bad.

We have seen that Aquinas touches on many of the most neuralgic points in the doctrine of original sin, but naturally he did not consider explicitly all of the issues that confront us. The most serious new objections come from modern biblical interpretation,[4] and evolutionary theory.[5] Both sets of issues in a sense concern the historicity of the first parents and their first sin—something that Aquinas not only assumed but took to be fundamental to the Catholic doctrine of the economy of salvation.

It has become commonplace to construe modern biblical criticism as entailing the view that the account of the first sin in Genesis is a myth that conveys a universal truth[6] rather than, with classical exegesis, as a history-like narrative conveying factual truths. While it is clear that we cannot regard Genesis as strict history, we must nonetheless regard it—as did Aquinas and all traditional exegetes and theologians—as a symbolic rendering of something that really happened, utilizing mythic elements in a kind of history-like or "realistic narrative,"[7] or "the history of the first human beings in the manner of traditional narratives."[8]

Another exegetical issue has arisen with regard to Romans 5:12–21, a passage that is central to canon 4 of the Council of Trent's

4. Hans W. Frei, *The Eclipse of Biblical Narrative* (New Haven, CT: Yale University Press, 1974).

5. See Jerry D. Korsmeyer, *Evolution and Eden: Balancing Original Sin and Contemporary Science* (New York: Paulist Press, 1998); Jean-Michel Maldamé, OP, "*Que peut-on dire du péché originel à la lumière des connaissances actuelles sur l'origine de l'humanité: Péché originel, péché d'Adam et péché du monde,*" *Bulletin de littérature ecclésiastique* 97 (1996): 3–27; Daryl P. Domning and Monica K. Hellwig, *Original Selfishness: Original Sin and Evil in the Light of Evolution* (Aldershot: Ashgate, 2006).

6. As, for example, Leon R. Kass, *The Beginning of Wisdom: Reading Genesis* (New York: Free Press, 2003) and, in a different way, Elaine Pagels, *Adam, Eve and the Serpent* (New York: Random House, 1988).

7. Frei, "The 'Literal Reading' of Biblical Narrative in the Christian Tradition: Does It Stretch or Will It Break?" in *Theology and Narrative: Selected Essays*, ed. George Hunsinger and William C. Placher (New York: Oxford University Press, 1993), 142–43.

8. Benedict Ashley, OP, *Theologies of the Body* (Braintree, MA: The Pope John XXIII Center, 1985), 373.

decree on original sin. Most scholars agree that the Vulgate rendering of *eph ho* as "*in whom* all men have sinned" is inaccurate. It seems to suggest that all men were *contained* in Adam when he sinned and participated in his act—a reading that Aquinas rejects as well. But the Council of Trent does not employ the text to teach this controversial position. Rather, it seeks to exclude the notion that original sin consists merely in an *imitation* of Adam's sin.

Beyond exegetical issues, the theology of original sin also needs to take account of the results of evolutionary science regarding human origins and thus the historicity of the first human beings who figure in the Genesis narrative. There has been an overwhelming preference in Catholic tradition for some form of historical monogenism. According to Catholic doctrine, the first human being began to exist for a supernatural destiny in accordance with a freely established divine plan, possessing a body like ours and a spiritual soul. He lost this destiny for himself and for his posterity, to be redeemed in Christ the New Adam. Faith teaches us to expect that this supernatural history of salvation overlaps with the evolutionary history of the human race. How this can be explained remains for the time being unclear.

In his splendid discussion of the historicity of Adam and Eve, Fr. Nicanor Austriaco points to the strong evidence, not for a multiregional model for human origins, but for an out-of-Africa model with a population of *anatomically* modern humans evolving into *behaviorally* modern humans much. He hypothesizes that "it would be fitting for God to have given the original speaking bipeds—our original parents—grace and preternatural gifts that they would have needed to attain their destiny of sharing the life of the Triune God."[9] This approach points to a promising line of theological explanation, provided that it could demonstrate why their rejection of the gift of grace should have had consequences for their posterity.

Modern biblical interpretation and evolutionary science clearly

9. Nicanor Austriaco, OP, "The Historicity of Adam and Eve/ Part IV: A Theological Synthesis" (https://www.thomisticevolution.org/disputed-questions/).

pose challenges to the Catholic doctrine of original sin. But the approach of Aquinas in addressing difficulties of this kind, in contrast to much secular thinking, teaches us to take our methodological orientation from the criterion of intelligibility rather than the criterion of reasonableness. It is a theology that arises from faith seeking understanding. It does not put God to the test, as if he could be called to the bar of human reason. Rather, it is a theological approach that acknowledges the limits of human rationality and the unlimited character of the intelligibility of divine truth and the divine plan in which it is manifested.

It is in this light that Aquinas offers his explanation of our membership in the human race as a way of understanding, in line with Catholic doctrine, how original sin could be said to have been transmitted—how sin and death entered the world through one man—and how, "as sin reigned unto death, so also grace might reign by justice unto life everlasting, through Jesus Christ our Lord." While the criterion of reasonableness allows only what makes sense to us, the criterion of intelligibility draws the human mind into the fullness of divine truth.

DIVINE EXPLANATION FOR THE EXISTENCE OF MORAL EVIL: ORIGINAL SIN AS REVEALED

G. K. Chesterton famously remarked: "Certain new theologians dispute original sin, which is the only part of Christian theology which can really be proved."[10] Although embedded in a complex argument, this often-quoted remark is one that people find appealing. The evidence for original sin is all around us, they seem to say, in the moral evil we can "see in the street."

But the doctrine of original sin, precisely *qua* doctrinal, is not the conclusion of observation and reflection on the presence of moral evil in the world. The most compelling *empirical* explanation for this undeniable feature of the human landscape is simply that

10. G. K. Chesterton, *Orthodoxy* (London and New York: John Lane, 1909), 22.

people commit morally bad actions that faith sees as sinful. There is in principle no need to appeal to a theory of inherited sin. A persistent problem is the confusion of original sin with the fact of actual sins committed by human beings and the cumulative consequences of these personal sins as they ramify through history and society. In the Catholic tradition, especially as expounded by Thomas Aquinas, original sin figures as a causal factor in this dismal situation only as contributing to the defective character of human moral agency, a lack of facility in choosing the good. Its causality is indirect.

In fact, the doctrine of original sin is a *datum* of revelation. We learn about the peril of our state—the alienation from God that is the human condition—and our need for Christ the Savior only through the witness of the Sacred Scriptures and the constant Tradition of the Church.[11] The Genesis account is a divinely inspired narrative that depicts in symbolic but realistic form the causes of moral evil. It constitutes, as it were, a divine explanation for the existence of moral evil in the world. Although apologetics might appeal to empirical evidence to support the doctrine, it does not depend on such evidence. As a revealed doctrine, it can only be known by faith—that is, it can only be known by faith that the moral evil in the world can be traced to the personal actual sin of the first human beings.

Note that the endeavor to account for the existence of moral evil is not restricted to cultures influenced by the Christian doctrine of original sin. There are a variety of religious and philosophical accounts that developed independently of Christianity. A sense that something is amiss is has been widespread, pace James Boyce, in all human cultures, not just in the West. And, in the West, neither rejection nor ignorance of the Christian doctrine of original sin guarantee the formation of a more positive outlook on the human condition. As it happens, pessimistic accounts of the human condition, resting on some notion of a primordial or ancestral fault are common everywhere.

11. See André-Marie Dubarle, OP, *The Biblical Doctrine of Original Sin* (London: Geoffrey Chapman, 1964).

It is important to understand that the revealed explanation of the existence of evil offers a correction, or at least an alternative, to common theories, religious and otherwise, about the source of moral evil. The account of creation and the fall in Genesis itself is clearly intended to counter prevailing dualistic views in ancient near eastern cultures. Features of the Genesis account "give to the Hebrew concept of Creation a fundamentally optimistic character which paves the way ... to the solution of the problem of the origin of evil."[12] Genesis affirms the essential goodness of creation as "the unique sovereignty of God over what he has made, a power limited by no antagonistic primordial principle"[13] with "no suggestion that material nature is imperfect."[14] Moreover, with regard to creation and fall of man, Genesis clearly affirms that "God is not the author of evil and that his creatures were not defectively made in the first place."[15] The exclusion of these erroneous theories remains a critically important aspect of Catholic proclamation.

In short, the Catholic doctrine of original sin is needed today precisely in order to counter the pessimism and dualism—not to mention the dystopian pessimism—that have become endemic to popular culture. The book of Genesis recounts something that really happened. Writing under the inspiration of the Holy Spirit, the authors seek to convey to us the truth of divine revelation that the source of moral evil we see around us lies in the human will of a single moral agent who failed to embrace the offer of divine communion intended by God to define the supernatural destiny of human nature. Good and evil are not equally matched forces locked into an eternal struggle. The goodness of creation and the omnipotent goodness of God are not undone. Foreseeing the fault, God out of love foreordained the remedy. And, for the record, we are not born bad.

12. Leo Scheffczyk, *Creation and Providence* (New York: Herder & Herder, 1970), 9.
13. Scheffczyk, *Creation and Providence*, 6.
14. Scheffczyk, *Creation and Providence*, 9.
15. Scheffczyk, *Creation and Providence*, 8–9.

CONCLUSION: THE HARROWING OF HELL

In Western art, the Resurrection is typically depicted with Christ in the very act of rising from the tomb, surrounded by prone soldiers who are either asleep or amazed at what they are witnessing. But in Eastern iconography what is depicted is not the Resurrection as such, but Christ at the moment when he breaks open with his Cross the gates of hell and reaches out to Adam and Eve, with St. John the Baptist—his precursor even here—standing to the side. The scene is perfectly described in a passage from an ancient homily for Holy Saturday: "[The Lord] has gone to search for our first parent, as for a lost sheep. Greatly desiring to visit those who live in darkness and in the shadow of death, he has gone to free from sorrow the captives Adam and Eve, he who is both God and son of Eve. The Lord approached them bearing the cross, the weapon that had won him the victory."[16]

Foreseeing Adam's disobedience, God chose to send his only-begotten Son, out of the stock of Abraham, to be the Redeemer who reconciles Adam and Eve, and each of us, so that we could again share in this marvelous gift of His grace. That Adam and Eve, who lost this gift, should be the first to have it restored to them provides a profound insight both into the nature of their fault and into that of the divine remedy. At the center of the whole history of divine love is Christ, who by His perfect obedience to the Father overcomes the sin and death that result from the human unwillingness to receive from God what He would freely bestow and now graciously restores in His Son. The already-quoted ancient homily puts into the mouth of Christ words directed not only to Adam and Eve but also to us: "Awake, O sleeper, and rise from the dead, and Christ will give you light. I am your God, who for your sake have become your son. Out of love for you and your descendants I now by my own authority command all who are held in bondage to come forth, all who are in darkness to be enlightened, all who are sleeping to arise.... I did

16. Liturgy of the Hours, vol. II, Office of Readings, 497.

not create you to be held a prisoner in hell.... Rise, let us leave this place. The enemy led you out of the earthly paradise. I will not restore you to that paradise, but I will enthrone you in heaven. I forbade you the tree that was only a symbol of life, but see, I who am life itself am now one with you."[17]

17. Liturgy of the Hours, vol. II, Office of Readings, 497–98.

CHAPTER 14

The Fundamental Unity of the Embodied Person

Theological and Pastoral Reflections on the Sexual Revolution

GNOSTICISM REAPPEARS

As this address is billed as the keynote of our conference, perhaps a wonderful old Jesuit-Dominican joke would not be out of order. It runs as follows: A man comes upon a Dominican and a Jesuit in conversation and asks them to identify themselves. When each replies by naming his religious community, the next question requests that they identify their founders:

> "St. Dominic Guzman," replies the Dominican.
> "St. Ignatius of Loyola," says the Jesuit.
> "Why were your orders founded?"
> The Dominican replies, "To convert the Albigensians."
> While the Jesuit says, "To convert the Protestants."
> "And have you been successful?"

This chapter is also set to appear in *The Body as Anticipatory Sign: Commemorating the Anniversaries of Humanae Vitae and Veritatis Splendor*, ed. David S. Crawford (Washington, DC: Humanum Academic Press, forthcoming).

At this point in the joke, a dramatic pause is customary to prepare the way for the cheeky Dominican riposte: "Well, when is the last time you ran into an Albigensian?"

The joke still provokes laughter, of course, perhaps because we sense that the punch line really doesn't work anymore—that we are, in fact, surrounded by Albigensians and may indeed be closet Albigensians ourselves, and that, under the cover of the sexual revolution, there prevail various gnostic dualisms that Albigensians would happily have embraced.

This awareness dawned on me for the first time in 1976 after reading a review essay by the Canadian Catholic philosopher J. M. Cameron that appeared in *The New York Review of Books*, tellingly entitled "Sex in the Head." Regarding one of the seven books under review in his essay, Cameron wrote: "There is a lot of Gnosticism, a false spirituality, an excessive concern with what Lawrence called 'sex in the head' (this is characteristic of the entire sexual revolution)."[1]

Cameron continued:

The belief is that in a union of love between two people, personal, nonsexual relations are fundamental and that to these relations, between males and females, males and males, females and females, there may be added sexual relations, as relaxation, play, signs of affection on occasion as means to procreation. In the biblical tradition, by contrast, it is the sexual relation between man and woman that constitutes the relation of marriage, and the love of friendship—this can exist outside of marriage and without sexual relations and is an added grace that belongs to the perfection of marriage but isn't constitutive of it.[2]

These days it has become almost commonplace to discern gnostic-like elements in the ideology of the sexual revolution. George Weigel recently wrote with particular insight that "contemporary Gnosticism ... is most powerfully embodied in the sexual

1. J. M. Cameron, "Sex in the Head," *New York Review of Books* (May 13, 1976); reprinted in *Nuclear Catholics and Other Essays* (Grand Rapids, MI: Eerdmans, 1989), 22. The phrase comes from a sentence in a letter of D. H. Lawrence: "The tragedy is when you've got sex in the head instead of down where it belongs."
2. J. M. Cameron, "Sex in the Head," *New York Review of Books*, 24–25.

revolution." Beneath "a cult of sensuality … in which sexual gratifi-
cation, in any form among consenting adults, is the highest of goods
and the most inalienable of personal liberties," there lies "a deeper
dimension of the new Gnosticism … the conviction that there are
no Things As They Are" and that "*everything* in the human condition
is plastic and malleable."[3]

Even when they do not draw an explicit parallel with gnostic
themes, many analysts have observed in the dualisms associated
with the sexual revolution elements that irresistibly bring Gnosticism to mind. Rooted in a fateful separation of sexuality and procreation, the ideology of the sexual revolution drives a wedge between
the realms of spirit and matter, between soul and body, between reason and emotion, between nature and freedom, between the procreative and unitive ends of marriage, and even between sexuality and
intimacy. These dualisms lend support to the notion central to the
sexual revolution that the human body can be instrumentalized for
the satisfaction of any type of sexual desire as long as one's intentions remain lofty, or, as an Albigensian might say, "pure." It sounds
a lot like sex in the head.

Christians have not been alone in recognizing that these are
ideas with dangerous consequences for the body as much as for the
soul. For one thing, what you do with your body can hurt your soul,
lofty intentions to the contrary notwithstanding. But far more seriously, from the perspective of an authentic Christian humanism, the
divorce of physical and spiritual desire and fulfillment short-circuits
the natural tendency of desire to seek the divine Good through the
enjoyment of created goods like sexual pleasure in marriage.

THE BODY AS ANTICIPATORY SIGN

Where the sexual revolution has over the past fifty years sown a series of gnostic-like separations in the nature and relationships of

3. George Weigel, *The Fragility of Order: Catholic Reflections on Turbulent Times* (San
Francisco: Ignatius Press, 2018), 127–28.

human persons, the Catholic magisterium has sought to recover and reaffirm the fundamental unity of body and soul in the human person and in human sexual relationships. It comes as no surprise in these circumstances that the Pontifical John Paul II Institute for Studies on Marriage and Family should mark the concurrent anniversaries of *Humanae Vitae* (1968) and *Veritatis Splendor* (1993) with a symposium under the theme "The Body as Anticipatory Sign."

This immensely significant phrase is drawn from paragraph 48 of the encyclical *Veritatis Splendor* of Pope St. John Paul II: "The person, by the light of right reason and the support of virtue, discovers in the body the anticipatory signs, the expression and promise of the gift of self, in conformity with the wise plan of the Creator." The argument of this paragraph of the encyclical is directed against the "objections of physicalism and naturalism [that] have been leveled against the traditional concept of the natural law, which is accused of presenting as moral laws what are in themselves mere biological laws" (§47).

While in *Veritatis Splendor* these objections are considered in the general context of the whole of Catholic moral teaching as it draws upon the natural law, the *specific* context of sexual morality is explicitly in play in these paragraphs. It was precisely objections of this kind that proved to be most damaging to the correct understanding and reception of the teaching of Pope St. Paul VI's encyclical *Humanae Vitae* regarding the immorality of artificial contraception.

Charles Curran led the charge here fifty years ago, but his complaint that *Humanae Vitae* employed a natural law methodology that he termed "physicalist" has become the rallying call for Catholic theologians and faithful who reject the Church's teaching on the immorality of contraception.[4] It can be said without exaggeration that a principal objective of Pope John Paul's theology of the body was precisely to refute the charge of physicalism lodged against the

---

4. For a trenchant examination of this objection to the teaching of *Humanae Vitae*, see Thomas Petri, OP, *Aquinas and the Theology of the Body* (Washington, DC: The Catholic University of America Press, 2016), 79–91.

teaching of *Humanae Vitae* and to do so within the framework of a highly sophisticated and original retrieval of Christian anthropology. Indeed, the main elements of Pope John Paul's defense of the teaching of *Humanae Vitae* can be found in synthesis in paragraphs 47 and 48 of *Veritatis Splendor*.

Against a theory that would grant a merely "pre-moral" status to the body and its inclinations, *Veritatis Splendor* poses the classical Christian view that the body in fact stands as anticipatory sign for an authentic understanding of the moral life of the free human person. The body is not simply raw material, "devoid of any meaning and moral values until freedom has shaped it in accordance with its own designs." In such a theory, "human nature and the human body appear as presuppositions or preambles materially necessary for freedom to make its choice, yet extrinsic to the person, the subject and the human act, ... not reference points for moral decisions, because the finalities of these inclinations would be merely physical goods" (§48).

According to the analysis of *Veritatis Splendor*, these premises constitute the core of the faulty theological anthropology that lies behind the charge that the Church's teaching on sexual morality is based on a crude physicalism. Catholic teaching is caricatured as if it elevated biological laws to the level of universally valid moral norms, and thus "on the basis of a naturalistic understanding of the sexual act, contraception, direct sterilization, autoeroticism, premarital sexual relations, homosexual relations, and artificial insemination were condemned as morally unacceptable" (§47).

It is alleged that "a morally negative evaluation of such acts fails to take into consideration both man's character as a rational and free being, and the cultural conditioning of moral norms" (§47). Behind the charge of physicalism lies a profound failure to understand the significance of the unity of the body and soul within the constitution of the human person. This failure is evident, according to *Veritatis Splendor*, in the view that "the workings of typically human behavior, as well as so-called natural inclinations, would establish at most a general orientation towards correct behavior, but cannot determine the moral assessment of human acts" (§47).

As *Veritatis Splendor* bluntly states: "This moral theory does not correspond to the truth about man and his freedom" (§48). Against it can be adduced the most basic teachings of the Church in the area of theological anthropology. *Veritatis Splendor* cites dogmatic definitions regarding the unity of the human person, "whose rational soul is *per se et essentialiter* the form of his body."[5] "The spiritual and immortal soul is the principle of unity of the human being, whereby it exists as a whole—*corpore et anima unus*—as a person."[6] According to these definitions, the body not only shares in resurrection and glory, but also possesses sense faculties that are intrinsically linked with reason and free will in the course of human action. "The person, including the body, is completely entrusted to himself, and it is in the unity of body and soul that the person is the subject of his own moral acts" (§48).

It is in this sense that we can say that the body is the anticipatory sign of the unity of the moral actions of the person whose soul *and* body play their distinctive roles in grasping "the specific moral value of certain goods towards which the person is naturally inclined" (§48).

Against the gnostic-like conception of the body, as raw material, as presupposition, as preamble, as pre-moral, as general orientation, as generally extrinsic to the person, Pope John Paul presents us in *Veritatis Splendor* with the body as anticipatory sign and invites us to view the teaching of *Humanae Vitae* in this light. Where the Christian doctrinal and theological tradition draws distinctions, Gnosticism drives separations. Bodily structures and inclinations form part of a comprehensive series of distinctive but integrated elements in moral action. The whole person acts. In assessing the morality of actions, attention to the physical or biological features of the whole

---

5. Cf. Ecumenical Council of Vienne, Constitution *Fidei Catholicae: DS*, 902; Fifth Lateran Ecumenical Council, Bull *Apostolici Regiminis: DS*, 1440.

6. Second Vatican Ecumenical Council, Pastoral Constitution on the Church in the Modern World *Gaudium et Spes*, 14.

person who acts does not distract from the properly rational and volitional aspects but completes the full profile of human action. In the Christian vision of the human person and the moral life articulated by *Veritatis Splendor*, there is continuity and integration all that way up and all the way down.

It is in this light that the Catholic teaching about the immorality of artificial contraception must be understood. In the words of *Humanae Vitae*, "this particular doctrine, often expounded by the magisterium of the Church, is based on the inseparable connection, established by God, which man on own initiative may not break, between the unitive significance and the procreative significance which are both inherent to the marriage act. The reason is that the fundamental significance of the marriage act, while uniting husband and wife in closest intimacy, also renders them capable of generating new life—and this as a result of laws written into the actual nature of man and of woman. And if each of these essential qualities, the unitive and the procreative, is preserved, the use of marriage fully retains its sense of true mutual love and its ordination to the supreme responsibility of parenthood to which man is called" (§11–12).

Expounding this passage particularly in the light of the book of Genesis and the Gospel of St. Matthew, Pope John Paul's catecheses on the theology of the body unfolded a deep extended commentary on the teaching of *Humanae Vitae*, as he himself stated towards their conclusion.[7]

"Such a commentary seems very necessary," declared Pope John Paul in the final catechesis. "In giving an answer to some questions of today in the sphere of conjugal and family morality, the encyclical, in fact, also raised other questions of a biomedical nature. However, the questions are also (and first of all) of a theological nature; they belong to the sphere of anthropology and theology that we have called 'theology of the body.'"[8] When read in their entirety,

7. Pope John Paul II, *Man and Woman He Created Them: A Theology of the Body*, trans. Michael Waldstein (Boston: Pauline Books, 2006), 617–63.

8. Pope John Paul II, *Man and Woman He Created Them*, 661.

these catecheses supply the key to the interpretation of *Humanae Vitae* that is articulated in paragraphs 47 and 48 of *Veritatis Splendor*. To affirm the inseparability of the unitive and procreative meanings of the conjugal act is not to fall into physicalism but to recognize in the body the anticipatory signs of the spiritual dimensions of the whole human person.

MORAL NORMS

As things turned out, the unity of the embodied person that is so absolutely central to the teachings both of *Veritatis Splendor* and of *Humanae Vitae* has proved very difficult to accept for many people, including many Catholic theologians and faithful. In the case of *Humanae Vitae*, the opposition was widespread and dramatic, while with *Veritatis Splendor* what might be called a broad non-reception of its reform of moral theology on the part of the discipline's academic practitioners has been pervasive but more subtle. Although he was fully aware of the potential unpopularity of the teaching of *Humanae Vitae*, Paul VI nonetheless wrote: "We believe that the human beings of our day are particularly capable of seeing the deeply reasonable and human character of this fundamental principle" [viz., the unity of the unitive and procreative meanings of the conjugal act] (§12). Commenting on this sentence, Pope John Paul wrote in the catecheses on the theology of the body that, given the "deep conformity" of this teaching "with all that is transmitted from the biblical sources ... it seems entirely reasonable to look in the 'theology of the body' for the foundation of the truth of the norms concerning such a fundamental issue of man as body: 'the two will be one flesh'(Gn 2:24)."[9]

Another point about the reasonableness of the teaching of *Humanae Vitae* advanced by Pope John Paul suggests that a factor in its continued rejection has been the failure of moral theologians to grasp the argument of *Veritatis Splendor*. Consider this important

9. Pope John Paul II, *Man and Woman He Created Them*, 622.

passage of John Paul's catechesis 119: The reasonable character of the teaching of *Humanae Vitae*

concerns not only the truth in the ontological dimension, that is, what corresponds to the real structure of the conjugal act. It concerns also the same truth in the subjective and psychological dimension, that is to say, the right understanding of the innermost structure of the conjugal act, that is, the adequate rereading of the meanings that correspond to this structure and their inseparable connection in view of morally right behavior. In this consist the moral norm and the corresponding ordering of human acts in the sphere of sexuality. In this sense, we say that the norm is identical with rereading the "language of the body" in the truth.[10]

Norms of sexual morality have an ontological basis that at least in principle can be subjectively grasped in the very experience of men and women engaged in sexual activity.

This comment expresses an understanding of the moral life that is advanced by *Veritatis Splendor* precisely in order to correct the prevailing and deeply engrained view that moral norms are more or less arbitrary constraints according to which certain things are permitted and certain things are forbidden, irrespective of the bearing of these injunctions on human goodness and flourishing. This idea has a long history stretching back to the nominalist theology that took hold in the fourteenth century and remained influential in the Catholic manualist tradition.[11] It served to foster what has come to be regarded and experienced as a *culture of legalism* in Catholic moral theology that was decisively rejected by the Magisterium in the encyclical *Veritatis Splendor*, but not before it had contributed in large part to the rejection of the teaching of *Humanae Vitae* and provided the ideology of the sexual revolution an enormous advantage in its conquest of once-Christian societies in the West.

Following the lead of *Veritatis Splendor*, it is of critical importance to insist on the priority of the categories of good and evil for assessing

10. Pope John Paul II, *Man and Woman He Created Them*, 621.

11. For excellent accounts of this history, see Petri, 11–44, and John Grabowski, *Sex and Virtue: An Introduction to Sexual Ethics* (Washington, DC: The Catholic University of America Press, 2003), 14–19.

the rightness and wrongness of particular actions. Whereas manualist moral systems at least imply that actions are good (and thus right)
because permitted, and bad (and thus wrong) because forbidden,
the authentic Catholic moral tradition recovered by *Veritatis Splendor* maintains that a certain course of action is forbidden and wrong
because it is *bad* for the agent, while another course of action is permitted and right because it is *good* for the agent. The requirements
enjoined by moral norms are not indifferent to human goodness and
happiness but advance the flourishing of the human person in accord
with natural order embedded in creation by a loving God.

In the legalistic moral doctrine typical of the manualists, the
principal virtue is obedience: one obeys the moral norms, whatever the content, because they are enjoined by God. But in the classical Catholic moral tradition, the observance of the moral norms is
meant to foster the specific virtues with which they are concerned
and thus the overall good of the acting person. In other words, moral norms treat primarily of good and evil rather than of the permitted and the forbidden. Obedience is just one of the virtues. Moral
norms thus express an order established by divine wisdom—as St.
Thomas Aquinas and *Veritatis Splendor* insist—in which the moral
law accords with the divinely created finalities of human nature and
is given to make human persons good and virtuous. Here we have
not the violation or restraint of authentic freedom, but its enablement. Freedom is the God-given capacity by which human persons
attain happiness. Unlike the subrational and nonpersonal creatures
"with whom we share the universe ... only persons are free to join
their hearts and souls to the endeavor to realize their true good—
which ... is the authentically personal good of ultimate communion"
with the Blessed Trinity.[12]

Moral norms are thus much more like an athlete's daily exercise
and diet regimen than they are like the traffic regulations. Traffic

12. J. A. Di Noia, OP, "*Veritatis Splendor*: Moral Life as Transfigured Life," in *Veritatis
Splendor and the Renewal of Moral Theology*, ed. J. A. Di Noia, OP, and Romanus Cessario,
OP (Princeton, NJ: Scepter Press, 1999), 8.

laws require that we stop on red and go on green, but it could just as well be the other way around. But the athlete follows the daily regimen enjoined by his or her coach in order to achieve and maintain a certain level of performance otherwise unattainable. There is a fit between the regimen and the outcome. Moral norms are like that. They involve nonarbitrary injunctions that guide human persons steadily toward the good in every action and thus toward our ultimate Good.

Created in the image of God, human persons are meant to grow into the image of Christ. As they become increasingly conformed to the perfect man Jesus Christ, the fullness of their humanity is realized. There is a "finality built into human nature as such, and, although its realization is possible only with the assistance of divine grace, this realization is in a real sense continuous with the tendencies and aspirations of human nature."[13]

It is only in the light of the authentic Christian vision of the moral life of human persons, articulated in *Veritatis Splendor,* that the reasonableness of the teaching of *Humanae Vitae* can be fully appreciated. Norms of sexual morality in their totality have a basis in the structure of human nature, "in the real structure of the conjugal act." And, as Pope John Paul insists, this same truth has a subjective and psychological dimension because it is open to a right understanding on the part of human persons. The innermost structure of the conjugal act can be "read" in the language of the body through an "adequate rereading of the meanings that correspond to this structure and their inseparable connection in view of morally right behavior." The norm of sexual morality and the corresponding ordering of human acts in the sphere of sexuality are "identical with rereading the 'language of the body' in the truth."[14] The norms of sexual morality are thus not extrinsically imposed on the human person but correspond to the spousal meaning of the body that is there to be read out, especially in the light of faith.

13. J. A. Di Noia, OP, "*Imago Dei, Imago Christi:* The Theological Foundations of Christian Humanism," *Nova et Vetera,* English edition 2 (2004): 270.

14. Pope John Paul II, *Man and Woman He Created Them: A Theology of the Body,* 621.

OBSTACLES

Three factors in particular have converged to make it difficult to read out the spousal meaning of the body from objective and subjective dimensions of man and woman in the conjugal act.

For one thing, the vision of Christian sexuality presupposed by *Humanae Vitae* and later articulated in *Veritatis Splendor* was eclipsed by manualist moral theology. In the authentic Christian understanding of the moral life, a rightly ordered desire and love for the good things of this world and the good of other persons, through the guidance of moral norms and the assistance of divine grace, already involves a participation in the Good which is God himself. Authentic Christian morality resists the misreading of Scripture and Tradition that claims to see in Christian faith the suppression of the ordinary enjoyments of human earthly life, particularly human intimacy and love, in favor of a good beyond life. On the contrary, for Christian faith the whole range of desire—or, to use more technical language, the inclination to the good embedded in the very structures of human existence—finds its fulfillment in beatitude, in the love of the triune God, and nothing less. This unity and continuity between *eros* and *agape* has been called "the sanctification of desire." It is to this end that moral norms in the area of sexuality direct us.

But instead of falling mainly on good soil formed by this understanding of the Christian moral life, the teaching of *Humanae Vitae* fell largely among the thorns and rocky ground of manualist legalism. In the place of the tradition's stress on grace, beatitude, virtue, and personal transformation, manualist moral theology had substituted obligation, freedom, conscience, and decision. In addition to external social and intellectual factors of considerable complexity, the resources with which to absorb and receive the teaching of *Humanae Vitae* thus barely existed broadly within the Catholic Church. Instead, as John Grabowski points out, in the prevailing conceptions fostered by the manualist tradition, morality was viewed "as a struggle between an undirected and privatized freedom and law imposed by external authority." In the case of *Humanae Vitae*, "it was the freedom of individual conscience to avail itself of new sexual opportunities afforded by twentieth-century attitudes and technology" that were set against the papal teaching. [15]

Thus it transpired that, "just as the sexual revolution was unleashed around them, Catholics found themselves in a Church that seemed paralyzed by argument [about contraception] and, at least on the local level, seemed to lapse into an uneasy silence about sex."[16] This "silence about sex" is a second factor in obscuring the spousal meaning of the body. It has resulted in a significant failure to communicate the Church's teaching on sexuality through catechesis, preaching, and adult formation. The reasonableness of the teaching that Pope John Paul later confidently expounded under the rubric of the theology of the body has not been explained to the faithful.

Reporting the results of a survey on the influence of religious beliefs on teenage sexual behavior, sociologist Mark Regnerus concluded in 2007: "The majority of religious interviewees with whom we spoke, the ones who might possibly own some sort of religious ethic concerning human sexuality, could articulate nothing more about what their faith has to say about sex than a simple no-sex-before-marriage rule. For most of them, this is the sum total of Christian teaching on sex. For the most part, congregations are doing a terrible job of fashioning distinctively Christian sexual ethics."[17] And in an important recent book, Regnerus's research leads him to acknowledge that Catholics

have access to more robust and developed ... conservative teachings on sexuality and marriage than do Protestants, but suffer from a profound "supply chain" problem. Average Catholics are unaware of their Church's own teachings or are insufficiently trained in them, due to Catholicism's historically poor theological education system. American Catholics also tend to approach religious life with a spirit of independence and an

15. Grabowski, *Sex and Virtue*, 19.

16. Grabowski, *Sex and Virtue*, 20.

17. Mark Regnerus, *Forbidden Fruit: Sex and Religion in the Lives of American Teenagers* (New York: Oxford University Press, 2007), 214.

anti-authoritarian streak, out of step with the hierarchical nature of the Magisterium. As a result, the average Catholic's sexual behavior looks (and is) more permissive than the average evangelical Protestant's.[18]

A third and perhaps decisive factor is the sexual revolution that has prevailed everywhere in the West—a massive social and cultural transformation that has resulted from the widespread uptake of artificial contraception. Fifty years on, the embrace of hormonal and other forms of contraception, even among Catholics, and with it the fateful separation of sexuality and procreation, seems irreversible. This transformation has so greatly altered the way in which people conceive of sexuality and the relationships between men and women as to render the spousal meaning of the body almost unintelligible.

As Anthony Giddens has suggested:

Effective contraception meant more than an increased capability of limiting pregnancy; it signaled a deep transition in personal life. For women—and, in a partly different sense, for men also—sexuality became malleable, open to be shaped in diverse ways, and a potential "property" of the individual. Sexuality came into being as part of a progressive differentiation of sex from the exigencies of reproduction. With the further elaboration of reproductive technologies, that differentiation has today become complete. Now that conception can be artificially produced, rather than only artificially inhibited, sexuality is at last fully autonomous. Reproduction can occur in the absence of sexual activity; this is the final "liberation" for sexuality, which thence can become wholly a quality of individuals and their transactions with one another.[19]

Other writers have sought to chart the various outcomes of this "deep transition in personal life"—notably Hanna Rosin in *The End of Men and the Rise of Women* and Mark Regnerus in *Cheap Sex*. Helen Alvaré calls this transformed conception of sexuality "sexual expressionism" and shows how it has become enshrined in law and government regulations in her recent *Putting Children's Interests First*.[20]

18. Mark Regnerus, *Cheap Sex: The Transformation of Men, Marriage, and Monogamy* (New York: Oxford University Press, 2017), 191.

19. Anthony Giddens, *The Transformation of Intimacy* (Cambridge: Polity Press, 1992), 27.

20. Hanna Rosin, *The End of Men and the Rise of Women* (New York: Riverhead

These three factors—the persistent influence of manualist moral theology, the deficiency of moral and sexual catechesis, and the emergence of sexual expressionism—together have made it difficult for the ordinary faithful to understand and accept the teaching of *Humanae Vitae* and indeed the entire Christian tradition of sexual morality. Taking the lead from the recent magisterium, it is of critical importance to recover and proclaim the Christian vision of the fundamental unity of the embodied human person. This would serve as the basis from which to address the gnostic-like dualisms that divide sexuality from procreation, spirit from matter, body from soul, reason from emotion, nature from freedom, and sexuality from intimacy. The concurrent anniversaries of *Humanae Vitae* and *Veritatis Splendor* afford a moment for a recommitment to the endeavor to present a robust Christian alternative to "sex in the head." This effort will require a deep theological and pastoral analysis of the social and cultural transformation of sexuality that followed upon the widespread uptake of artificial contraception in the West.[21]

Pope John Paul was moved to declare in *Familiaris Consortio*: "In the context of a culture which seriously distorts or entirely misinterprets the true meaning of human sexuality, because it separates it from its essential reference to the person, the Church more urgently feels how irreplaceable is her mission of presenting sexuality as a value and a task of the whole person, created male and female in the image of God" (§32). Despite the considerable challenges posed by the sexual revolution, the Church can no more abandon this mission than she could the task of evangelization itself.

Books, 2013); Helen Alvaré, *Putting Children's Interests First in U. S. Family Law and Policy: With Power Comes Responsibility* (Cambridge: Cambridge University Press, 2018).

21. See, in addition to works already cited, Edward O. Laumann, et al. *The Social Organization of Sexuality: Sexual Practices in the United States* (Chicago: University of Chicago Press, 1994).

PART III

———:———

The Way of the
Church in Dialogue
with Others

CHAPTER 15

The Prospects for
Catholic Theology of Religions
Observations on Some Recent Developments
in Catholic Magisterium

INTRODUCTION

When I published a book on the theology of religions twenty-five years ago, I tried, in a concluding bibliographical essay, to survey the most significant literature and the prevailing theological positions.[1] For the developments since then, we now have the Gavin D'Costa's masterful *Christianity and World Religions: Disputed Questions in the Theology of Religions.*[2] This flourishing of the theology of religions to which these books bear witness can be traced to the massively

---

This chapter began as a paper presented on October 6, 2017 at a conference on Theology of Religions hosted by the Newman Institute in Uppsala, Sweden. [ed. note: Other papers from this conference became the contents of a book, Philip Geister, SJ, and Gosta Hallonsten, eds., *Faithful Interpretations: Truth and Islam in Catholic Theology of Religions* (Washington, DC: The Catholic University of America Press, 2021), to which Di Noia contributed a brief foreword.]

1. J. A. Di Noia, OP, *The Diversity of Religions: A Christian Perspective* (Washington, DC: The Catholic University of America Press, 1992), 171–94.

2. Gavin D'Costa, *Christianity and World Religions: Disputed Questions in the Theology of Religions* (London: Wiley-Blackwell, 2009).

influential teachings of the Vatican Council II in this area.[3] Just as over fifty years ago the Church's magisterium at work in this momentous ecumenical council inspired a lively theological discussion regarding Catholic relations with other religions, so in recent years some major magisterial interventions will have important consequences for the future shape of Catholic theology of religions. These interventions were prompted by two key theological issues: the tension between dialogue and evangelization, and the affirmation of the unique salvific role of Jesus Christ. A careful examination of the relevant magisterial interventions affords both an overview of the entire post-conciliar discussion of Catholic relations with other religions as well as a glimpse at the direction this discussion is likely to take in the future.

REDEMPTORIS MISSIO AND DIALOGUE AND PROCLAMATION

The first magisterial development was prompted by a tension left unresolved by the Second Vatican Council, namely, that between the commendation of interreligious and intercultural dialogue in *Nostra Aetate*, on the one hand, and, on the other, the even more forceful mandate to engage in mission and proclamation in other key conciliar documents. The lingering tension in post-conciliar theology and pastoral practice occasioned the momentous encyclical of Pope John Paul II, *Redemptoris Missio*, in 1991, and in the same year a joint document of the Congregation for the Evangelization of Peoples and the Pontifical Council for Interreligious Dialogue entitled *Dialogue and Proclamation*.

In order to understand this problematic, we need to consider the remote origins of the religious use of the notion of dialogue in the work of existentialist and personalist thinkers in the first quarter of

3. See Gerald O'Collins, SJ, *The Second Vatican Council and Other Religions* (Oxford: Oxford University Press, 2013).

the twentieth century, notably Martin Buber, whose enormously influential book, *I and Thou*, appeared in 1923.

But it was only after World War II, according to Eric Sharpe, that the concept came to be applied to interreligious relations. To be sure, interreligious conversations have a very long history and the rubric of "dialogue" embraced a genre of literary conventions for constructing conversations about philosophical and religious differences. Nonetheless, for a variety of reasons, as such contacts came to be more actively pursued in the early twentieth century, the term "dialogue" was used to describe them. The discrediting and collapse of colonial empires spelled the resurgence of non-Western religious cultures and religions. Particularly in those former colonies that lie within the ambit of major religious traditions (like Islam, Buddhism and Hinduism), the missionary enterprise found itself forced to adopt an increasingly defensive posture. Sharpe asserts that "it was in this atmosphere that the word *dialogue* began to emerge as the only workable term with which to describe the proper attitude of one group of believers over against another."[4]

At the outset, the term "dialogue" and the stance of mutual respect and tolerance it connoted were championed principally by liberal Christians. Conservatives, according to Sharpe, "found the term unacceptable, since it implicitly placed religious traditions on a par with one another, or at least was less than explicit when it came to affirming the claims of Christianity."[5] But since the mid-twentieth century, and particularly over the past fifty years, the notion of interreligious dialogue has steadily gained legitimacy within mainstream Christianity. It is commonplace to note that *Nostra Aetate* marked a decisive moment in this legitimation not only in the Catholic Church but also with regard to policies later adopted by the World Council of Churches.

But the Second Vatican Council's embrace of a dialogical attitude

4. Eric J. Sharpe, "Dialogue of Religions," in *Encyclopedia of Religions*, ed. Mircea Eliade (London: Macmillan, 1987) 4:344.

5. Sharpe, "Dialogue of Religions," 4:344.

to other religions by no means dispelled the tension that such an embrace involves—logically and existentially—for Catholic faith and practice. How the appropriation and endorsement of interreligious dialogue could be consistent with a commitment to the mission *ad gentes* was not specified.

In effect, Vatican II simply juxtaposed the commitment to mission and dialogue without undertaking to show how, doctrinally speaking, they could be reconciled with one another. This task was left to the magisterium and to subsequent theological reflection. The question is: does engagement in dialogue and the attitudes it entails undermine or support evangelization? A voluminous theological literature attests to the variety and ingenuity of the strategies that have been deployed in pursuit of a satisfactory answer to this question.[6]

In such a situation, it is not surprising that the magisterium would undertake to provide an authoritative response. The encyclical *Redemptoris Missio* resolves the tension by its forthright subsumption of dialogue within or under mission. This marks a critical development in the way that the Church understands its participation in interreligious dialogue. Among the activities of the mission *ad gentes*, dialogue is listed along with proclamation and witness as one of the "paths of mission" presented in Chapter 5 of the encyclical—at one stroke combining a strong affirmation of the Church's commitment to mission with a clear endorsement of participation in interreligious dialogue. The document *Dialogue and Proclamation*, issued in the same year, follows the lead of *Redemptoris Missio* when it asserts that "proclamation and dialogue are ... component elements and authentic forms of the one evangelizing mission of the Church" (§2).

The importance of these two documents cannot be overstated. In the light of the history of the concept of dialogue over the course of the last century, these documents represent what might be called

---

6. For extensive bibliography and thorough discussion of this issue, see Karl J. Becker and Ilaria Morali, eds., *Catholic Engagement with World Religions: A Comprehensive Study* (Maryknoll, NY: Orbis Books, 2010).

the complete "domestication" of the previously alien or at least marginal notion of dialogue within the Catholic mainstream. From having been a maverick concept, interreligious dialogue now became "an integral element in the Church's evangelizing mission" (*Dialogue and Proclamation*, §38).

We can express the doctrinal and theological premises behind this move in the following way. The single purpose of the triune God in creation and redemption is to bring the whole human race into community with the Blessed Trinity and in this way to consummate its ecclesial unity. The principal agent of this participation in the communion of the Blessed Trinity is Jesus Christ, in whose image all are created and by whose blood all are redeemed. This purpose continues to be actively pursued in history by the Holy Spirit at work through the Church which proclaims, "God's wisdom, mysterious, hidden, which God predetermined before the ages for our glory" (1 Cor 2:7) and affords access to the riches of God's grace. The Church's mission is to proclaim this purpose to the ends of the earth. In pursuing this mission, the Church understands that the Spirit is at work in the hearts of all human beings and that through the Spirit all are called to fellowship with God in the blood of Christ. Hence the Church believes that, in the course of the mission *ad gentes*, the Spirit's presence and action will in principle be recognizable.

Moreover, the mission will in part consist in bringing this presence and action to light in the minds of those to whom it is directed. Christian respect for the values enshrined in other religious traditions arises from these convictions about the universal scope of God's activity in inviting human persons into communion with himself and with one another in him. This respect in turn impels Christians to engage in dialogue with persons who, while they do not share explicit Christian faith, must be supposed to be touched by the Spirit and striving according to their lights to respond to this grace, although they are not aware of this. It is in this complex sense that dialogue can be said to be integral to the Church's evangelizing mission: mission and dialogue express the single, though differentiated,

Christian participation in the single, though diversely advanced, purpose of the triune God. In dialogue the Christian seeks to identify and explicate the truth that the Holy Spirit plants in the dialogue partner.

From a world-historical perspective, the Christian espousal of interreligious and intercultural dialogue in *Nostra Aetate* also represents a realistic assessment of and adaptation to the new situation facing the Church in its encounter with the major world religions. In the past, Christian mission met with most of its success among peoples of indigenous religions (in the Americas and Africa). But as its focus shifts increasingly to the adherents of major religious traditions, the context of mission alters dramatically. John Milbank has written that

every major religion is *already* the result of confronting the fact of religious differences and an attempt to subsume such differences.... By comparison, genuinely local [indigenous] religions ... may scarcely have had to confront the question of whether their beliefs and practices are relevant beyond the confines of their own society; this is presumably why they are so liable to conversion by or accommodation with the terms of a major religion, which is in part the result of such a confrontation. The major religions are notoriously not so susceptible to conversion or accommodation, precisely because they already embody a more abstract, universal, deterritorialized cultural framework, although they do not usually succumb to the temptation of trying to found this universality in a reason independent of all particularized memory.[7]

Milbank's astute observation implies that it is only through interreligious dialogue that Christians can relate to the major religions and in this way realize the Church's evangelizing mission in the context of societies within their ambits—India (Hinduism) or Malaysia (Islam) or Sri Lanka (Buddhism), for example. The forms of dialogue with which Christians have become familiar—dialogue with other Christians or with atheistic thinkers—are in marked contrast to the situation posed by interreligious dialogue. Here the Church

---

7. John Milbank, "The End of Dialogue," in *Christian Uniqueness Reconsidered*, ed. Gavin D'Costa (Maryknoll, NY: Orbis Books, 1990), 180.

confronts, not disagreements arising from a fundamentally shared faith or from common philosophical or cultural assumptions, but massive and enduring bodies of religious wisdom and highly ramified systems of doctrines derived from ancient scriptural canons. One can see immediately that the challenges posed by this kind of encounter come not from religiously skeptical individuals but from religious communities advancing well-developed alternative conceptions of the ultimate aim of life and the pattern of life directed to the attainment of this aim.[8] This recognition does not imply simply a strategic redirection of missionary energies, but, as the theological justification for dialogue indicates, a recovery of the doctrine of the universal salvific will of God and the universal scope of the action and presence of the Holy Spirit. The need to adapt missionary strategies to a new situation may be regarded as the providential occasion for the retrieval and reaffirmation of truths latent in and, to be fair, never far beneath the surface of the doctrinal and theological traditions of Christianity. The lasting significance of *Nostra Aetate* and of the rich subsequent developments of the Church's magisterium is to have permanently opened up the way to this new path of mission and proclamation.

DOMINUS IESUS: JESUS CHRIST, THE UNIQUE SAVIOR

A second development in the Church's responds to an issue that has arisen in some post-conciliar theology of religions, namely, the notion that it is arrogant to claim that Jesus Christ is the unique mediator of salvation. According to this notion, to ascribe a uniquely salvific role to Jesus Christ seems to constitute a denial of the salvific role of other religious founders and thus could be an affront to their communities.

In part this notion arises from preoccupation with the issue of the salvation of non-Christians and the classification of theological

8. See Di Noia, *The Diversity of Religions*, passim.

positions on the relation of the Church to other religions solely on
the basis of their account of this issue (exclusivism, inclusivism, and
pluralism). This is an important issue, but it is largely internal to
Catholic theology and attention to it frequently blurs the significant
differences in what other religions teach about the ultimate aim of
life and the way to attain it.[9]

The more problematic positions in an inclusivist vein actually
attribute intrinsic salvific value to the scriptures, rituals, symbols,
and ethics of other religious traditions even when these elements
form the basis of a pattern of life directed to an ultimate aim entirely
different from what Christians mean by "salvation." Pluralists, as we
shall see, tend to ascribe to all religions a certain equivalence as paths
to an unknowable beyond more or less equally attainable by way of
the diverse patterns of life they recommend. Both inclusivists and
pluralists tend in this manner to understate the unique salvific role
of Jesus Christ as savior of the human race.[10]

In order to address these fundamental errors in some recent theology of religions, the Congregation for the Doctrine of the Faith in
2000 published the Declaration *Dominus Iesus*. The ferocious reaction to this document amply demonstrated how widespread is the
misunderstanding of the unique salvific role of Jesus Christ, even
within the Church.[11]

We might note here that the origins of these errors lie deep in
the mentality of post-Enlightenment modernity and its multifar-
ious theological progeny. According to this mentality, all religions
express some experience of the absolute or ultimate or transcendent

9. See William A. Christian, Sr., *Meaning and Truth in Religion* (Princeton, NJ:
Princeton University Press, 1964); *Oppositions of Religious Doctrines* (New York: Mac-
millan, 1972); and *Doctrines of Religious Communities* (New Haven, CT: Yale University
Press, 1987).

10. See D'Costa, "Theology of Religions," in *The Modern Theologians*, 3rd ed., ed.
David Ford (Oxford: Wiley-Blackwell, 2005), 626–44, and George R. Sumner, *The First
and the Last: The Claim of Jesus Christ and the Claims of Other Religious Traditions* (Grand
Rapids, MI: Eerdmans, 2004).

11. See Angelo Amato, SDB, "La recezione della *Dominus Iesus*," in *Gesù, identità del
Cristianesimo: conoscenza ed esperienza* (Vatican City: Libreria Editrice Vaticana, 2008).

reality—however it is named and described—that encompasses worldly existence. No religion can claim to possess a privileged description of a reality incomprehensible and ineffable to all equally, nor to afford unique access to a realm in principle available to all equally. In order to address this challenge, we need in the first place to make clear that our faith in Christ's uniqueness does not entail a devaluation of the world's religions. The religions of the world are monuments to the human search for God. As such, they are worthy of respect and study because of the immense cultural richness of their witness to the desire for God planted in every human heart. But the Christian faith attests not only to the human search for God, but principally to God's search for us.

What God wants to share with us is nothing less than a communion of life, a share or participation in the divine trinitarian life. This is the basic starting point for understanding the unique role of Jesus Christ in the salvation of the human race. For the idea that God wants to share the communion of his life with persons who are not God cannot come from anyone but God himself. The initiative here comes from God's side, both to reconcile us because of sin and to make possible a kind of life that would not only be impossible for us but unthinkable as well.

Salvation in this comprehensive sense is not something that can be arranged or organized by human beings. It cannot come from the created order, for the created order has neither the resources to achieve nor the imagination to conceive such a destiny for human persons. Arians, neo-Arians, and their fellow travelers throughout history are willing to acknowledge that Jesus is a savior but then it seems that "salvation is nothing more than a minor adjustment internal to the contingent order. Salvation is something that one creature performs in relation to others."[12]

Given that salvation in the Christian sense of the term involves

---

12. Alan Torrance, "Being of One Substance with The Father," in *Nicene Christianity: The Future for a New Ecumenism*, ed. Christopher R. Seitz (Grand Rapids, MI: Baker, 2001), 57.

both reconciliation of sinners and the elevation of creaturely persons to a new kind of life, it cannot come from within this world. Saviors are a dime a dozen when one fails to grasp what's really at stake. We need to be delivered not just from error, or suffering, or desire, or injustice, or poverty.

To understand what the Christian faith means and promises by salvation, we must grasp the peril of the human condition as well as the glory that is human destiny in the economy of salvation. God desires nothing less than to share his life with us. If the salvation that the triune God wills for the entire human race entails communion with the Father, Son, and Holy Spirit, then the creaturely and sinful obstacles to this communion must be overcome.

It has never been claimed of anyone but Jesus Christ that he could and did overcome these obstacles, and that he could and did make us sharers in his divine life. Through him we are both healed of sin and raised to an adoptive participation in the life of the Blessed Trinity—and nothing less.

The obstacles to this participation are either overcome or not. If they are not overcome, then Christians have nothing for which to hope, for themselves or for others. In that case, they will hawk an empty universal salvation on the highways of the world. If Christians abandon the proclamation of Christ's unique mediatorship as the divine, only-begotten Son of the Father, they will have no other mediatorship with which to replace it. We need the Savior who is not just any savior.

How persons who are not now explicit believers in Christ can actually come to share in the salvation that God desires for the human race and that Christ alone makes possible is too large a topic for this presentation.[13] But surely it must be evident that if Christians—in the wholly admirable desire to be respectful of non-believers and optimistic about their chances of salvation—no longer confess Christ's

13. See Francis A. Sullivan, SJ, *Salvation Outside the Church? Tracing the History of the Catholic Response* (New York: Paulist Press, 1992), and Ralph Martin, *Will Many Be Saved? What Vatican II Actually Teaches and Its Implications for the New Evangelization* (Grand Rapids, MI: Eerdmans, 2012).

unique mediatorship in making ultimate communion with the Blessed Trinity a real possibility for created persons, then the problem of how non-Christians can share in it is not resolved: it simply evaporates. For Christians to have a truly universal hope and confidence in the salvation of persons who are not Christians, they have to affirm the unique role of Christ in bringing this salvation about, not just for themselves but for others as well.

CONCLUSION

As it happens, this international conference on the theology of religions in a Catholic perspective falls at the start of what will likely be the last year of my fifteen-year tenure in the Holy See as a theologian in direct service of the magisterium. It occurred to me that this keynote address should properly provide you with the "view from Rome" as it were—an account of the ways that the magisterium has evolved to address some of the challenges posed for theology by the Second Vatican Council's teachings on the Church's relations with other religions.

In part in order to sharpen the focus of this paper and to allow time for questions and discussion, I have left many things out. Among these, the most serious omission is the absence of a discussion of the significant developments in theology of the relations of the Catholic Church and the Jewish people. This is something I very much regret. To have done justice to these developments would have required another paper and a very different kind of paper. In my defense, I can say that I have risked this serious omission only because in many ways the tremendous progress in this area represents perhaps the most remarkable outcome of the Second Vatican Council. In a real sense, this is perfectly appropriate. As is well known, what became the conciliar decree *Nostra Aetate* was at first intended as a statement devoted entirely precisely to the relations between the Church and the Jewish people.[14] In the aftermath, the pontificate and

14. See Arthur Kennedy, "The Declaration on the Relationship of the Church to

magisterium of Pope John Paul II were especially significant.[15] Not only has the Church adopted a posture of dialogue with our Jewish brothers and sisters, but she has forcefully repudiated antisemitism as well as those interpretations of her teaching that may contribute to anti-Judaism and antisemitism. The enormity of this challenge, both for the Church but also for Western thought, was demonstrated by David Nirenberg in a brilliant book on anti-Judaism.[16] Perhaps most theologically significant has been the acknowledgement of the irrevocable character of the First Covenant, a development that continues to prompt lively theological discussion.

Another omission is the resurgence of indigenous religions as a component of the reassertion of the historical ethnic and cultural identities of communities of original populations in many parts of the world: among Native Americans in the United States, the Indios of South America, the First Nations in Canada, Aboriginal Australians, the Sami here in the Nordic countries and in Russia, and so on. At times, these populations experienced Christian evangelization as an aspect of colonialization and/or subjugation and even ethnic cleansing. The challenges posed for the Church by this new awakening of indigenous religions vary from country to country—as we hear from the bishops who come to Rome regularly on their *ad limina* visits. But from a theological point of view, there are certain common themes—for example, Earth-centered piety—and certain issues—for example, the relation of Christianity and culture—that merit attention in the theology of religions rather than simply in the classical locus of the theology of mission.[17] It may well happen that the concerns of bishops will prompt some developments in the Church's magisterium regarding indigenous religions.

Non-Christian Religions, *Nostra Aetate*," in *Vatican II: Renewal Within Tradition*, ed. Matthew Lamb and Matthew Levering (New York: Oxford University Press, 2008), 397–409.

15. See David G. Dalin and Matthew Levering, eds., *John Paul II and the Jewish People: A Jewish-Christian Dialogue* (Lanham, MD: Rowman and Littlefield, 2008).

16. David Nirenberg, *Anti-Judaism: The History of a Way of Thinking* (New York: W. H. Norton, 2013).

17. See James L. Cox, ed., *Critical Reflections on Indigenous Religions* (New York: Routledge, 2016).

How the developments in the Church's universal magisterium that I have considered in this paper—namely, those regarding the compatibility of dialogue and proclamation and those regarding the unique salvific mediatorship of Jesus Christ—will come to shape the future of Catholic theology of religions remains to be seen. The preoccupation of much of the field with the question of the salvation of non-Christians continues to be, in my view, a distraction. Perhaps a small dose of what Catherine Cornille has called "soteriological agnosticism"[18] might serve us well here if it helps us both to respect the distinctiveness and integrity of what other religions actually teach and at the same time to hold firmly to fundamental truths of our own faith.

18. Catherine Cornille, "Religious Pluralism and Christian Faith: A Case for Soteriological Agnosticism," *Actualidad Teologica* vol. 40–41 (2012): 50–71.

CHAPTER 16

Christian Universalism
The Nonexclusive Particularity of Salvation in Christ

Is Jesus Christ the unique mediator of salvation? I was one of five panelists assigned to address this question at a recent meeting of Catholic theologians. I was the first to speak and, as it turned out, the only panelist prepared to advance an unqualified affirmative response to the question. Why is this? Why would a group of Catholic theologians decline to affirm what, until recently, would have been considered an unquestionable tenet of ecumenical Christian faith?

As the session unfolded, it became clear that their reluctance to do so was motivated at least in part by a desire to avoid giving offense to religious people of other traditions. The underlying premise of their remarks, and of the ensuing discussion, seemed to be this: To ascribe a uniquely salvific role to Jesus Christ would constitute a denial of the salvific role of other religious founders (like the Buddha and Muhammad) and thus would be an affront to their communities.

The way that many theologians think about this issue has been influenced by the pluralist theology of religions popularized by John

Originally published in *Either/Or: The Gospel of Neopaganism*, ed. Carl E. Braaten and Robert W. Jenson (Grand Rapids, MI: Eerdmans, 1995), 37–48. Reprinted by permission of the publisher.

Hick, Paul Knitter, and others.[1] Indeed, Paul Knitter was one of the panelists at the session I mentioned above. In a nutshell, pluralists claim that in one way or another all religions aim at salvation. In John Hick's influential definition, salvation is the movement from self-centeredness to "Reality-centeredness." Since, according to pluralists, ultimate Reality is incomprehensible and ineffable, no one religious description can claim primacy over rival descriptions, and no tradition can claim exclusive rights to the means of salvation.

In the pluralist perspective, therefore, each religious founder must be regarded as in some sense a savior. Exclusive or unique status, with respect to the knowledge of, provision for, or access to, salvation can no more be claimed for Jesus of Nazareth than it can be claimed for Gautama the Buddha or for Muhammad. Naturally, pluralists do not deny that these founders were unique historical personalities. What they deny is that any one of them could provide a uniquely privileged or exclusive access to salvation.

It follows for pluralists that Christian theologians cannot give a simple affirmative answer to the question, Is Jesus Christ the unique mediator of salvation? On the basis of their study of religious traditions, pluralist philosophers and theologians contend that salvation, though diversely mediated, is nonetheless universally accessible. It is not just in order to avoid giving offense to other religious people that pluralists have championed this view. Pluralists argue on empirical and philosophical grounds that a soteriological structure underlies all religious traditions and thus variously orients their adherents to "Reality" as it is diversely figured in these traditions. Only in this way can Christian theologians affirm the universality of salvation

1. Paul Knitter has advanced his position on this issue in a widely read book called *No Other Name? A Critical Survey of Christian Attitudes toward Other Religions* (Maryknoll, NY: Orbis Books, 1985). John Hick has recently restated his position in *An Interpretation of Religion: Human Respondents to the Transcendent* (New Haven, CT: Yale Univ. Press, 1989). With Paul Knitter, Hick edited an influential volume of essays, *The Myth of Christian Uniqueness: Toward a Pluralistic Theology of Religions* (Maryknoll, NY: Orbis Books, 1987), in which the pluralist case is pressed from a variety of standpoints. For responses to these essays and to pluralism generally, see *Christian Uniqueness Reconsidered: The Myth of a Pluralistic Theology of Religions*, ed. Gavin D'Costa (Maryknoll, NY: Orbis Books, 1990).

and of religious truth, at least as possibilities, without giving offense to other religious people.

To be sure, pluralists are not the only theologians who have been concerned with the salvation of persons who are not Christians. According to the typology prevailing in current theology of religions, the chief alternative positions on this issue are represented by exclusivism and inclusivism. In contrast to pluralists, both exclusivists and inclusivists would have no difficulty in giving an affirmative answer to the question, Is Jesus Christ the unique mediator of salvation? For all their sharp differences, exclusivists and inclusivists concur in their avowal of the uniquely salvific role of Christ. But exclusivists deny the possibility of salvation for non-Christians who do not before death explicitly profess faith in Christ. Inclusivists, on the other hand, allow for the possibility of salvation chiefly on the grounds of some form of implicit faith in Christ, combined with a morally upright life, on the part of non-Christians.[2]

The Christian concern not to give offense to other religious people is a praiseworthy one, while the concern to allow for the possibility of their salvation is a doctrinally crucial one. But suppose that, far from being an affront to other religious traditions, a strong Christian affirmation of the uniqueness of Christ's salvific role were fundamental to traditional Christian universalism. Suppose, in other words, that the particularity of salvation in Christ were non-exclusive. Suppose, further, that an affirmation of this nonexclusive particularity of salvation in Christ were not an obstacle to but a condition for genuine respect for other religious people.

I have argued this position at length elsewhere.[3] It rests not only on central Christian doctrines but also on the suggestion that

2. For a historical perspective on this debate, see Francis A. Sullivan, SJ, *Salvation Outside the Church? Tracing the History of the Catholic Response* (New York: Paulist, 1992). For a reliable survey of the current discussion, though from a largely inclusivist vantage point, see Gavin D'Costa, *Theology and Religious Pluralism* (Oxford: Basil Blackwell, 1986).

3. See J. A. Di Noia, OP, *The Diversity of Religions: A Christian Perspective* (Washington, DC: The Catholic University of America Press, 1992).

"salvation" is not a term that encompasses what all religions seek, but is a properly Christian designation for that which should be sought above all else in life. Salvation has a distinctively Christian content: transformation in Christ with a view to ultimate communion with the triune God. Even where other religious communities employ the term "salvation," their conceptions of the aim of life differ from one another and from that espoused by Christian communities. By framing the agenda of theology of religions primarily in terms of the possibility of extra-Christian salvation, pluralists and inclusivists often fail to give enough weight to the specificity and distinctiveness of religious aims. Inclusivists fail to notice their distinctiveness because they tend to reinterpret non-Christian patterns and aims in Christian terms. More at the center of my attention in this essay, however, are pluralists who make salvation an all-encompassing designation for the variety of aims that religious traditions espouse and commend.

If the issues here were framed differently, it might turn out that to affirm Christ's unique role in salvation is not to exclude persons who are not Christians but to embrace them. In other words, it might turn out that we could give a strong affirmative answer to the question, Is Jesus Christ the unique mediator of salvation? and still both show respect for other religious people and include them in the final consummation of all things for which we have reason, only in Christ, to hope.

In order to reframe these issues, and at the same time to identify what seems to be the weakness especially of typical pluralist approaches to them, I want to engage in an experiment. I will compare the question, "Is Jesus Christ the unique mediator of salvation?" with the question, "Is the Buddha the unique revealer of the Dharma?"

Suppose that I pose this second question to a Buddhist friend. Along with most other Buddhists, she will answer it affirmatively. The Dharma comprises all that concerns Nirvana and its attainment. Even though Buddhists commonly insist that knowledge of the Dharma is in principle accessible to anyone, still they regard

Gautama's discovery and teaching of the Dharma as unique in this era.[4]

Consider how the conversation might proceed at this point. If my Buddhist friend should caution me that I will never attain Nirvana by following the course of life laid out for me by the Christian community, I do not feel anxious about this. I have not been persuaded that seeking Nirvana is what I should be doing. If I did begin to be persuaded of this, then I should undertake to discover the path and try to make my way along it. I would, in other words, have begun to be a follower of the Buddha. I might then even join a Buddhist community, or at least become an inquirer. Some Catholics I know have done this very thing. But if I continue to be convinced that it is salvation that I should be seeking and that Christ is the unique mediator of this salvation, then I would continue on the Christian path.

One thing to notice about this hypothetical encounter between me and my Buddhist friend is that I have not felt affronted by her warning that I shall not attain Nirvana unless I follow the Excellent Eightfold Path taught uniquely by the Buddha. On the contrary, my initial reaction is that what she has said to me makes perfect sense. If the Excellent Eightfold Path is the way to Nirvana, and if I do not choose to pursue this path, then it follows that I may not reach Nirvana. But, since I have as yet no desire to attain and enjoy Nirvana, I am not offended by this reasoning. I have not been persuaded that Nirvana is what I should be seeking.

Without trying to field a "definition" of religion—something that has proven notoriously difficult to do—I could say that the Christian community and the Buddhist community (with their various subcommunities) both seem to have some conception of an ultimate aim of life and have developed a pattern of life geared toward attaining it. Other major religious communities share this tendency as well.[5] What is ultimate, whether it be a transcendent agent or

4. See, e.g., the discussion of the uniqueness of the Buddha's discovery and teaching of the Dharma in Sangharakshita, *A Survey of Buddhism,* 5th ed. (Boulder, CO: Shambhala Publications, 1980), 37–38.

5. In his *Doctrines of Religious Communities* (New Haven, CT: Yale University Press,

as-yet-unrealized state of being, invades life at every moment, and summons the community's members to order and shape their lives in view of this aim. The world's religious communities differ in their descriptions of the aims that are ultimate in this sense (e.g., the extinction of the self or communion with the triune God) as well as in their provision for the cultivation of patterns of life ordered to the attainment and enjoyment of such aims (e.g., the Dharma or the gospel). But they seem to agree in espousing and commending comprehensive aims of life, and in striving to shape the lives of their members with a view to those aims.

I can now formulate a preliminary result of the consideration of the hypothetical conversation between me and my Buddhist friend. If the assertion "The Buddha is the unique revealer of the Dharma" is not offensive to me, then why should the assertion "Jesus Christ is the unique mediator of salvation" be offensive to Buddhists, or, for that matter, to Muslims, Vedantists, or Jews? A Jewish rabbi once said to me, revealingly: "Jesus Christ is the answer to a question I have never asked." This remark suggests that we might be on the right track in our reflections. Salvation in the Christian sense, it implies, is not what the rabbi is seeking. Asking the question to which Jesus Christ is the answer commits oneself to an inquiry (logically speaking) that may lead to the adoption of a Christian way of life. At least in part, this will mean that what Christians aim for, as expressed by the umbrella term "salvation," has begun to look appealing or even ultimately important. One might conclude: *This* is what I should be aiming for in my life. But what would *this* be?

When Christians try to answer this question, we find ourselves becoming quite specific. When we try to say what comprises salvation, we find ourselves talking about the triune God; the Incarnation, Passion, Death, and Resurrection of Jesus Christ; grace, sin, and justification; transfiguration and divinization; faith, hope, and

---

1987), William A. Christian, Sr., has observed: "There seems to be a deep-seated tendency in the major religious communities to develop a comprehensive pattern of life … which bears on all human interests … and on all situations in which human beings find themselves" (186).

charity; the commandments and the moral virtues; and many other characteristically Christian things as well. We should not be surprised if, in trying to answer a cognate question, a member of another religious community, say a Buddhist, should also become very specific about Nirvana and all that bears on its attainment. We should not be surprised, furthermore, if the descriptions of salvation and Nirvana do not coincide. But, for the moment, let us continue the experiment by sketching some of the things that a Christian description of salvation might have to include.

Allowing for variations across its various subcommunities, we can understand the ecumenical Christian community to teach that the ultimate aim of life is a communion of life—a communion of life with the Father, through the Son, and in the Holy Spirit. According to ecumenical Christian faith, this is a truth proclaimed by Christ and a destiny made possible for us by his Passion, Death, and Resurrection. This is what Christians mean by salvation: The term embraces both the goal of ultimate communion and the empowerment to attain and enjoy it.

Human persons are called to nothing less than communion with the Father, Son, and Holy Spirit, and with each other in them. Indeed, Christianity affirms that the triune God could not bring about a more intimate union with created persons than that which has already been initiated in Baptism and will be fulfilled for us in Christ. Ultimate communion involves nothing less than becoming part of the trinitarian family. The principle and agent of this communion for us is Christ. Just as Christ is Son by nature—a member of the divine family of the Trinity in virtue of his being the Son of the Father—so human persons are to be sons and daughters by adoption. Our fellowship with Christ and with each other in him brings us into the divine trinitarian family.

But if we are destined to enjoy this ultimate communion, then we must change. We must become fit for it. Interpersonal communion with God is only "natural" to uncreated persons; for created persons, who are also sinners, such communion is possible only through justification and grace. Through the redeeming grace of Christ and, specifically, through the transformation that this grace makes possible, we are rendered "fit" participants in the communion of the Father, Son, and Holy Spirit. Our transformation will be a conformation: The more we become like Christ, the more surely do we discover our true selves, the unique persons created by the triune God to share in the divine life and to enjoy the personal life of the Trinity. As Catholics pray in one of the Sunday prefaces: "Father, … [y]ou sent him as one like ourselves, though free from sin, that you might see and love in us what you see and love in him."[6]

However, this conformation does not amount to a mere conformity. The conformation to Christ that is the principle of our transformation is not a mere cloning but the realization of our distinctive and unique personal identities. This must be so, for otherwise the communion to which this transformation is directed could not be consummated. The image of God in us consists precisely in the spiritual capacities for knowing and loving that make interpersonal communion possible. But authentic interpersonal communion presupposes the full realization of the individual persons who enter into it. Thus, if Christ is to be the principle and pattern of our transformation, in being conformed to him we must each discover and realize our own unique identities as persons, and be healed of the sinful dispositions that obstruct the flourishing of our true selves.

This is the force of the astonishing saying of Christ:

If a man wants to be my disciple, let him deny himself and take up his cross and follow me. For whoever wants to save his life will lose it, and whoever loses his life for my sake will find it. For what will it profit a man if he gains the whole world but loses his life? Or what will he give in return for his life? (Mt 16:24–26)

None of us, whether as teachers, parents, or pastors—no matter how inflated our conceptions of ourselves or how confident our sense of our abilities—would ever dare to say to anybody in our charge that

6. Sundays in Ordinary Time, Preface VII, *The Sacramentary* (New York: Catholic Book Publishing Co., 1974), 443.

they will find their true selves by imitating us. In effect, Christ asserts that an indefinite number of human persons will find their distinctive identities by being conformed to Christ. A moment's reflection shows us that only the Son of God could make such an assertion. No mere human could do so. Only the inexhaustibly rich, perfect Image of God who is the person of the Son in human nature could constitute the principle and pattern for the transformation and fulfillment of every human person who has ever lived.

When Christians affirm that Jesus Christ is the unique mediator of salvation, something like the above can stand as a summary of what they mean. Leave aside for a moment the question whether such a description includes or excludes persons who are not Christians. What we need to consider first, as we continue to reflect on my hypothetical conversation with a Buddhist friend, is whether such a description of what Christians mean by salvation is offensive to persons who are not Christians—Buddhists, for example. Informed of what a Christian means by salvation, would there be reason for a Buddhist to feel excluded by the assertion that Jesus Christ is the unique mediator of salvation?

We have seen that salvation has a specific content for Christians: It entails an interpersonal communion, made possible by Christ, between human persons and the Father, Son, and Holy Spirit. At least at first sight, this seems to be something very different from what Buddhists can be supposed to be seeking when they follow the Excellent Eightfold Path that leads them on the way to realizing enlightenment and the extinction of self in Nirvana.[7] At least on the face of things, what Buddhists mean by "Nirvana" and what Christians mean by "salvation" do not seem to coincide. This does not

7. The statement of my argument here is deliberately hypothetical. My purpose is not to present an account of Buddhism, though I have striven to be accurate about Buddhist doctrines. Rather, it is to render plausible the claim, fundamental to my argument, that "Nirvana" and "salvation" seem to designate significantly different aims of life, and thus call forth distinctive patterns of life in the members of Buddhist and Christian communities respectively, and to render implausible the pluralist claim that salvation encompasses what Christians mean by ultimate communion with the triune God and what Buddhists (seem to) mean by Nirvana.

mean that they are opposed; it remains to be seen whether seeking salvation and seeking Nirvana are complementary to each other or related in some as yet unspecified manner.[8] However, it seems clear that interpersonal communion is a very different thing from the extinction of the self entailed in Nirvana. Many forms of Buddhism are concerned to cultivate dispositions that increasingly unmask the illusoriness of personal identity. As I noted above in my sketch of what most Christians mean by salvation, Christians understand personal identity to be of permanent, indeed eternal, significance because eternity centrally involves interpersonal communion.

Let us return to my hypothetical conversation with a Buddhist friend. You will recall that we left the conversation at the point when she cautioned me that I would not reach Nirvana unless I followed the Excellent Eightfold Path. This warning was not disturbing to me, for I do not want to attain Nirvana. Suppose that when the conversation resumes I offer a description of what Christians mean by salvation, a description not unlike the one presented above. Would we be surprised to find that my Buddhist friend wants no part of this? It is difficult for us to understand and accept that what we regard as most important—more so than anything else, absolutely speaking—other religious people challenge or repudiate. Buddhist communities in all their variety possess highly ramified teachings about the true aim of life and about the means to attain it. These teachings do not, at least on the surface, coincide with what Christians teach about these very matters. Buddhists do not want ultimate communion; they do not seek it, and, insofar as they think about it, they may regard us as misguided for wanting and seeking it. For, by wanting and seeking ultimate communion we remain, from a Buddhist point of view, incorrigibly attached to the very conceptions of personal identity that constitute the chief obstacle on the way to Nirvana.

8. For a philosophical analysis of religious disagreements, see William A. Christian, Sr., *Oppositions of Religious Doctrines* (New York: Seabury, 1972). For a discussion of the kinds of arguments that such disagreements might give rise to in interreligious dialogue, see Paul J. Griffiths, *An Apology for Apologetics: A Study in the Logic of Interreligious Dialogue* (Maryknoll, NY: Orbis Books, 1991).

Gautama the Buddha is the authority on these matters. He discovered and taught the Dharma, and through it attained enlightenment. His role, in revealing the Dharma to others is regarded by most of his followers as something original, at least in the present epoch. Hence, while it makes good sense for Buddhists to affirm that the Buddha is the unique revealer of the Dharma, it makes little sense for them to be offended when Christians describe Jesus Christ as the unique mediator of salvation. Buddhists regard Christian beliefs about this as misguided and perhaps only partially true, but they will not be anxious or offended by such a Christian affirmation. They are not interested in seeking and attaining salvation as Christians understand it.

To be sure, some people—pluralists in particular—want to define "salvation" so broadly that it includes both what Christians mean by it and what Buddhists mean by Nirvana. On this account of things, my hypothetical encounter with a Buddhist friend would not present either of us with a choice between seeking Nirvana and seeking salvation. Some would say that to think that there is a serious choice here is, religiously speaking, overly literalistic and even simpleminded. Indeed, pluralists contend, precisely at this juncture the superiority of pluralist theology of religions is displayed. Pluralists argue that all religious communities advance their members toward specific aims—communion or enlightenment, as the case may be—that are surpassed or transcended by a more ultimate, but indescribable, aim. All religious communities seek this yet more ultimate aim with varying degrees of clarity and success. Not only is this conception closer to the truth of the matter, it also provides the basis for the sympathetic understanding, fruitful dialogue, and mutual respect that are desperately needed today.

In fact, however, this basic premise of pluralist theology of religions will not stand up under close scrutiny. Even if religious communities were prepared to accept some such description of what they are about—something few of them show any inclination to do—it still remains true that they espouse and commend specific aims that differ from one another. Furthermore, these specific aims call forth distinctive patterns of life in each of the major religious traditions and in local traditions as well. Certain kinds of life are understood to foster the enjoyment of certain kinds of ends of life, and others to obstruct this enjoyment. This seems to be an ineradicable feature of the characteristic discourse and ethos of most religious communities. Individual lives come to be shaped by the ultimate aims that are sought. So even if the true aim of life were one that transcended the particular aims of all religious traditions—something stipulated by pluralists—no one could seek it. No one could undertake to order life in such a way as to attain and enjoy an ultimate aim of life of which no description could be given.

But this goes directly against the grain of characteristic religious affirmation and conviction. Religious people, by and large, believe themselves to be in possession of understandings, incomplete though they may be, of what is ultimately important in life and how to orient life in its direction. Significant disagreements obtain among the major and local religious traditions about these matters. Pluralist theology of religions does not so much explain these disagreements as explain them away. In this way, pluralism seems to offer a massive redescription, rather than an interpretation, of religious beliefs and practices, and of the arresting differences among them.

Thus, the following statements are not problematic in the way that many people, like those I joined on the theological panel, seem to think: "Jesus Christ is the unique mediator of salvation" and "The Buddha is the unique revealer of the Dharma." Were representatives of Christian or Buddhist communities to retreat from advancing such claims, it is not clear what they would have to offer to the world. There would be no compelling, or even interesting, reasons to persevere in membership in these communities, or indeed to seek it.

The great challenge facing present-day Christian theology of religions and interreligious conversation is to avoid minimizing the distinctive features of the major religious traditions through a well-intentioned universalism. Christian confidence in the universal scope of salvation rests on convictions about the historical career and perduring agency of Jesus Christ. Only if his identity is affirmed in its fullness—in accord with the holy Scripture, the great councils, and the church's liturgy—as the Son of God who became man and died for us, can the hope of Christians for themselves and for others be sustained. "For in him all the fullness of God was pleased to dwell, and through him God was pleased to reconcile all things, whether on earth or in heaven, by making peace through the blood of his cross" (Col 1:19–20).

If the salvation that the triune God wills for the entire human race entails ultimate communion with the three persons, then the creaturely and sinful obstacles to this communion must be overcome. It has never been claimed that anyone but Jesus Christ could overcome these obstacles. Through him we are both healed and raised to an adoptive participation in the life of the Trinity. The obstacles to this participation are either overcome or not. If they are not overcome, then Christians have nothing for which to hope, for themselves or for others. In that case, they will hawk an empty universalism on the highways of the world. When Christians abandon the proclamation of Christ's unique mediatorship, they have no other mediatorship with which to replace it. How persons who are not now explicit believers in Christ are to share in the salvation he alone makes possible is a large topic that I have not addressed in this paper. But if Christians no longer confess Christ's unique mediatorship in making ultimate communion a real possibility for created persons, then the problem of how non-Christians can share in it is not resolved. It simply evaporates. True Christian universalism depends on the affirmation of the nonexclusive particularity of salvation in Jesus Christ.

CHAPTER 17

———————— : ————————

"By Whom All Things Were Made"

Trinitarian Theology of Creation as the Basis for a Person-Friendly Cosmology

"[W]e are the product of 15 billion years of an expanding, evolving universe and 3 billion years of an ineluctable evolution from primitive living organisms to the most complex entity known to exist, the human brain. But that evolutionary path was not a straight and narrow one."[1]

The path, scientists generally agree, goes back about 15 billion years: it was then that the universe erupted in an explosion called the Big Bang and has been expanding and cooling ever since. Working backward to the moment of this eruption, scientists have attempted to map the first three minutes after the Big Bang occurred in order to explain the background for the gradual emergence of the conditions necessary for the formation of atoms at about three hundred thousand years later, the condensation of galaxies and stars at about one billion years later, and the formation of planets at about 10 billion

Originally published in *Nicene Christianity: The Future for a New Ecumenism*, ed. Christopher Seitz (Grand Rapids, MI: Brazos Press, 2001), 63–73. Excerpt from *Nicene Christianity* by Christopher R. Seitz, ed., copyright © 2001. Used by permission of Brazos Press, a division of Baker Publishing Group

1. George Coyne, SJ, "The Universe: Scientific Understanding and Theological Implications," *Origins* 26 (1997): 480.

years later. Recent observations of the behavior of supernovas tend to confirm the Big Bang theory and to point, somewhat unexpectedly, to an accelerating rate of cosmic expansion, in which a balance between inflationary and contracting forces will be maintained.

In our own solar system and on earth, which were formed about 4.5 billion years ago, the conditions have been favorable to the emergence of life. While there is little consensus among scientists about how the origin of this first microscopic life is to be explained, there is general agreement among them that the first organism dwelt on this planet about 3.5 to 4 million years ago.[2] They are virtually certain that all living organisms have descended from this first organism.[3] This represents a considerable development since Charles Darwin first advanced his account of the evolution of species more than one hundred years ago. Although Darwinian and neo-Darwinian versions of evolutionary theory have been subjected to vigorous criticism, particularly with regard to the role of natural selection in evolution, converging evidence from many studies in the physical and biological sciences furnishes mounting support for the evolutionary

2. In his recent book, *The Fifth Miracle: The Search for the Origin and Meaning of Life* (New York: Simon & Schuster, 1999), Paul Davies states: "What remains to be explained—what stands as the central unsolved puzzle—is how the first microbe came to exist" (29).

3. In "Biological Evolution and Christian Theology—Yesterday and Today," *Darwinism and Divinity*, ed. John Durant (New York: Blackwell, 1985), 115, A. R. Peacocke summarizes the evidence for evolutionary relations among living organisms: "Twentieth-century biochemistry, notably in its phase of molecular biology, has now demonstrated fundamental similarities at the molecular level between all living organisms from bacteria to man. Not only is nucleic acid (DNA or RNA) the prime carrier of hereditary information in all living organisms but the code that translates this information from base sequences in DNA, via messenger RNA, to amino acid sequences in proteins (and thence to their structure and function), is the *same* code in *all* living organisms. This code is arbitrary with respect to the relations of the molecular structures involved and its universality is comprehensible only as the result of evolution: the code now universally operative is the one which happened to be present in the living matter that first successfully reproduced itself fast enough to outnumber other rivals. Molecular biology has provided another independent and powerful confirmation of evolutionary relations through its ability to compare amino acid sequences in proteins with the same chemical function (e.g. cytochrome C) in widely different organisms. The striking fact is that such comparisons entirely and independently confirm ... the evolutionary relationships previously deduced on morphological and paleontological grounds."

hypothesis.[4] Among scientists, there is controversy over the pace and mechanisms of evolution but not over the general explanatory efficacy of evolutionary theory.

Set within this broad history of biogenesis, the story of human origins is extremely complex and is regularly revised on the basis of new discoveries.[5] While there is considerable disagreement among scientists over the interpretation of the prehuman (and, indeed, prehominid) fossil record, lines of evidence in physical anthropology and molecular biology combine to make a convincing (but by no means universally accepted) case for the origin of the human species in Africa at about forty thousand years ago in a humanoid population descended from a common genetic lineage. Over the next thirty thousand years, modern humans spread from Africa to Asia and beyond. However it is to be explained, the decisive factor in human origins was a continually increasing brain size, culminating in that of *Homo sapiens*, "which is acknowledged to be a feat of fantastic difficulty, the most spectacular enterprise of life since its origin, a unique instrument of as many as one billion nerve cells, ... a network of incredibly complex neural circuits."[6] Furthermore, with the development of the brain, the nature and rate of evolution were permanently altered: with the introduction of the uniquely human factors of consciousness, intentionality, freedom and creativity, biological evolution was recast as cultural and social evolution.[7]

---

4. See, for example, Michael Denton, *Evolution: A Theory in Crisis* (Bethesda, MD: Adler & Adler, 1985) and Michael J. Behe, *Darwin's Black Box* (New York: Simon & Schuster, 1996). For a brief summary of the issues, see Ian G. Barbour, *Religion and Science: Historical and Contemporary Issues* (San Francisco: HarperCollins, 1997), 221–25. See also Kenneth D. Miller, *Finding Darwin's God: A Scientist's Search for Common Ground Between God and Evolution* (New York: HarperCollins, 1999).

5. For a summary account, see Richard Fortey, *Life: A Natural History of the First Four Billion Years of Life on Earth* (New York: Alfred Knopf, 1998), 289–315.

6. Christopher F. Mooney, SJ, *Theology and Scientific Knowledge* (Notre Dame, IN: University of Notre Dame Press, 1996), 138.

7. See Peter Medawar, *The Threat and the Glory* (New York: HarperCollins, 1990), 144–77. More recently, in *NonZero: The Logic of Human Destiny* (New York: Random House, 2000), Robert Wright has argued for the continuity between biological and cultural evolution, pointing to the marked tendency in both toward increasing complexity.

BY WHOM ALL THINGS WERE MADE

"By whom all things were made"? Indeed yes. To be sure, it may have been easier to comprehend and maintain this affirmation of the Nicene Creed when the universe was a cozier place and our position within it more secure. Nonetheless, ours is a moment when the Nicene confession must continue to define the contours of Christian faith, and is urgently relevant to address a cosmology and an account of human origins that has permanently dispelled the coziness of the universe. The immense age and unimaginable vastness of the universe have made it increasingly difficult to paint a significant niche for human persons in the big picture. Indeed, far from viewing the universe as centered on the flourishing of human persons, some environmentalists seem to regard us as interlopers and spoilers. In these circumstances, religious communities like Buddhism, that affirm the radical impersonality of the universe and whatever lies beyond it, are at an apologetic advantage in comparison with Christian communities.

We need to recover and articulate the Christian understanding of the cosmos as a person-friendly place. A trinitarian theology of creation is essential to—indeed requires and entails—this recovery and reaffirmation. Central to this project is what Cohn Gunton has termed a "theology of relatedness."[8] This vast, ancient, and seemingly impersonal universe exists for one reason alone: because of the divine desire to share the communion of trinitarian life with persons who are not God.

Before proceeding to consider the contemporary relevance of this clause of the second article, let us briefly review what the clause affirms and what was at stake in this affirmation.

---

8. Colin E. Gunton, *The One, the Three and the Many: God, Creation and the Culture of Modernity* (Cambridge: Cambridge University Press, 1993), 155–79.

What does the clause affirm?

The clause draws directly upon a scriptural idiom. "In the beginning was the Word … and the Word was God…. All things were made through him, and without him was not anything made that was made" (Jn 1:1–3 RSV). God created everything by the eternal Word. In him, "all things were created, in heaven and on earth … all things were created through him and for him. He is before all things, and in him all things hold together" (Col 1:16–17 RSV). The Triune God created the world. As St. Irenaeus says, "he made all things by himself, that is by his Word and his Spirit."[9] Although the third article of the Nicene Creed is to be covered by other speakers, we should note here that the Catechism takes the phrase "giver of life" to affirm the part of the Holy Spirit in creation—*Veni Creator Spiritus*. Creation is a free, personal act of the Blessed Trinity, operating through Word and Wisdom.

What was at stake?

The question of what was at stake is more fully discussed in Alan Torrance's chapter. We may note briefly here that the Arian notion, as summarized by J. N.D. Kelly, entailed the view that "the created order could not bear the weight of the direct action of the increate and eternal God."[10] As Jaroslav Pelikan puts it: "Only he who had created the universe could save man, and … to do either or both of these he himself had to be divine and not a creature."[11]

What is at stake now?

Addressing the topic of evolution recently, Pope John Paul II stated that "new knowledge leads to the recognition of the theory of evolution as more than a hypothesis. It is indeed remarkable that this

9. Quoted in the *Catechism of the Catholic Church*, §292.

10. J. N. D. Kelly, *Early Christian Creeds*, 3rd edition (New York: David McKay, 1972), 232.

11. Jaroslav Pelikan, *The Emergence of the Catholic Tradition (100–600)* (Chicago: University of Chicago Press, 1971), 203.

theory has been progressively accepted by researchers following a series of discoveries in various fields of knowledge." In view of this growing consensus among scientists, Pope John Paul II went on to state that the concern of the Church with the question of evolution focuses particularly on "the conception of man" who, as created in the image of God, "cannot be subordinated as a pure means or instrument either to the species or to society." As a person created in the image of God, he is capable of forming relationships of communion with other persons and with the Triune God. Pope John Paul encouraged philosophers and theologians to continue to collaborate with scientists in addressing the questions that scientific studies of human origins raise about human beings within the perspective of God's plan.[12] What is at stake now in the Nicene confession that all things were made in Christ can be stated simply: the history of the evolving universe since the moment of creation can only be seen in its complete reality in the light of faith, as a *personal history of the engagement of the Triune God with creaturely persons.*

The truth that human persons are created by God in the image of the Triune God illumines all aspects of the concrete human reality. It provides the indispensable foundation for the dialogue between science and theology about the origins of the universe and of the place of human persons within the universe.

The new ecumenism furnishes the resources to approach this dialogue with science about the place of human beings in the universe confident that, since the God who created the world also created the human desire and capacity to know this world, scientific truth and divine truth cannot be in opposition (cf. *Fides et Ratio*). Scientific inquiry is itself an exercise of the dominion and stewardship of human persons created in the image of the Triune God. To be sure, in the conversation between science and theology, there is always the possibility that particular scientific questions might challenge and even

12. Pope John Paul II, Message to Participants in the Plenary of the Pontifical Academy of Sciences, 22 October 1996 (https://www.vatican.va/content/john-paul-ii/fr/messages/pont_messages/1996/documents/hf_jp-ii_mes_19961022_evoluzione.html), §4, 5, and 6.

oppose the affirmations of the faith. But both scientists and theologians have increasingly recognized that the relationship between science and theology should be viewed neither as one of permanent conflict nor of mutual irrelevance, but rather as one of dialogue and, where appropriate, integration.[13]

It is important to take advantage of the new recognition of the possibilities afforded by dialogue between science and theology. Christian theology in this new ecumenical moment cannot be satisfied with a situation in which scientific and religious understandings are regarded as either contradictory or irrelevant to one another. For one thing, the great Catholic tradition insists on the complementarity of faith and reason, and on the possibility that inquiries undertaken in science and under faith can be mutually illuminating. In addition, the present atmosphere is quite favorable for positive dialogue between scientists and theologians. A growing number of scientists regard developments in biology and astrophysics as opening the way to a more fruitful kind of dialogue with theologians than might have been possible even in the recent past. Theologians for their part are challenged to keep abreast of these developments, and to consider both their implications for the Christian understanding of creation and the light which Christian faith throws on accumulating scientific discoveries about cosmic and evolutionary history. We cannot withdraw from this discussion, leaving it to a variety of New Age strategies that seek "salvation" through the cultivation of spiritual powers in an otherwise closed universe. Speaking from within my own tradition, I should note that the Catholic theology of creation approaches the dialogue with the science of evolution and the origins of the universe with considerable experience and resources. In particular, there is a long tradition of biblical exegesis of the first books of *Genesis* that has generally sought to keep pace with developing

---

13. For a discussion of these ways of relating science and religion, see Barbour, *Religion and Science*, 77–105. See also, Avery Dulles, SJ, "Science and Theology," in *John Paul II on Science and Religion*, ed. Robert John Russell, William R. Stoeger, SJ, and George V. Coyne, SJ (Vatican City: Vatican Observatory, 1990), 9–18.

scientific understandings of the world.[14] I believe that these resources are accessible to many of the Christian traditions represented at
this gathering. In general, while Catholic theologians and philosophers have been critical of the materialistic and naturalistic positions
that some scientists and intellectuals have thought evolutionary theory to entail, faith in the doctrine of creation has been seen as generally open to the idea of evolution. It is significant that Catholic
theologians have not on the whole espoused the systematic opposition to evolutionary theory that has emerged in some Christian
circles under the rubric of "creation-science."[15] Notwithstanding the
tentative character of scientific understanding of the universe, it remains true that emerging theories of evolution and the origin of the
universe possess particular theological interest and relevance for the

14. See the survey by Ernan McMullin, "Evolution and Creation," in *Evolution and
Creation*, ed. Ernan McMullin (Notre Dame, IN: University of Notre Dame Press, 1985),
1–56. On the classical exegesis of the hexaemeron, see E. Mangenot, "Hexaméron," in *Dic-
tionnaire de Théologie Catholique*, I, 2335–39; William A. Wallace, OP, Appendices 7–10, in
Thomas Aquinas, *Summa Theologiae*, Blackfriars Edition (New York: McGraw-Hill, 1967),
Vol. 10, 202–29. The need for exegesis to keep informed of scientific developments was
emphasized by Pope John Paul II in his address to the plenary assembly of the Pontifical
Academy of the Sciences in 1992 (*Acta Apostolicae Sedis* 85 (1993): 764–72). For a general
orientation to these issues, see the Pontifical Biblical Commission, *The Interpretation of the
Bible in the Church* (Vatican City: Libreria Editrice Vaticana, 1993).

15. Impelled partly by a certain biblical literalism and partly by acknowledged dis-
crepancies in evolutionary theory, "creationism" or "creation-science" tries to show
that it can furnish a more adequate explanation of the scientific evidence than can
"evolution-science." In her essay, "Let There Be Light: Scientific Creationism in the
Twentieth Century," in *Darwinism and Divinity*, 181–204, Eileen Barker draws the following definition of creation-science from an Arkansas statute enjoining its balanced
treatment: "'Creation-science' means the scientific evidences for creation and inferences
from those scientific evidences...that indicate: (1) Sudden creation of the universe, energy and life from nothing; (2) the insufficiency of mutation and natural selection in
bringing about the development of all living things from a single organism; (3) changes
only within fixed limits or originally created kinds of plants and animals; (4) separate
ancestry for man and apes; (5) explanation of the earth's geology by catastrophism, including the occurrence of a worldwide flood; and (6) a relatively recent inception of the
earth and living kinds" (191). For more complete and recent studies of creation-science,
see Ronald Numbers, *The Creationists: The Evolution of Scientific Creationism* (New York:
Knopf, 1998), and Robert T. Pennock, *Tower of Babel: The Evidence Against the New Creationism* (Cambridge, MA: MIT Press, 2000). For a Catholic critique, see Stanley L. Jaki,
The Savior of Science (Grand Rapids, MI: Eerdmans, 2000), 224–41.

doctrines of the creation *ex nihilo* and the creation of man in the image of God.[16]

THE COSMOS AS THE PLACE OF PERSONAL COMMUNION

The Nicene confession that all things were made through Christ teaches us that the cosmos is the stage upon which the Triune God enacts a great drama of communion by sharing the divine life of the Father, Son and Holy Spirit with persons who are not God.

Human beings are created in the *image of God*. This likeness to God in nature is the basis for a likeness to God in grace. Human persons are created in the image of God in order to become partakers of the divine nature (2 Pt 1:3–4) and thus to share in the communion of trinitarian life and in the divine dominion of the created universe. At the heart of the divine act of creation is the divine desire to make room for created persons in the communion of the uncreated Persons of the Blessed Trinity through adoptive participation in Christ. What is more, the common ancestry and natural unity of the human race are the basis for a unity in grace of redeemed human persons under the headship of the New Adam, the ecclesial communion of human persons united with one another and with the uncreated Father, Son, and Holy Spirit. Through the eyes of faith, then, the likeness to the divine nature that is enjoyed by spiritual creatures endowed with intellect and will turns out to be a likeness to the divine Trinity enjoyed by created persons who, in grace, know and love the Father, Son, and Holy Spirit, and one another in them. The likeness of man to God rests not only in his possession of an intellectual capacity, but even more in his vocation, as Pope John Paul II has said, "to enter into a relationship of knowledge and love with

16. On this topic in general, see the important essay by Ernan McMullin, "How Should Cosmology Relate to Theology?" in *The Sciences and Theology in the Twentieth Century*, ed. A .R. Peacocke (Notre Dame, IN: University of Notre Dame Press, 1981), 17–57; on the tentative character of scientific reasoning in relation to theology, see especially 49–52.

God himself, a relationship which will find its complete fulfillment beyond time."[17]

Human beings are *created* in the image of God. The gift of natural life is the basis for the gift of the life of grace (cf. *Evangelium Vitae*). Where the central truth concerns a person acting freely, it is impossible to speak of a necessity or an imperative to create, and it is, in the end, inappropriate to speak of the Creator as a force, or energy, or ground. Creation *ex nihilo* is the action of a transcendent *personal* agent, acting freely and intentionally, with a view toward the all-encompassing purposes of personal engagement. The history of the doctrine of the origin of human beings is guided by the determination to secure and maintain the revealed truth of this fundamentally relational or personalist understanding of God and of human nature. The exclusion of pantheism and panentheism in the doctrine of creation, and of emanationism and traducianism in the doctrine of the creation of human beings can be interpreted at root as a way of protecting this revealed truth. The doctrine of the immediate or special creation of each human soul, which is central to the present discussion, must be viewed in this light: it not only addresses the ontological discontinuity between matter and spirit, but it also establishes the basis for a divine intimacy that embraces every single human person from the first moment of existence.[18]

A properly trinitarian theology of creation, such as the Nicene confession warrants, entails a singular affirmation of the truly personal character of creation and its order toward a personal creature who is fashioned as the *imago Dei* and who responds not to a ground, force or energy, but to a personal creator. The Nicene confession teaches us that the existing universe is the setting for a radically personal drama, in which the Triune Creator calls out of

17. Pope John Paul II, Message to Participants in the Plenary of the Pontifical Academy of Sciences, October 22, 1996, §5.

18. Although it was reaffirmed by Pope Pius XII in *Humani Generis* (1950) in response to materialist evolutionary theories (*DS*, 3896), the doctrine of the immediate creation of the human soul has been continuously held by the Church and was not originally formulated with a view to issues raised by evolutionary theories (see *DS*, 190; 201; 285; 360; 455; 685).

nothingness those to whom He then calls out in love. Here lies the profound meaning of the words of *Gaudium et Spes:* "Man is the only creature on earth that God has wanted for his own sake" (§24). Created in God's image, human beings assume a place of stewardship and dominion in the physical universe. Under the guidance of divine providence and acknowledging the sacred character of the created order, the human race reshapes the natural order and becomes itself an agent in the evolution of the universe itself. The physical and ontological structures that support the possibility of the personal engagement in and with the Triune God, as well as the role of stewardship and dominion under God, on the part of creaturely persons can be the object of study in science and philosophy. In the light of faith, the history of the evolving universe is a history of the Triune God's engagement with created humanity.

It is within this perspective that, while rejecting all reductionistic accounts of the human persons, Christian theology in the ecumenical vein must consider scientific accounts of the origins of the universe and of evolution and human origins. Catholic theologians recognize that scientific reasoning concerning evolution and the origin of the universe does not in the main directly conflict with the doctrine of creation.

TRINITARIAN *CREATIO EX NIHILO*

Granting the hypothetical and tentative character of theories concerning cosmic history— particularly the Big Bang theory and the anthropic principle—and of theories concerning the origin of human life, theologians can well ask whether recent theories do not in fact lend a certain indirect support, and at least do not conflict with, the doctrines of the *imago dei* and the *creatio ex nihilo.*[19]

19. In addition to Catholic (and other Christian) authors already cited, the following works are worthy of note for their synthetic scope: Benedict Ashley, OP, *Theologies of the Body* (Braintree, MA: Pope John XXIII Center, 1985) and Jacques Arnould, OP, *La théologie après Darwin: Eléments pour une théologie de la création dans une perspective évolutionniste* (Paris: Editions du Cerf, 1998).

The Big Bang theory can be construed as supplying indirect support for the doctrine of *creatio ex nihilo* insofar as it can be said that "there is nothing scientifically or philosophically inadmissible about the supposition of an absolute beginning."[20] To be sure, it must be recognized that Catholic theology has generally held that the knowledge that the universe has an absolute beginning in time is given only by the divine revelation of creation and thus knowable only by faith. Since the Big Bang theory does not in fact exclude the possibility of an antecedent stage of matter, it can only be asked whether the theory does not appear to provide *indirect* support for the doctrine of *creatio ex nihilo*: "if an absolute cosmic beginning *did* occur, it could look something like the horizon-event described in the Big Bang theory."[21]

CONTINUING TRINITARIAN ACTION

A properly trinitarian account of divine causality in creation understands that, as universal transcendent personal agent, the Triune God, in his Word and Wisdom, is the cause not only of existence but also the cause of causes.[22] This agency is utterly unique: there are no natural analogs for it. For this reason, divine causality can never be seen to be at the same level or in competition with created causes, whether they act necessarily, contingently, or freely. God's action does not displace or supplant the activity of creaturely causes; rather he enables creaturely causes to act according to their natures and, nonetheless, to bring about the ends he intends.[23]

Two implications of this account of divine agency are

---

20. Ernan McMullin, "How Should Theology Relate to Cosmology?," 38.

21. Ernan McMullin, "How Should Theology Relate to Cosmology?," 38.

22. The writings of St. Thomas Aquinas have been influential in the development and articulation of this account of divine causality. Among the many texts that could be cited, see especially, *Summa theologiae* I, qq. 14, 19, 45, and 105; *Summa Contra Gentiles* III, Chs. 66, 67, and 70; *De Potentia* II, 7.

23. On this account, as Brian Hebblethwaite has put it in his essay "Providence and Divine Action," *Religious Studies* 14 (1978): 226, "the whole web of creaturely events is to be construed as pliable or flexible to the providential hand of God."

fundamental to the perspective that Nicene Christianity affords when it ponders current scientific understandings of cosmic history and human origins. First, the traditional distinction between primary and secondary causality entails that the Triune God as primary cause (absolutely speaking) makes use of secondary or subordinate causes in bringing about the states of affairs he intends.[24] Secondly, "the creator of the world can act beyond the causal powers granted to created things ... and thus both bring about particular effects in the world and preserve the immanent structures of nature."[25]

According to this account of divine agency at work in a plan exhibiting divine Word and Wisdom, it in no way detracts from the doctrine of the *creatio ex nihilo* to affirm that in freely willing to create and conserve the universe the Triune God wills to activate and to sustain in act all those secondary causes whose activity contributes to the unfolding of the law-governed natural order that he intends to produce. It is entirely in accord with the divine wisdom that God should will that through the activity of natural causes operating both necessarily and contingently there should gradually arise those conditions required for the emergence and support of living organisms, and, furthermore, for their reproduction and differentiation. While scientists have generally insisted that the purposiveness of these developments cannot be *scientifically* established, they are increasingly ready, as we have seen, to acknowledge that these developments have de facto favored the emergence and flourishing of life.

Within the broad areas of agreement concerning the origin of the universe and the evolution of human life, many unresolved and disputed questions continue to stimulate inquiry and research and

24. See discussions of the relevance of this understanding of divine causality for issues of science and religion in Ernan McMullin, "Evolution and Creation," *passim*, and in his essay, "Natural Science and Belief in a Creator: Historical Notes," in *Physics, Philosophy and Theology*, ed. Robert John Russell, William R. Stoeger, SJ, and George V. Coyne, SJ (Vatican City: Vatican Observatory, 1988), 49–79.

25. Thomas F. Tracy, "Particular Providence and the God of the Gaps," in *Chaos and Complexity: Scientific Perspectives on Divine Action*, 2nd ed., ed. Robert John Russell, Nancey Murphy, and A. R. Peacocke (Notre Dame, IN: University of Notre Dame Press, 1997), 311. Tracy's entire essay (289–324) is indispensable for the consideration of the issues under discussion here.

to provoke controversy among scientists. One question of particular interest to theology of creation concerns the so-called anthropic principle.[26] Granted that, as is generally agreed, the universe evolved in the direction of increasing complexity, and that steadily developing physical conditions favored the emergence of life, and in particular, of human life, still scientists ask whether these developments can be regarded as purposive and thus directed to the emergence of human life as such, as the anthropic principle is understood to maintain? While it is generally agreed that the sequence, timing, duration, and nature of these cosmic developments exhibit a definite degree of fine-tuning favorable to the subsequent emergence of life, the significance of these developments is much disputed. The already-mentioned discovery of the accelerating rate of cosmic expansion and the resultant "cosmological constant" has been seen by some scientists (e.g., Stephen Hawking) as unlikely to be susceptible of a non-anthropic explanation and by others (e.g., John Polkinghorne) as confirming the relevance of anthropic reasoning, if not of the anthropic principle itself. Additional support for anthropic reasoning comes from what has recently been called the "rare Earth" hypothesis which argues that, while simple life may be widespread in the universe, the conditions for complex life, such as are instantiated in our solar and terrestrial world, are extremely rare.[27]

26. See J. D. Barrow and F. J. Tipler, *The Anthropic Cosmological Principle* (Oxford: Oxford University Press, 1986). At the beginning of his new book, *Nature's Destiny: How the Laws of Biology Reveal Purpose in the Universe* (New York: Free Press, 1998), the biologist Michael Denton expresses a strong version of this principle when he states that his aim is "first, to present the scientific evidence for believing that the cosmos is uniquely fit for life as it exists on earth and for organisms of design and biology very similar to our own species.... and, second, to argue that this 'unique fitness' of the laws of nature for life is entirely consistent with the older teleological religious concept of the cosmos as a specially designed whole, with life and mankind as its primary goal and purpose" (xi). See also William A. Dempski, *Intelligent Design: The Bridge Between Science and Theology* (Downers Grove, IL: InterVarsity Press, 1999), and, for a preliminary theological analysis, Jean-Michel Maldamé, OP, *Le Christ pour l'univers* (Paris: Desclée, 1998), 91–126.

27. See Peter D. Ward and Donald Brownlee, *Rare Earth: Why Complex Life is Uncommon in the Universe* (New York: Copernicus/Springer-Verlag, 2000). A complementary perspective can be found in Martin Rees, *Just Six Numbers: The Deep Forces that Shape the Universe* (New York: Basic Books, 2000).

Despite the tentative character of these findings, Catholic theologians can ask whether anthropic lines of reasoning in scientific accounts of cosmic history can be construed as consistent with teleological lines of affirmation entailed by faith in divine creation and divine providence. Such questions are suggested by the Christian conviction that, in the providential design of creation, the Triune God intended to make a place for human beings not only in the universe, but also, and ultimately, in his own trinitarian life.

At the same time, this account of divine agency involves the affirmation that particular actions of the Triune God bring about effects that transcend the capacity of created agents operating according to their natures. The appeal to divine causality to account for genuinely *causal* as distinct from merely *explanatory* gaps does not involve a reversion to the rightly discredited physicotheology that inserted divine agency to fill in the "gaps" in human scientific understanding (thus giving rise to the so-called "God of the gaps").[28]

But both in a scientific perspective and certainly in a theological perspective, the structures of the world can be seen as open to divine action in directly causing events in the world. Thus, it must be recognized that the emergence of the first members of the human species, whether as individuals or in populations, represents an event that is not susceptible of a purely natural explanation and that can appropriately be attributed by faith to divine intervention.[29] Acting indirectly through causal chains operating from the beginning of cosmic history, God prepared the way for what Pope John Paul II has called "an ontological leap.... the moment of transition to the spiritual."[30] Although scientific investigation of evolution can observe

28. See McMullin, "Evolution and Creation," esp. 27–32; and Tracy, "Particular Providence and the God of the Gaps."

29. For a theological defense of this position, see Karl Rahner, *Hominisation* (New York: Herder & Herder, 1965); and Ashley, *Theologies of the Body*, 307–44. For a recent philosophical discussion of the origin of the soul, see Richard Swinburne, *The Evolution of the Soul* (Oxford: Clarendon Press, 1986), 174–99. For the classical discussion of this issue, see St. Thomas Aquinas, *Summa theologiae* I, qq. 90–92.

30. Pope John Paul II, Message to Participants in the Plenary of the Pontifical Academy of Sciences, October 22, 1996, §6.

and perhaps eventually chart with precision the developments that led to the threshold of this "transition to the spiritual," theologians ask whether the event itself can explained entirely by appeal to the operation of natural causes. Scientific understandings of human origins must be complemented by philosophical and theological reflection. Philosophy can study the distinctive spiritual conditions of human consciousness, freedom, and creativity and thus account for the ontological discontinuity between matter and spirit. But it falls to theology to locate this account of the special creation of the human soul within the overarching plan of the Triune God to share the communion of trinitarian life with human persons who are created out of nothing in the image and likeness of God, and who, in his name and according to his plan, exercise a creative stewardship and dominion over the physical universe.

Scientific understandings of the origins of the universe and of human life must be viewed in the light of Nicene faith—that is, a robustly trinitarian faith—to offset their tendency to conceive these processes in entirely deterministic and impersonal terms, with which only Buddhism or New Age religiosities will feel at home. The Nicene confession—whose relevance must be fully recovered in the new ecumenism—sees the evolving universe since the moment of creation as a personal history of the engagement of the Father, Son, and Holy Spirit with creaturely persons. We must never settle for less.

CHAPTER 18

---·---

The Church in the Gospel
Catholics and Evangelicals in Conversation

At the conclusion of *Evangelicals and Catholics Together: Toward a Common Mission*, the Catholic Richard John Neuhaus exhorts evangelicals to "reflect on the ecclesial dimensions of their faith and life" and to recognize that "the Church is an integral part of the gospel." He expresses the hope that "the 'Church in the gospel' can then be given fuller articulation" in evangelical theology.[1]

THE EVANGELICAL-CATHOLIC CONVERSATION ABOUT THE CHURCH

How can the conversation fostered by the statement "Evangelicals and Catholics Together" contribute to the desired "fuller articulation" of the Church in the gospel?

The conversation to date seems to demonstrate that evangelicals do not deny what Neuhaus calls "the inescapably ecclesial character

Originally published under the same title in *Pro Ecclesia* 13 (2004): 58–69. Used according to the SAGE Publications Author Archiving and Re-Use Guidelines, https://us.sagepub.com/en-us/nam/journal-author-archiving-policies-and-re-use, accessed 10/17/2023.

1. Richard John Neuhaus, "The Catholic Difference," in *Evangelicals and Catholics Together: Toward a Common Mission*, ed. Charles Colson and Richard John Neuhaus (Dallas: Word Publishing, 1995), 222.

of Christian existence."[2] In *Evangelicalism and the Future of Christianity*, for example, evangelical theologian Alister McGrath states that "the 'community of Christ' is integral to an evangelical understanding of the Christian life." When he writes that the Pauline image of the Church as the body of Christ "points to a corporate rather than individualistic conception of Christian life," he seems almost to echo Neuhaus's remark that "becoming a Christian and living as a Christian is an intensely personal matter, but it is not a private matter."[3] McGrath is not alone here. J. I. Packer, for example, in listing the principles basic to evangelicalism states that "the Church is essentially a fellowship of believers in Christ with Christ."[4] Charles Colson writes: "If we don't grasp *the intrinsically corporate nature of Christianity* embodied in the church, we are missing the very heart of Jesus' plan."[5]

Yet, despite what appears to be a fundamental agreement between Catholics and evangelicals about the "inescapably ecclesial character of Christian existence," it is commonplace to list (as does Donald A. Carson, for example[6]) the nature of the Church among the topics about which evangelicals are understood to disagree with Catholics.

It is not clear that evangelicals are in complete agreement with one another about the nature of their *disagreement* with Catholics on this matter. Packer states that the Catholic Church "misconceives the nature of the Church as the New Testament writers explain it" by giving institutional form to a "sacramental and juridical organization

2. Richard John Neuhaus, "The Catholic Difference," 223.

3. Alister McGrath, *Evangelicalism and the Future of Christianity* (Downers Grove, IL: InterVarsity Press, 1995), 78–79.

4. J. I. Packer, "Crosscurrents among Evangelicals," in *Evangelicals and Catholics Together*, 151.

5. Charles Colson, *The Body: Being Light in Darkness* (Dallas: Word Publishing, 1992), 271 (emphasis in original).

6. Donald A. Carson, "Evangelicals, Ecumenism and the Church," in *Evangelical Affirmations*, ed. Kenneth A. Kantzer and Carl F. H. Henry (Grand Rapids, MI: Zondervan, 1990), 347–85. For discussion, see Alister McGrath, "What Shall We Make of Ecumenism?" in *Roman Catholicism: Evangelical Protestants Analyze What Divides and Unites Us*, gen. ed. John Armstrong (Chicago: Moody Press, 1994), 199–217.

sustained by priests channeling divine life through set rituals."[7] But McGrath states that "evangelicalism has never been committed to any single model of the church, regarding the New Testament as being open to a number of interpretations in this respect."[8] Still, it may be supposed that some "models" exceed or contravene what the New Testament may be construed to permit, even on McGrath's generous evangelical reading. Packer and McGrath would agree, it seems, that, while, in McGrath's words, "evangelicals are at liberty to defend and develop any doctrine of the church that is well-grounded in Scripture and carefully thought through in practice,"[9] Catholic institutional doctrine and practice fail to measure up to this standard.

Within the ongoing conversation fostered by the ECT statement, the Catholic participants have sought to demonstrate that, in point of fact, Catholic institutional doctrine and practice are grounded, as Avery Dulles states, "in the order of the apostolic Church as attested by the New Testament."[10]

In his contribution to the book, *Evangelicals and Catholics Together*, Cardinal Dulles supports this contention in the course of an admirably concise summary of the basic elements of the Catholic understanding of the Church.[11] In the New Testament, according to Cardinal Dulles, the Church is a universal community "existing sociologically in the form of a multiplicity of congregations." Among the structures that emerged to safeguard the unity of the early Church, as attested by the New Testament, Cardinal Dulles lists the following: (1) a body of teaching common to all local congregations; (2) extended oral traditions; (3) a growing body of written literature; (4) hierarchical vigilance by the apostles and their associates; and (5) common practices of worship. According to Cardinal

7. Packer, "Crosscurrents among Evangelicals," 161

8. McGrath, *Evangelicalism and the Future of Christianity*, 81

9. McGrath, *Evangelicalism and the Future of Christianity*, 79

10. Avery Dulles, "The Unity for Which We Hope," in *Evangelicals and Catholics Together*, 130

11. Avery Dulles, "The Unity for Which We Hope," 125–34.

Dulles, the "Catholic system" continues to embody these elements: "The members of the Church are in communion with one another to the extent that they enjoy the same sacramental life, profess the same faith and acknowledge the same authoritative leadership."[12]

If I have understood them correctly, evangelicals would be inclined to lodge at least two objections against this Catholic understanding of the Church. In the first place, evangelicals would challenge the assumption that, according to McGrath, the New Testament stipulates "with precision any single form of church government that can be made binding on all Christians."[13] Secondly, evangelicals deny the claim of the Catholic Church to embody this scripturally normed ecclesial polity—the claim to be, as Packer puts it, "the only institution that can without qualification be called the Church of Christ."[14]

But these significant areas of disagreement between evangelicals and Catholics about whether the gospel warrants a particular form of the Church and what that form would be do not seem to contravene our agreement about "the inescapably ecclesial character of Christian existence." The passages we have been considering suggest that disagreement about the nature of the Church in the gospel does not rule out the shared conviction that there is a Church in the gospel.

Throughout McGrath's admittedly brief sketch of the evangelical understanding of the Christian community, the "nature of the Church" for the most part seems to refer to Church order, government, structures, or polity.[15] He insists that an evangelical commitment is consistent with membership in denominations representing diverse forms of church order and government. Despite their membership in local churches (evangelical or otherwise), in McGrath's description of what we might term their "ecclesial situation," evangelical Christians share in a unity with each other that transcends

12. Avery Dulles, "The Unity for Which We Hope," 134.
13. McGrath, *Evangelicalism and the Future of Christianity*, 82.
14. Packer, "Crosscurrents among Evangelicals," 161.
15. McGrath, *Evangelicalism and the Future of Christianity*, 72–85.

the denominations and communities to which they belong. Although McGrath does not make this point explicit, he clearly believes that this understanding of the unity shared by Christ's disciples is warranted by the New Testament. Packer describes this unity nicely when he states that, in the evangelical perspective, the Church in the New Testament is "a worldwide fellowship of believers who share in the resurrection life of the Lord Jesus Christ and enjoy unity with each other by virtue of the spiritual union with Christ himself that their baptism proclaims."[16] Despite his contention that the New Testament "does not stipulate ... any single form of church government," Alister McGrath would presumably embrace Packer's formulation of the evangelical understanding of the Church in the gospel.

But, what neither Packer nor McGrath acknowledge in the passages under consideration here is that Catholics would have no difficulty embracing this formulation as well. Consider the unmistakably parallel description of the Church in the New Testament provided by Avery Dulles: "Christianity in the lifetime of the apostles was in some sort a universal religion, embracing in a single fellowship adherents of every race, nation and linguistic group."[17]

These evangelical and Catholic theologians, at least, agree that there is a Church in the gospel and concur in its description at crucial points. A Catholic theologian (especially one of Thomist leanings like myself), desiring to contribute in some modest way to evangelicalism's "fuller articulation" of the Church in the gospel, could not fail to notice this agreement and to strive to exploit its theological potential.

THE PRIMACY OF GRACE IN
CHRISTIAN FELLOWSHIP

One of the tasks of ecclesiology, as Catholics pursue it, is to provide a theological account of this basic description of the Church

---

16. Packer, "Crosscurrents among Evangelicals," 161.
17. Dulles, "The Unity for Which We Hope," 125.

as a universal fellowship centered on Christ. It is true that Catholic ecclesiology, particularly in response to Reformation critiques of the late medieval church, came to be preoccupied with questions of order and the basis of order in the New Testament, sometimes to the neglect of more fundamental questions about the nature of the Church. It was not always so in churchly theology. Patristic and scholastic theologians sought to articulate the nature of fundamental unity of the Church, chiefly in terms of the grace of communion with the Father through Christ and in the Holy Spirit. While surely not independent of the visible Catholic institutions that embodied this communion and safeguarded its temporal unity, this account of the ecclesial dimensions of the "theological life" of the baptized was nonetheless seen as the basis of the sacramental, doctrinal and governmental structures of the Church.[18] The central themes of this classical ecclesiology continue to be actively recovered in present-day Catholic ecclesiology and in large measure provided the impetus for the renewal of the doctrine, practice and theology of the Church at the Second Vatican Council and in its aftermath.

Both Catholics and evangelicals have a lot to learn from these developments—different things no doubt, but important things nonetheless—if they are to reach an understanding of the Church that will both contribute to a renewed ecclesiology in their communities and sustain a common commitment to Christian mission in the third millennium. In particular, there are resources in the classical doctrine of the Church that can be deployed in articulating the nature of the universal fellowship in Christ which, if my analysis has been correct, constitutes what both evangelicals and Catholics understand the Church in the gospel to be.

18. For general orientations to the history of ecclesiology, see: Johann Auer, *The Church: The Universal Sacrament of Salvation* (Washington, DC: The Catholic University of America Press, 1993), esp. Part One, and Louis Bouyer, *The Church of God* (Chicago: Franciscan Herald Press, 1982) esp. Part I. My own understanding of these issues has been influenced especially by Yves Congar, "The Idea of the Church in St. Thomas Aquinas," in *The Mystery of the Church* (Baltimore: Helicon Press, 1960), 97–117, and Avery Dulles, "The Church According to Thomas Aquinas," in *A Church to Believe In* (New York: Crossroad, 1982), 148–69.

The first thing that needs to be said at this point has already been said in what Richard John Neuhaus has termed "the most important affirmation of the ECT: "All who accept Christ as Lord and Savior are brothers and sisters in Christ. Evangelicals and Catholics are brothers and sisters in Christ. We have not chosen one another, just as we have not chosen Christ. He has chosen us, and he has chosen us to be his together."[19]

Fundamental to the Catholic doctrine of the Church is the conviction that the Church is a divinely created fellowship or communion. As Stanley Hauerwas puts it, Christians gathered in worship "rightly confess their belief in the Church. They do so since confession is the practice necessary to remember that the Church is God's creation, not our own."[20]

Our churchly fellowship with each other in Christ is not the result of our joining together to establish community with like-minded people who share our belief in Christ and who want to give corporate expression to it. Rather, according to "catholic" ecclesiology, this fellowship is, in the first place, the result of a divine action that transforms us in the depths of our being and constitutes a renewed human community sharing in the life of God. Our fellowship with each other arises from our fellowship with the triune God. "For the Catholic Church ... the communion of Christians is none other than the manifestation in them of the grace by which God makes them sharers in his own communion, which is his eternal life" (*Ut Unum Sint*, §9).

This fundamental truth has been a constant refrain in recent official Catholic teaching about the nature of the Church. The Second Vatican Council was clear in stating it: "The eternal Father, in accordance with the utterly gratuitous and mysterious design of his wisdom and goodness, created the whole universe, and chose to raise up men to share in his own divine life.... He determined to call

19. Neuhaus, "The Catholic Difference," 178.
20. Stanley Hauerwas, *In Good Company: The Church as Polis* (Notre Dame, IN: University of Notre Dame Press, 1995), 9.

together in a holy Church those who should believe in Christ" (*Lumen Gentium*, §2). In commenting on the nature of the Church as a communion, the Congregation for the Doctrine of the Faith stated: "It is essential to the Christian understanding of communion that it be recognized above all as a gift from God, as a fruit of God's initiative carried out in the paschal mystery."[21] The new ecumenical directory, promulgated by the Pontifical Council for Promoting Christian Unity in 1993, framed the same fundamental truth in terms of the Paschal Mystery when it stated: "God sent into the world his only Son, who was raised up on the cross, entered into glory and poured out the Holy Spirit, through whom he calls into unity of faith, hope and charity the people of the new covenant which is the church."[22]

The importance of such texts for understanding the primacy of grace in any properly "catholic" ecclesiology cannot be overestimated.[23] All the structures and activities of the Church result from the grace of God active in the community of the people he has made his own. Sacraments, doctrine, governance, and mission are all rooted in this source and derive their effectiveness from the gift of divine fellowship which constitutes the Church in her very being. The human community of the Church is constituted by the saving and gracious action of the triune God who first called Israel to be a people out of the nothingness of its slavery in Egypt and continues to call and confirm the new Israel in its faithfulness to Christ and its unceasing mission to the world in his name. "His divine power has granted to us all things that pertain to life and godliness, through the knowledge of him who called us to be his own glory and excellence, by which he has granted to us his precious and very great promises, that through these you may

21. "Some Aspects of the Church Understood as Communion," (1992), §3 (https://www.vatican.va/roman_curia/congregations/cfaith/documents/rc_con_cfaith_doc_28051992_communionis-notio_en.html).

22. "Directory for the Application of Principles and Norms on Ecumenism" (1993), §11 (http://www.christianunity.va/content/unitacristiani/en/documenti/testo-in-inglese.html).

23. The discussion in this and the following section depends at many points on Thomas Aquinas's theology of grace, esp. *Summa theologiae* I, q. 43, a. 3; q. 62; qq. 93 & 95; I-II, q. 62; I-II, qq. 109–114; II-II, qq. 1–46; III, q. 8; qq. 46–49; qq. 53–57; qq. 60–62.

escape from the corruption that is in the world because of passion, and become partakers of the divine nature" (2 Pt 1:3–4 RSV).

The Church learns this great truth about the gracious gift at the heart of her existence from the announcement of the angel Gabriel to Mary as recorded in St. Luke's Gospel (1:26–38). At the very beginning of our salvation comes the news that God will accomplish something which does not—and indeed *could not*—depend upon a prior human readiness. Thus, when the angel informs Mary that she will bear a son whom she will name Jesus, her response is, in effect, that she has not fulfilled the necessary conditions for this to occur: she has no husband yet. The angel, again in effect, dismisses this precisely human protest of unreadiness by affirming the priority of the divine action in bringing about an event for which there are no relevant conditions (except, of course, those which God himself undertakes to put into place in creation and grace). Mary's readiness is profoundly a divinely constituted readiness: according to the Catholic doctrine of the Immaculate Conception, she was preserved from sin in virtue of the foreseen benefits of the Passion, Death, And Resurrection of her Son.

In the mystery of the Annunciation, the Church learns the fundamental truth that her existence is not a human achievement but a divine gift: the human community that is the Church arises from the communion with the Father, Son and Holy Spirit that is their gift to those who have died and risen in Christ. The universal fellowship that evangelicals and Catholics concur in discerning as the Church in the gospel has its ground in the shared life that flows, like sap, from the vine of Christ to the branches united with him and with one another in him. Nothing less than communion with the Father, Son and Holy Spirit lies at the heart of the community that is the Church of Christ.

Father Neuhaus draws out the ecumenical consequences of this fundamental truth: "Our purpose is not to create a unity among Christians that does not already exist. Indeed, we cannot create Christian unity at all. Unity is God's gift, not our creation.... In the

Catholic view, the problem posed by the division between Catholics and evangelicals is not that we are *not* united. *The problem, indeed the scandal, is that we are united but live as though we were not.*"[24]

It is central to my purpose in this paper to explore those aspects of Catholic ecclesiological doctrine that have direct bearing on the fuller articulation of the nature of the Church in the gospel and that have resonances with evangelical understandings of the Church. We are ready to take another step along the path of this inquiry.

To affirm the primacy of grace in the constitution of the Church is, furthermore, to affirm the centrality of the gift of trinitarian communion. As Pope John Paul II has written: "The faithful are one because, in the Spirit, they are in communion with the Son and, in him, share his communion with the Father: 'Our fellowship is with the Father and his Son Jesus Christ' (1 Jn 1:3)" (*Ut Unum Sint*, §9).

A central feature of the achievement of the Second Vatican Council was to have recovered and underscored the significance of "the ecclesiology of communion" for a proper understanding of the nature of the Church.[25] The following passages from *Lumen Gentium* and *Gaudium et Spes* are typical of many that could be cited: "The universal Church is seen to be 'a people brought into unity from the unity of the Father, the Son, and the Holy Spirit'" (*Lumen Gentium*, §4). "The Lord Jesus, when he prayed to the Father 'that they may be one ... as we are one' ... opened up vistas closed to human reason. For he implied a certain likeness between the union of the Divine Persons, and the union of God's children in truth and charity" (*Gaudium et Spes*, §24; quoted in *Ut Unum Sint*, §25). It is understandable that Walter Kasper would term this theme the "guiding ecclesiological idea" of the council.[26]

---

24. Neuhaus, "The Catholic Difference," 187.
25. "The Final Report of the 1985 Synod of Bishops," *Origins* 15 (1985): 448.
26. Walter Kasper, "The Church as Communion," in *Theology and Church* (New

The fundamental core of the narrative the Church recounts is that the triune God has undertaken to be in communion with humankind. Christ himself affirms this: "If a man loves me, he will keep my word, and my Father will love him, and we will come to him and make our home with him" (Jn 12:23 RSV). The ultimate communion in which we are called to share is a personal one: each person is invited to enjoy the communion of the Persons of the blessed Trinity and, in this way, a transformed communion with other persons.

The Church's narrative of human history and society, which is nothing less than the continuing story it shares with the people of Israel, is essentially trinitarian in structure.[27] It recounts the stages by which this ultimate communion has been pursued and achieved by God, and where its final consummation lies. To employ a central Pauline motif, through Christ human persons come to enjoy by adoption the triune familial life that Christ the Son enjoys by nature. Since the grace that comes through Christ overcomes human finitude and sin, it entails both enablement and restoration. It involves enablement because enjoyment of trinitarian communion is "natural" only to the uncreated Persons; created persons can enjoy it only by grace. Thus, human life in grace is life lived at a new level, one enabled by the triune God for the sake of communion in the trinitarian life. The grace of Christ involves restoration as well. No sinner

---

York: Crossroad, 1989), 148–65. The most thorough discussion of this theme can be found in J.-M. R. Tillard, *Church of Churches: The Ecclesiology of Communion* (Collegeville, MN: Liturgical Press, 1992). See also: Joseph Ratzinger, *Called to Communion: Understanding the Church Today* (San Francisco: Ignatius Press, 1996), and Susan K. Wood, "Communion Ecclesiology: Source of Hope and Controversy," *Pro Ecclesia* 2 (1993): 424–32. For some ecumenical perspectives on communion ecclesiology, see, for example: George Lindbeck, "The Structure of Communio," in *Consensus and Communion* (Geneva: Lutheran World Federation, 1992), 28–40; David Yeago, "Memory and Communion: Ecumenical Theology and the Search for a Generous Orthodoxy," in *Reclaiming Faith*, ed. Ephraim Radner and George R. Sumner (Grand Rapids, MI: Eerdmans, 1993), 247–71.

27. In his "Communion Ecclesiology: A Cautionary Note," *Pro Ecclesia* 4 (1995): 442–53, Nicholas Healy warns us that an emphasis on the ecclesiology of communion can involve "a reduction of the primary constitutive element of the church to a purely spiritual, invisible reality" and thus, in effect, suppress "the importance of the church's particularity" (448). My account here strives to avoid this pitfall.

can enjoy ultimate communion without reconciliation and conversion in continual conformity to the cross and resurrection of Christ.

But if this communion is personal, it also must be *inter*personal. It affords nothing less than human engagement and communication with the triune God in knowledge and love. Faith, hope and charity are properly "theological virtues" because they permit precisely this level of engagement with God. The "theological life" of faith, hope and love in grace is the life of ultimate communion begun here on earth.[28]

Those raised up with Christ and in Christ are joined to each other by the Holy Spirit. Hence the "inescapably ecclesial character of Christian existence." No merely human community can have the depth of communion of those called in Christ to share the life of the Spirit in the Church. Only Christ can overcome the sinfulness that corrupts human communities through pride, factionalism, and self-ishness. In Catholic ecclesiology, through the sacramental and liturgical life of the Church, Christ's grace remains a permanent source of vitality and renewal for the community that is, in a true sense, his body. Church governance and magisterium—the structures of communion—have no other purpose than to safeguard and serve this unity.[29] In this way, ultimate communion becomes the foundation of authentic human community.

Part of the Church's mission in the world is to summon all human persons to share in this communion and to resist the social and political constraints that obstruct its cultivation. The Church has a story to tell not only to its members but to the whole human race. It is a story whose divinely assured happy ending will come only when the entire human race is united in communion with the triune God.

The universal fellowship which we have identified as the Church in the gospel is nothing less than "the communion of each human

---

28. See the book by Romanus Cessario, *Christian Faith and the Theological Life* (Washington, DC: The Catholic University of America Press, 1996).

29. See J. A. Di Noia, "Communion and Magisterium: Teaching Authority and the Culture of Grace," *Modern Theology* 9 (1993): 403–18 [reprinted in this volume as Chapter Two].

being with the Father through Christ in the Holy Spirit, and with others who are fellow sharers in the divine nature, in the passion of Christ, in the same faith, in the same spirit."[30]

A COMMUNION WILLED AND ESTABLISHED
BY JESUS CHRIST

Earlier in this paper, we took note of Alister McGrath's statement of the conviction of evangelicals that they "are at liberty to defend and develop any doctrine of the church that is well-grounded in Scripture and carefully thought through in practice."[31] If I have been correct in my analysis, McGrath's comment can be taken to refer to the diversity of church orders that can be authorized by appeal to the New Testament. Although there are long-standing disagreements between (and among) the Catholic Church and the traditions of the Reformation centering on attempts to find explicit warrant for particular church structures in the New Testament, it is beyond the scope of this paper to examine these competing construals of the New Testament. I have tried to focus my efforts here on teasing out the implications of what seem to be shared convictions on the part of evangelicals and Catholics on the fundamental nature of the Church in the gospel.

I take these shared convictions about the nature of the Church to extend to a further conviction about the intrinsic connection of the Church with, in Colson's words "the very heart of Jesus' plan."[32] It may be supposed, therefore, that evangelicals would embrace Pope John Paul's statement that "Jesus himself, at the hour of his Passion, prayed 'that they may all be one' (Jn 17:21). This unity, which the Lord has bestowed on his Church, and in which he wishes to embrace all people, is not something added on, but stands at the very heart of Christ's mission.... God wills the Church, because he wills

---

30. "Some Aspects of the Church Understood as Communion," 108.
31. McGrath, *Evangelicalism and the Future of Christianity*, 79.
32. Colson, *The Body: Being Light in Darkness*, 271.

unity, and unity is an expression of the whole depth of his *agape*" (*Ut Unum Sint*, §9).

At the Second Vatican Council, both the Constitution on the Church and the Decree on Ecumenism underscored this fundamental Christian conviction: "The mystery of the holy Church is already brought to light in the way it was founded. For the Lord Jesus inaugurated his Church by preaching the Good News, that is, the coming of the kingdom of God, promised over the ages in the scriptures" (*Lumen Gentium*, §5). "After being lifted up on the cross and glorified, the Lord Jesus poured forth the Spirit whom he had promised, and through whom he has called and gathered together the people of the New Covenant, which is the Church, into a unity of faith, hope and charity" (*Unitatis Redintegratio*, §2).

The 1993 ecumenical directory echoes these conciliar statements: "It is the will of Jesus Christ that through the faithful preaching of the Gospel, the administration of the sacraments and through government in love exercised by the apostles and their successors under the action of the Holy Spirit, this people should grow and its communion be made ever more perfect."[33]

I believe that these passages express basic convictions about Christ and the Church in the gospel that Catholics and evangelicals share. I quote them at length to prepare the way for a final brief methodological observation concerning the Scriptural basis of the doctrine of the Church sketched in this paper.

The enthusiastic appropriation of the historical-critical method among a number of Catholic biblical scholars and the application of these methods to the study of the texts of Scripture have served to challenge the traditional conviction, expressed in the passages quoted above, that Christ willed to "found" the Church.[34] It has been noted that this way of framing the issue is itself entirely a product

---

33. "Directory for the Application of Principles and Norms on Ecumenism," 132.

34. See, for example, Frederick J. Cwiekowski, *The Beginnings of the Church* (Mahwah, NJ: Paulist Press, 1988), or Raymond Brown, et al., "Church in the New Testament," *The New Jerome Biblical Commentary* (Englewood Cliffs, NJ: Prentice Hall, 1990), 1339–46.

of a style of interpretation associated with modernity.[35] But, however the issue comes to be framed, it remains decisive for a properly theological interpretation of the Scriptures to affirm Christ's intention, through his preaching of the kingdom of God and his Passion, Death and Resurrection, to constitute his brethren in the communion of everlasting love of the Father, Son and Holy Spirit. That the community of his followers only came to understand and record *after his Resurrection* the full significance of Christ's enacted intention with regard to this communion does not undermine the conviction, arising from faith, that he willed to do just what the narratives of the Scripture recount. As Francis Watson has expressed it: "The actions of Jesus, as narrated in the gospels, must be interpreted ... against the background of the soteriological, Christological and eschatological claims of the narratives as a whole."[36]

This is not the place for an extended discussion of the place of historical studies in theology or of the relation of historical-critical exegesis to theological inquiry.[37] But it is important for evangelicals and Catholics together to affirm, in the context of a discussion of the Church in the gospel, that it is only in the light of faith that the events of Christ's life can be understood in their historical reality as such. For, a complete account of the events narrated in the Gospels must include a reference to the divine agency and intentions at work in them. There is a Church because the triune God willed to share his divine life with human persons and to establish this communion

35. See the excellent accounts of the history and central issues of this debate in Auer, *The Church*, 131–47, and, more extensively, in Francis Schüssler Fiorenza, *Foundational Theology: Jesus and the Church* (New York: Crossroad, 1984), 60–107.

36. Francis Watson, *Text, Church and World: Biblical Interpretation in Theological Perspective* (Grand Rapids, MI: Eerdmans, 1994), 247.

37. For a fuller discussion of these issues, see J. A. Di Noia and Bernard Mulcahy, "The Authority of Scripture in Sacramental Theology: Some Methodological Observations," *Pro Ecclesia* 10 (2001): 329–45 [reprinted in this volume as Chapter Four]. See also Aidan Nichols, *The Shape of Catholic Theology* (Collegeville, MN: Liturgical Press, 1991), 99–162. I have been greatly influenced in the thinking about these issues by Hans Frei's *The Eclipse of Biblical Narrative* (New Haven, CT: Yale University Press, 1974) and George Lindbeck's "Scripture, Consensus and Community," in *Biblical Interpretation in Crisis*, ed. Richard John Neuhaus (Grand Rapids, MI: Eerdmans, 1989), 74–101.

through the incarnation, passion, death, and resurrection of the only begotten Son. The Church in the gospel is not the invention of the post-Easter community, but a divine creation effected by the Father through Christ and in the Spirit in order to establish our communion with them and with one another in them—and nothing less than this.

Index

337